SEVEN HUNDRED AND FIFTY COPIES OF THIS BOOK HAVE

BEEN SET IN GRANJON TYPES AND PRINTED ON

SPECIALLY MADE PAPER AT THE WALPOLE

PRINTING OFFICE, MOUNT VERNON

THIS COPY IS NUMBER 325

newspapers and magazines. But Poe's work was well done, and Lord chose the Church for his life work. His poetry was virtually forgotten.

Lord had his ardent champions. He was represented in anthologies and libraries, but the public recognition he so richly deserved was long absent. However, in the last few years, there has been a growing consciousness on the part of Americans in their literary tradition, and particularly in Lord himself. It was then discovered that the original editions (now exceedingly rare and mostly in the hands of collectors) were by no means sufficient to fill the increasing demand for his works. Random House has undertaken, in this volume, again to make the poetry of Lord available, in the hope that this time he will come into his proper inheritance.

This book contains all Lord's familiar works, and a quantity of new material, much of which is as fine as anything the author ever published. The introduction and critical notes are by Professor Thomas Mabbott of Hunter College. The edition is limited to 750 numbered copies and has much in it to make it valuable as a piece of Americana. It is an interesting chapter in the story of Lord's poetical fortunes, a story which is unique in the history of American letters.

POETICAL WORKS OF
W. W. LORD

THE COMPLETE

POETICAL

WORKS

OF

W. W. LORD,

Edited and with an
Introduction by
THOMAS OLLIVE
MABBOTT

RANDOM HOUSE · NEW YORK

MCMXXXVIII

INTRODUCTION

WORDSWORTH, on reading the earliest poems of William
W. Lord, wrote to Bishop Doane, "I have to thank you
for several specimens of the abilities of a young poet, which
seem to me of high promise. They are full of deep emotion,
and not wanting in vigorous and harmonious expression.
Pray convey to him my best wishes for his health and happiness and success in that department of literature in which
it becomes every day more difficult to obtain and secure
attention, however well it may be deserved." There is also
a tradition that when Wordsworth heard of Lord's decision to devote himself rather to the ministry than to a
career of poetry alone, he expressed regret, a tribute indeed
to his regard for the abilities of the American poet, when
it is considered with what reverence Wordsworth regarded the Church. Lord's decision was made, and it is not for
us to regret a career which was eminently useful and distinguished in the field he himself felt his true calling. But,
since Lord, while not putting himself forward as a poet
after his youth, did not wholly forget the Muses, and wrote
occasional poems throughout his life, it seems only fitting
that the work of which one of the greatest poets thought
so highly should be collected. This is particularly desirable,
because Lord's gift seems to have grown with the years.
It is in those poems which have been hitherto inaccessible,
that at times the prophecy of Wordsworth was fulfilled.
The reader must judge for himself how far Lord did fulfill
his promise, but we must remember that his life was not
devoted to poetry alone, and the poems are rather the
fragments of a stately edifice than the edifice itself.

These fragments are here collected, and since Dr. Lord
is not with us to make a selection, every authentic poem
of which we now possess a copy is included. It may be
added that all save two or three were preserved by the
poet himself, who spoke little of his verse in later life, but
seems to have been careful to keep it.

As Stedman said in a letter written in 1890, "That first

book of Lord—which Edgar Poe attacked so savagely—
proved him to be a true poet and man of genius. But he
scarcely achieved the career expected of him."

Wordsworth has spoken of deep emotion, vigorous and
harmonious expression. To these we may add dignity and
occasional fire, especially in the "Ode to England" and in
"Niagara," and deep religious feeling. Lord, we think, did
not mature fully until after the Civil War, and it is by two
or three lyrics of this period and of his later life that the
true measure of his powers should be judged. Always clas-
sically restrained, at this time he produced one or two
lyrics of chiseled perfection, and faultless calm.

William Wilberforce Lord was born on October 28,
1819, in Madison County, New York. His father, the Reverend John Way Lord, was a Presbyterian clergyman and
a descendant of the Lord family of Lyme, Connecticut.
His first ancestor, Thomas Lord, whose coat of arms was
given in *Burke's Armory* as that of Laward, was an original proprietor of Hartford. His mother, Sarah Bryant
Chase Lord, was a lady of cultivation, a first cousin to the
late Chief Justice Salmon P. Chase. The poet was of the
seventh generation in America on two sides. He was edu-
cated at Geneseo High School and entered the University
of Western New York (now defunct) from which he is
said to have been graduated in 1837.

Griswold tells us that "during his college life his health
failed and his friends . . . committed him to the care of a
master of a whaleship, owned by a family friend of New
London. After being a few weeks at sea he grew weary of
the monotony of the cabin passage and . . . forced his way
into the forecastle where he soon became a sturdy seaman,
and during four years of service in the Pacific endured all
the hardships, privations and perils of that adventurous
life." He is also said to have been captured by cannibals
on the African coast and rescued by seamen from an
American man-of-war. There is reason to believe that this
ship was the one on which R. H. Dana had previously
served and had immortalized in *Two Years Before the
Mast*. On his return in 1841 Lord entered Auburn Theo-

logical Seminary, but on the death in 1843 of its president,
the Reverend Dr. Richards, he joined the senior class of
the Princeton Theological Seminary, from which he was
graduated in 1845.

He had from early youth been devoted to Shakespeare
and the Elizabethans, and he now became imbued with
ancient literature and the best German writers, although
philosophy was his favorite study. He also came under the
influence of Coleridge and Wordsworth. It was during
1844 that his poetical talents flowered and he composed
most of the poems which are included in his first volume
of verse, published in his twenty-sixth year. He had also
contributed to *Godey's Lady's Book* and to at least one
Annual under the pseudonym of Tristram Langstaff.

Lord's volume was published in May 1845. Bibliophiles
may like to know that a copy bearing the curious presen-
tation inscription, "To Miss Mary S. Kearny from *her*
friend, & *the* friend of the 'Mysterious Stranger in Black'
New York, June 13, 1845," now in the Huntington Library, is still in the original paper wrappers, printed in
green, red, and gold inks, one of the earliest surviving
"dust jackets."

The book was preceded by favorable notices in the press,
some of them rather extravagantly calling Lord "the
American Milton." Among Lord's sponsors were Charles
King (who later became president of Columbia College)
editor of the *New York American,* Charles Fenno Hoffman and others. Unfortunately some of these sponsors
were partisans of the *Knickerbocker Magazine* which was
engaged in a literary war with Edgar Allan Poe. As Poe's
personal feelings often swayed his critical powers, he was
predisposed against Lord. To make matters worse Lord's
"New Castalia" was a burlesque of "The Raven." Poe had
quarreled with one of his best friends for writing a parody
on "The Haunted Palace." From an unknown writer spon-
sored by people he did not like, the "New Castalia" was
unforgiveable and the result was a review in Poe's best
tomahawk style in the *Broadway Journal* of May 24, 1845,
followed up by another in the issue of October 24th. Poe

had been goaded by the Knickerbockers and undoubtedly believed Lord had begun the battle. One cannot altogether blame him for this, but when he chose to regard the "New Castalia" as a plagiarism and ended his review with the phrase "Good Lord, deliver us," he was fighting effectively and criticizing execrably. It is unfortunate that the fame of the critic has led many people to know Lord only through this review, usually without knowing of its place in a literary quarrel with a clique of which Lord was not really a member. This is the more regrettable, for Poe, returning to the attack in the *Democratic Review* for April, 1846, speaks of rereading Lord's poems in a way that suggests he was aware of his prejudice but could not overcome it. I have for many years believed that lines 54-67 of Lord's "Niagara" was the inspiration of a passage in Poe's poem, "To Helen" (Whitman) written in 1848. Poe was certainly familiar with this passage for he began a quotation of poetry he did not like with line 68 of "Niagara." One regrets that Poe did not live to read Lord's "The White Rose," or "The Lost Spring." We know enough of what Poe said of Lord, the only comment of Lord on Poe is more novel; in his old age he remarked to his grandson on one occasion, "Poe tried to prove I was not a great poet. It was really a compliment."

Because Poe found a number of echoes of earlier writers in Lord's youthful poems, it seems only fair to note that they were apparently intentionally introduced by Lord, in the fashion of the ancient writers. He knew an immense amount of poetry by heart, and apparently expected informed readers to recognize adaptations for what they were. He could quote at length from classical writers in all the chief ancient and modern languages. On one occasion later in life he sent a friend a copy of a poem of over a hundred lines, with the following note:

"The Diver" by Schiller: translated in Blackwood, many years before Bulwer's translations appeared, with its lumbering imitation of the German: and is a remarkable example of success in the use of the style of the old English ballad. An occasional hiatus in memory (for I possess no

copy) has been supplied by the imagination. W. W. L.

The verses appear to be substantially correct, and are hence not sufficiently Lord's work to require inclusion in this edition, but the anecdote may serve to illustrate the power of his poetic memory, which must have rivaled Dr. Johnson's.

There were a good many other reviews. That by Hoffman in the *New York Evening Gazette* for May 24 was favorable, as was that in *Godey's* for July. The *New York Alleghanian* of May 31, 1845, flew to Lord's defense with an amusing article called "The Poe-dom of Poetry," sympathizing with Lord "while suffering under the know-nothing-about-him-ativeness" of Poe. Other less interesting reviews may be found in the *Knickerbocker* for July, the *Democratic Review* for June, the *Southern Literary Messenger* for July and October, and the *Southern Quarterly Review* for October.

But Lord seems to have been rather discouraged by the whole affair, and at this time wrote from Princeton to his publisher:

Mr. Appleton: *Sept. 8, 1845.*
Dear Sir

Your interest in my little venture upon the high seas of literature, especially since it has met with some adverse winds, will perhaps make a piece of intelligence that you will not doubt gratified me, in some degree, gratifying to you. I have been favored with a communication from Bishop Doane, which contains the following extract from a letter to him by William Wordsworth.

[Here follows the quotation with which this memoir opens.]

I shall be happy to hear from you and learn something of the prospects of the Book.

                    Your ob't s'v't,
                    W. W. Lord

Mr. D. Appleton.

The words of Wordsworth seem to have been inserted in the newspapers at the time, though we have not met with any copy of them hitherto in print, and Lord wrote to Griswold on hearing that his biography was to appear in a new edition of *The Poets and Poetry of America:*

> *Princeton, Jan. 20, 1846.*
>
> *Dear Sir*
>
> *I have just become aware that a notice of my life, something lengthier and more minute than any performance of mine, or reputation acquired by it, will justify, has been transmitted to you by my friend Mr. Kinney. The life of a poet is in his book, and when men are but little interested in* that, *which is his real life and unconscious auto-biography, they will not be very curious about his inferior state of existence and development. If in conformity with your plan it is necessary to preface the selections you do me the honor to make with a sketch of my life I desire that it may be as brief as possible, and contain merely such facts as relate to birth, parentage, situation etc. It is not the least among the misfortunes of a young author that while it is still doubtful whether he can make good his title to fame he loses his right to obscurity.*
>
> > *With high respect,*
> > *Yours,*
> > **W. W. Lord**
>
> *Rev. R. W. Griswold.*

In 1845-1846 Lord was Boudinot Fellow at the College of New Jersey, as Princeton was then called. And he seems to have begun to lecture even before this. His subjects varied widely, one lecture, still preserved in manuscript, called "Three Eras in Literature," he delivered at Princeton College in 1845, Amherst in May, 1846, Columbia College in 1847, and repeated as late as 1867 at Charleston College in South Carolina. A very interesting lecture on Bunyan, worthy of publication lies before me as I write this. Of his lectures at Hope Chapel in New York in 1850 we have interesting notices in the *Literary World* for March 2 and December 7. The first course was on "The Heroes and Saints of the Middle Ages," and the reviewer chose that on St. Bernard for synopsis as one of the ablest, containing "fine examples of poetic painting" and of genuine, hearty, unaffected love of the old and beautiful and grand. He remarks, "What the lecturer thinks bursts forth in a vigorous and fiery rhetoric . . . earnest, manly, and effective. The later course was on the "Romantic Poets." One wishes that the Wordsworth lecture were accessible.

In 1847 Lord was Tutor in Mental and Moral Science at Amherst, and perhaps even before this had received the degree of Doctor of Divinity from the University of Alabama, where he was once invited to read a Phi Beta Kappa poem. Lord himself is the authority for these statements, and there is no reason to doubt them, although the records of the universities available fail to verify them.

About 1850 Lord made the acquaintance of E. C. Stedman, who wrote to his mother as appears in his *Life and Letters*:

Mr. Lord went over to New York with me the morning you sailed. I admire him, from the bottom of my heart. I have with great difficulty (they are so little known) procured a copy of his poems, and am lost, in ecstasy and wonder at the sublimity of his "Niagara"—the calm and holy and grand philosophy of his "Worship" and the majesty and elegance of his "Ode to England" especially his address to Wordsworth in it—whom he imagined to himself as old and blind.
"For so were Milton and Mæonides!" He says—speaking of Niagara.

> *"And joy was in my heart as of a God*
> *At birth of a new world!"*

What an intellect he has! Will this be my fate—to be forgotten and unknown?

Later for a time there seems to have been some aloofness between Stedman and Lord, who is said to have criticized, upon request, some of Stedman's poems and to have rejected and resented Stedman's efforts to induce him to write in a more popular manner. He was both sensitive and reticent. However, in later life the breach, if it ever existed, was healed. We find two references to Lord in *The Poets of America,* 1888, as well as a selection from his poems. Stedman said at one place:

"Occasionally a note of promise was heard, from some quaint genius like Ralph Hoyt, or some aspirant like Lord, of whom great things were predicted, and who, in spite of Poe's vindictive onslaught, was and is a poet."

And writing of Whittier's "Ichabod," Stedman remarked:

Among our briefer poems on topics of dramatic general interest, I recall but one which equals this in effect,—and that, coming from a hand less familiar than Whittier's, is now almost unknown. I refer to the "Lines on a Great Man Fallen," written by William W. Lord, after the final defeat of Clay, and in rebuke of the popular judgment that to be defeated is to fall. The merit of this eloquent piece has been strangely overlooked by the makers of our literary compilations.

It is also known that Stedman continued his interest in Lord throughout life and there was on his desk at the time of his death the unfinished manuscript of a study of Lord and his poetry which to our great regret we have not been able to consult.

Although trained as a Presbyterian, Lord felt a deep love and reverence for the Protestant Episcopal Church, and he was ordered Deacon in that Church in 1848, and ordained priest by Bishop Doane in 1850. His first post seems to have been as Assistant at Coventry, Somerset County, Maryland. Thence he moved to St. Peter's, Baltimore, where he served bravely during an epidemic of cholera in 1851. On February 18 of that year he married Margaret Stockton. They had a son who bore his name, and five daughters, one of whom, Nellie, who died in childhood, is the subject of some of Lord's poems.

Later in the same year he published his religious epic,

Christ in Hades. This was reviewed fairly widely, and one may consult W. R. Alger's review in the *Christian Examiner* for May; and other notices, usually anonymous, in the *Literary World* for May 3; the *Southern Quarterly Review* for October; *Graham's* for May; and the *Democratic Review* for April, 1851.

The following extract from an article in the *American Church Review* for January, 1853, represents the feeling of a number of Lord's great admirers among the more intellectual and classical scholars of his day.

For the present Christ in Hades *will not be a celebrity. It has none of the elements of immediate popularity—it wears no look fascinating to the common eye.... Hence it is that the lower orders of poetry are, in general, more immediately popular than the higher. They pass into instant favor—they are praised by booksellers, readers and paragraph critics.... Not so is it with the real issues of the shaping, creative mind. They purchase immortality at the expense of present neglect. Coming up out of souls, grand and deep as the moral life of man ... they are able to wait the verdict of future ages.... Their life ... is both lasting and hidden, because deep, central, self-poised. ... Our author has in a certain sense stood aside from his time.*

In 1852 Lord was assistant at St. Ann's at Annapolis and thence he transferred to Vicksburg, Mississippi, where in 1854 he became rector of Christ's Church. He was one of the educators who selected a site for the University of the South at Sewanee, Tennessee. Among his more intimate friends was Jefferson Davis. While in Vicksburg he published his last volume of verse, *André,* in 1856. The best comment on this book is found in the following letter which he received from R. H. Dana, Sr. to whom he had sent a copy:

Dear Sir:

I received your tragedy some six or eight weeks since. At the time & for a long while after, I was in no fit state to

*look into a new poetic work, & when better I put it off
from misgivings on account of the subject. I asked myself
if the events of our revolution could as yet be sufficiently
idealized to be taken as subjects for poetry. I remembered
too that tragedies written for the closet had more or less
of an air of stuffiness & artificiality & that genius moulded
into that form would act with freer motion & more power
in almost any other.*

*I have now read the tragedy &, with no little pleasure, at
finding how far you had overcome these real difficulties,—
It is rich in thought—in unforced, right thought—in poetic images, pathos & true passion, with a poetic turn of
phraseology, the language of a clear, distinct character—
a true refreshment to one in these days.*

*I could wish that you had ended with André's going
out to execution—3rd sc. It would have given a roundness
to the play which it now seems to me to lack—I would not
imply that there are not many things in what follows sc.
3rd, good in themselves, but that they affect the reader like
after work. His interest has "slacked off," & he can not
be wrought up again to his previous state of feeling by
anything however strong. Here, it is like telling us what
happened afterwards. Some portions following sc. 3rd
might perhaps have been worked in before it; other portions must have been sacrificed; but a writer like all his
fellow creatures must sacrifice many things which he loves.
Arnold's wife is a noble creature. I thank you for the real
satisfaction which the play has given me and for your
kindness in remembering me. Pardon an old man's criti-
cism and believe me, dear Sir,*

Sincerely yours,
Rich'd. H. Dana.

Boston, March 21, 1857.

*I enclose this to the care of your publisher as your place in
the Church Register does not agree with that you dated
from in your preface and I am in doubt as to which is the
right one.*

André has continued to attract the attention of students, and was reprinted by William Abbatt as Extra Number 179 of *The Magazine of History,* Tarrytown, N. Y., 1932. This is prefaced by a few words by Brander Matthews, praising Lord's blank verse.

When the Civil War broke out Lord continued his pastorate but became chaplain of the first Mississippi Brigade, and he worked tirelessly during the siege of Vicksburg. During this siege his possessions, including his library, said to have been the largest and most scholarly private collection in the southwest, were destroyed. At least two members of Lord's family have written descriptions of the hardships of the siege. Upon its conclusion General Grant offered him a passport to St. Louis but he refused this and went into the Confederacy where he continued his labors with the army. Soon after the war was over Lord became rector of St. Paul's Church, Charleston, South Carolina, where he remained several years. At Charleston he was also Principal of a Boarding and Day School for Young Ladies at the corner of Meeting and Charlotte Streets where the Latin classics, French and German were taught. The number of boarding pupils was limited to twelve.

At Charleston in the days of hardship after the war his poetic genius was again awakened and it was at this period of his life that he produced a few lyrics, restrained, dignified, deeply moving, which compare favorably with the poems of Timrod and seem to prove the rightness of Wordsworth's prophecy that Lord, devoting himself to poetry, might have attained, indeed, to major rank.

In 1871 he returned to Vicksburg, where he founded the Church of the Holy Trinity, on the lofty spire of which he affixed with his own hands the cross.

Of Dr. Lord at this time we have the following delightful reminiscences from General Maury's *Recollections of a Virginian* published in 1894. Maury had met Lord during the siege of Vicksburg and apparently knew nothing of his early reputation as a scholar and poet. He comments:

Dr. Lord was one of the most remarkable men I have ever known. . . .

Some time after the war, while I was the guest of Major Flowerree in Vicksburg, Dr. Lord was invited to dine with me. The night before I had been to see Ben de Bar play Falstaff—the best Falstaff I have ever seen. Dr. Lord took up the subject, and made the most interesting discussion of Shakespeare's greatest character I had ever listened to. He plainly proved that Falstaff was no coward, and when I asked for his exposition of the difference between wit and humor, he recapitulated the history of the Fat Knight, showing where he was witty, where humorous, and where both witty and humorous. We listened to him, absorbed, for an hour, when he left us to attend to some parochial duty. As soon as he had gone, I said to Flowerree, "I have never had such a treat; I seem to have struck upon Dr. Lord's specialty."

"You were never more mistaken in your life," he replied. "No matter what the subject is, he seems to have mastered it. Some years ago there was a club of intelligent gentlemen here in Vicksburg, who met to enjoy conversation. Dr. Lord was a member, and no matter what might be the question under discussion, he was the master of it. One day Dr. Crump received a new book upon whaling and other arctic experiences; I believe it was called Three Years Before the Mast. *He read the book and was charmed with it, and passed it around to several other gentlemen of the club, that they might also read it and introduce the subject at their next gathering, and for once know some-thing with which Dr. Lord was not familiar.*

"Accordingly, when the evening came, the subject of whale-fishing was taken up by these freshly informed gentlemen, with the expectation that their rector would for once be at a loss, but they reckoned without their host; for in a few minutes the reverend gentleman took up his parable, and instructed them all in facts about whales and the Arctic Circle, such as they had never heard of before, and finally informed them he had been a sailor on that very ship they had been reading about." He remained with

his people during the severe trials and dangers of their terrible siege, and ever bore with him their affectionate and grateful memories.

Lord's greatest popular fame was probably earned at the time of his work during the epidemic in Memphis. He was known throughout the South as "The Church Militant." A tall and strongly built man, he was the picture of intellectual, physical and moral vigor.

Lord's preaching was eloquent, richly intellectual, sound theologically, yet sometimes highly original in the views expressed. Several of his sermons and lectures were printed, and since some of the pamphlets are very rare, we give here a list of those with which we have met, in chronological order: *Our Citizenship in the Church,* Vicksburg, 1857; *Liberty and Law,* a speech made in Vicksburg at the laying of the corner stone of the court house of Warren County, Vicksburg, 1858; *A Discourse . . . in Honor of Capt. Paul Hamilton . . . Killed in the Battle of Chickasaw Bayou, Dec.* 29, 1863 . . . *Commemorated . . . January* 4, 1863, Vicksburg, 1863; *The Word Trinity and Other Words.* A sermon in St. Paul's Church Radcliffeboro', on Trinity Sunday, 1869, Charleston, South Carolina, 1869; *The Limits of Ritualism in the Protestant Episcopal Church,* Vicksburg, 1872; *Man, and the Record of his Origin,* New York, 1880 (a lecture on evolution); *Man Hereafter; or Heaven and Hell. Two Discourses in . . . Vicksburg,* New York, 1882; *Two Sermons . . . at the Close of His Rectorship,* Cooperstown, 1882.

At least one copy of each is known. Collections consulted include the Library of Congress, Brown University, New York Public Library, and the collection of his grandson Mr. R. R. Reed. A large number of other sermons are preserved in manuscript by Lord's descendants, as well as some of his lectures.

His interest in evolution was deep and intelligent, the lecture *Man and . . . his Origin,* referred to above, deserves attention as the prose companion of the curious serio-comic philosophical poem called *The Great Ascidian,* and is a more successful treatment of a topic that really fits ill with poetry, but which Lord perhaps attempted because of his interest in Browning, whom he admired, but not unreservedly, as his poem on that subject shows.

In 1876 Lord was called to Christ's Church, Cooperstown, New York where he served until his retirement from the ministry about 1883 when he was offered, but refused, the title of Rector Emeritus. After his retirement Dr. Lord resided at Cooperstown but spent a part of each winter in New York City. During 1890 he made a trip to the Holy Land which inspired two or three very fine poems on religious and classical subjects including "The Waiting of Judah," which he wrote when he actually stood upon the Mount of Olives. A minor interest is worth noting: he composed some verses, pleading that the daisy be made the national flower, in 1880. Although he seems to have lived very quietly, he enjoyed many pleasant friendships, among which may be mentioned one with Bishop Potter, to whom a brief familiar poem is addressed. The Spanish War called forth a few verses. He wrote the inscription for the monument to the Indians at Cooperstown and in the beginning of the present century still occasionally returned to the muses, once on seeing a young girl, and again to greet a young friend serving with the American forces in China. Dr. Lord, having reached the ripe old age of eighty-eight, died at the Clendening in West 103rd Street in New York City on Monday, April 22 ,1907, and was buried at Cooperstown, overlooking Otsego Lake, the sheer beauty of which was one of the chief joys of his later years and the scene of many happy days.

On a friend's tablet he had written, "A servant of God and a Friend of Man," which he might well have applied to himself. His own epitaph, however, reads simply, "Poet, Priest and Scholar."

THOMAS OLLIVE MABBOTT

April 12, 1938

POETICAL WORKS OF
W. W. LORD

CONTENTS

POEMS

POEMS,

BY

WILLIAM W. LORD.

NEW-YORK :
D. APPLETON & CO., 200 BROADWAY.
PHILADELPHIA :
GEO. S. APPLETON, CHESNUT-STREET.
MDCCCXLV

TO

PROFESSOR ALBERT B. DOD,

THESE POEMS,

THE OFFSPRING OF AN EARNEST

(IF INEFFECTUAL)

DESIRE TOWARD THE TRUE AND BEAUTIFUL,

WHICH WERE HARDLY MY OWN BY PATERNITY,

WHEN THEY BECAME HIS BY ADOPTION,

ARE INSCRIBED,

WITH ALL REVERENCE AND AFFECTION,

BY THE AUTHOR

"The Booke ytte moste bee ytts owne defense."

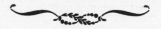

WORSHIP

FOR them, O God, who only worship thee
In fanes whose fretted roofs shut out the heavens,
Let organs breathe, and chorded psalteries sound:
But let my voice rise with the mingled noise
Of winds and waters;—winds that in the sedge,
And grass, and ripening grain, while nature sleeps,
Practise, in whispered music, soft and low,
Their sweet inventions, and then sing them loud
In caves, and on the hills, and in the woods,
—A moving anthem, that along the air
Dying, then swelling forth in fitful gusts,
Like a full choir of bodiless voices, sweeps,—
Yea, of the great earth that make an instrument,
Awakening with their touch, itself not mute,
Each different thing to difference of tone,
Long, harp-like shrillings, or soft gush of sounds;—
Waters,—to earth, as to the air the winds,
Motion and utterance, and that begin
Even at their source the gently murmured hymn,
Rise with the river, with the torrent swell,
And at the cataract's dizzy, headlong leap,
Break forth in solemn and deep bursts of song.
Yet what is all this deep, perpetual sound,—
These voices of the earth, and sea, and air,
That make it seem to us, as if our Earth,
Into the silent and unruffled deep
Led forth, with thunder-step, the choir of worlds?
All these,—what are they?—in the boundless void,
An insect's whisper in the ear of night,
A voice in that of death,—in thine, O God,
A faint symphony to Heaven ascending
Amid ten thousand, thousand songs of praise.
   Then what is one weak voice, the utterance
Of a thought as weak, an aspiration,

Struggling up to thee on wings that beat the air
With feebler motion still as they ascend?
O God! and dost thou hear, or do our lips
Mock, when we pray, a cold, unpeopled sky,
Beyond which is for us no eye, no ear,
No heart of love, no God?—Infinite One,
Eternal God, *Thou art!* O, not this sky,
These mountains, nor the solemn-sounding sea,
Have spoken it, but thou, thou to my soul
Hast spoken, and it knew thy voice:—Thou art!
Soul of all Being, Infinite God, Thou art!
And nought that is can be, and yet to thee,
Who art its life, be nought.

       Break forth ye Winds!
That in the impalpable deep caves of air,
Moving your silent plumes, in dreams of flight,
Tumultuous lie, and from your half-stretched wings
Beat the faint zephyrs that disturb the air;—
Break forth ye fiercer harmonies, ye storms!
That in the cavernous and unquiet sea
Lie pent, and like imprisoned thunders beat
Your azure confines, making endless moan;—
All sounds, all harmonies break forth! and be
To these my thoughts and aspirations, voice;—
Rise, rise, not bearing, but upborne by them,—
Rise through the golden gates uplift and wide!
In, through the everlasting doors! and join
The multitude of multitudes whose praise
With mighty burst of full accordant sound
Moves Heaven's whole fabric vast, as move the clouds
That from their swinging censers upward pour,
By wings of hovering seraphim disturbed,—
A sound so deep and loud, that at its might
The pillared heavens would fail, and all their frame
Of ancient strength and grandeur sink at once,
But for its soul of sweetness that supports,
And mightier harmony that builds them still:—

Ye Winds! ye Storms! all sounds and harmonies,
O thither rise! be heard amidst the throng;
Let them that dwell within the gates of light,
And them that sit on thrones—let seraphs hear,—
Let laurelled saints, and let all angels hear,—
A human soul knows and adores its God!

O Spirit! present in all sight and sound,
But never given to the eye or ear—
Who shall ascend to Heaven, or, winged with light,
Descend the abyss, or range the shoreless void
In search of Thee?—Here, here thou art, Most High!
These are thy courts, these valleys, and these hills;
Yea, we do always in the presence dwell
Of Godhead, and Eternal Majesty.
With Nature, day with night, from birth to death,
In a perpetual worship do we live—
A high solemnity.

He whose goings forth
Like thine are glorious, and of old like thine,
The symbol of thy strength, the mighty Sun,
Whether with day upon his wings he mounts,
Lifting the wide-spread splendor from the deep,
Or sinks beneath the alternating night,
Forever turns his burning eye on thee
With awful homage. Thee the bright host of Heaven,
The stars adore:—a thousand altars, fed
By pure unwearied hands, like cressets blaze
In the blue depths of night; nor all unseen
In the pale sky of day, with tempered light,
Burn radiant of thy praise.

Earth, fallen earth,
Still worships, but—alas for Eden lost!
Alas for sin, and for her children's shame!—
With stern and dreadful expiatory rites.
Of all that tread the earth or wing the air,
Of every plant and flower, she offers up

Her daily and perpetual sacrifice:
The clod beneath our feet, the soil that clothes
Her discontinuous valleys ridg'd and pierced
With naked mountains, is the kneaded dust,
Relics and ashes of her offered dead.
The clouds above that overhang the Earth,
And ancient hills that seem created old,
And stand like altars vast, are but the smoke
That from the mighty holocaust ascends
As the Sun's fires consume the accepted gift:—
The smoke of offerings blended with the sweet
Invisible incense of the golden flowers,
And with the vapory tribute of the seas,
That like a blessing falls in holy dews,
Or in the rain like full libations poured.

O multiform and glorious! can it be,
O thou so vast and varied, and with life
Instinct and active, Nature! can it be
That thou unto thyself art not alive?
Or worse, (as bolder apprehension hints,)
Art thou but as the void and shapeless mist,
On which the beam of heaven, the shaping thought,
Breaking like day upon the night-breathed fog,
Gives it its shape, its splendor, and its hues,—
Or when, advancing, on the cloudy east
He paints the gates from which he issued forth,
The gates and blazing pinnacles of Heaven?
Great Worshipper! hast thou no thought of Him
Who gave the Sun his brightness, winged the winds,
And on the everlasting deep bestowed
Its voiceful thunder,—spread its fields of blue
And made them glorious, like an inner sky
From which the islands rise like steadfast clouds,
How beautiful!—who gemmed thy zone with stars,
Around thee threw his own cerulean robe,
And bent his coronal about thy brows,
Shaped of the seven splendors of the light,—

Piled up the mountains for thy throne; and thee
The image of His beauty made, and power,
And gave thee to be sharer of his state,
His majesty, his glory, and his fear!

But if, Almighty Builder, for our use,
And ours alone, insentient Nature stands
With all her ordered forms and mighty frame,—
A shadow in the else unbroken light
Of thy pure being—then, O what neglect,
What desecration of our service high!
Unthoughtful of her forms and mysteries,
On altars and in places consecrate,
Like temple-haunting martlets do we build,
Than they less innocent, and heed it not!
There is a sacred meaning in all sights,
All sounds that Nature owns, but we, grown blind,
Who were the original priests of this
Her august temple, in its porches stand,
And with irrational and heedless eye
View all the moving symbol of the year.
The Seasons are a solemn service;—Spring,
Winter, and Summer, and the Harvest Moon,
Each have their meaning, and each changing day
Its worship, of high import to the whole.
The heedful ear may hear in every field,
On insect-haunted banks, among the leaves,
And in the rills, a thousand tinkling sounds,
That, here and there, confusedly distinct,
Like some sweet strain dissevered and unlinked
And broken into discords scarce less sweet,
Fill all the air—then hushed, then heard again,
Like mystic sounds that in cathedrals vast
Order the service, call the thoughtful soul
To worship meet. And sometimes in the wood,
At morn or even, or when the vernal rain
That fell thick-pattering among the leaves,
Stints suddenly, the birds ring out a peal

With such sweet chime and involution heard,
Of intricate swift strains and jangled bells,
As oft surprises cold unwilling hearts
To worship unawares: and oft above,—
As when the great bell thunders in its tower,
And to the villages and listening hills
Speaks with its deep and awful voice of God,—
So in the concave and o'er-hanging sky
The lightning's tongue strikes forth that dreadful peal,
To him that listens, yet half fears to hear,
—Made, like a child, sublime of thought—the voice
Of God himself! Groves have their worship;—there
Where fall the shadows, like the solemn awe
That on assembled worshippers comes down,
Great oaks their heaven-ward lifted arms stretch forth
In suppliance; nor have they not a voice
For praise and worship, as who hears may deem
What time the sea of air in which they stand
Moves in their depths.—The imperishable Hills
In visible and ceaseless worship rise:
Rooted in earth's foundations, through the earth
And sea, and air they rise, with place in each,
And bearing to the sky the praise of all.
The Fields beneath the eye of heaven outspread
In worship lie; nor do they lack a voice
Of praise from lowing herds and bleating flocks,
And the perpetual hum, that, day and night,
Whoever listens with hushed thoughts, may hear
Rise like the deep and quiet breathing of the Earth.
Each slightest thing, tuneful or mute, each leaf
Hath part in this great service, that for souls
Intelligent of God was first devised;
And though by them unheeded, still moves on
In unabated pomp of day and night,
And changing seasons, tilth, and herbs, and flowers.

Almighty God! surely we have not felt
The power, the awfulness of common things!

All sound is but the echo of thy voice,
Into reverberations infinite
Broke and prolonged among the worlds that rose
From the twinn'd gloom and silence at its sound.
The light in which we live, how dread the thought!
Is the same flood that, like the eternal Soul
Making itself first visible to the things
Created by its power, rushed on the world— •
And gave to that obscured in night before,
And undistinguished from its shapeless mass,
Reality,—and glorious beauty gave,
And twofold being, being in itself
And in the sight.

         All that we behold,
Mountains and forests, and the spreading seas,
The all-surrounding sky, its clouds and stars,
Existed still with thee, Eternal One,
And in thy soul had being, (ere revealed
In forms material to material sight,)
As thy conceptions of thyself; the thoughts
Of grace, magnificence and power,
That peopled, ere the earth or heaven rose,
Thine ancient night of realmless solitude.
Think! heedless one, or who with wanton step
Tramples the flowers, the flowrets are God's thoughts—
Beautiful thoughts! that, long before he gave
Their loveliness to bless thy thankless sight,
Perennials of an eternal year,
Blossomed and shed their fragrance in his soul,—
And ere beheld on earth, did garden heaven!
There is in nature nothing mean or base,
But only as our baseness thinks it so,
Making that common by the touch and sight,
Which, if as distant as the stars, would seem
As sacred and as marvellous as they.
O ye innumerous, to whom Heaven is pure
Because the high invisible domain

Of angels, and to mortals difficult!
Should your permitted feet but touch its floor
Of purest gold inlaid with lustrous gems,
'Twould turn to base and earthly mould, and all
Its towers of gold and amethyst would seem
Like a fantastic building in the air
Of clouds and sunlight; Know! that in this green,
Living, and voiceful, and all-glorious earth—
Whose dawn of unperfected beauty filled
The soul of God with passion, that called forth
His acclamation, amidst angel-shouts
Responsive, and antiphonies of Stars—
He that has ear and vision and can find
Of heaven naught, will find but earth in heaven.

Thus far with Nature has my spirit been,
Not doubtful of her teachings, and, unawed
Save by the spirit that inspires me, sung
Above all temples built by human hands,
Maker! thy six-days' work. And can it be
That I, who as I enter now, in thought,
At the low portals of thy house, with head
Bowed lowly and obedient steps, and hear,
Awe-struck, these mortal voices sing thy praise,
Am he, whose soul, making the winds its voice,
Entered the storm and sung it in thine ear,
And bade the harping choir of heaven be mute!—
That I who feel a clinging awe descend
From this dark roof, and dim, low-pillared aisle,
And to my knees persuade me, am the same
Who clad myself with nature, yea, put on
Her glory like a vestment, and with thought
Illimitable pervaded all her frame,
And in the earth and heavens clothed, stood up
And worshipped,—now naked, and with shame of soul
Afflicted, fear, and consciousness of guilt!
Is this thy dwelling, Lord! this dark, low roof
Thine earthly house? The place is like a tomb,

And like a tomb shuts out the earth and sun.
Yet Thou!—Sun without night, and unobscured,
And unobstructed by material forms,—
Thy glory fills the place!—I feel Thee here;
These are thy courts. The place is like a tomb,
But as our bodies to the tomb descend
Ere re-ascending, purged from mortal dross,
They pale the light of that last earthly day,
And with like difference, as of different stars,
Reflect thy glory, so the soul that hence
Goes purged by death and sepulture with Christ,
More bright reflects thine image in thy works.

Lord! thou art here, and fearful is the place!
This lowly roof, and these strict walls with awe
O'erwhelm me;—this darkness that shuts out the sky
Like the o'ershadowing of thy wings I feel,
And this envir'nment, that excludes the earth,
Like thy surrounding arm. I feel thee here;
And they who see thee not in all thy works,
Nor in themselves discern, but mountains climb
And scale the stars to find thee, deemed remote,
Here, doubted not, because no longer sought,
Feel thee in awfulness unspeakable descend.

ODE TO ENGLAND

Oh! England, England! shall it ever be
  That I, whose thoughts have daily pilgrims been
  To thy old-storied fanes, and fields of green,
The nurseries of sweet thoughts, and fancies free,
  Shall see, in other than the light,
    The shaping beam of trance and sleep,
  That from within informs the sight,
    Thy white cliffs rising from the deep?
Land of the blessing!—of the nations blest,

And blest with benediction from above;
Land of my fathers!—where their ashes rest,—
  The mother of my years—but daughter of my love!—
Like the sick yearnings of a child for home,
  Such is my longing to behold thy shore—
For fair as that fair isle, that through the foam
  To cradle the twin-gods its summit bore,
When to my dreaming eyes the visions come,
  Thou, Albion! risest from thine ocean frore.

Oh! might I see those white cliffs rise,
  Those storied fanes, those fields of green,—
    Although my head the snow
    Of wintry life might show,
And in my dim and fading eyes
  The sunset of the soul be seen;—
    Though quenched the lover's fire,
    And mute the poet's lyre,
That moment would revive in me,
    Like the phenix from her pyre,
    The youth that was a long desire
That moment's self to see:
And so my kindling eyes would beam
  With light of days whose suns have fled,
That Spring her first white flowers might deem
  The winter's snow upon my head;
And I unto myself should seem
    Immortal as the dead!
It is not, England! that the day and night
  Thy empire, in their equal reign, divide,—
It is not that the world's embattled might
  Quails at thy steadfast eye of pride,—
It is not, Island-daughter of the sea!
  Mother of navies! that, self-deified,
Thou, proud to reign where all by right is free,
  Dost grasp the trident in the realm of storms!—
  Nor is it, England, that the blood that warms
The heart within me had its source in thee,

Nor that my country brings her birth-right thence;
But thou my soul hast peopled with bright forms!
And vision hast bestowed those forms to see,—
Beings, whose presence makes its earth of sense
A heaven of thought and thought-created things,—
Conceptions, memories, imaginings,
High fancies, dreams, and god-like shapes, that dwell
In such complexity of being, there,
So equal-beauteous, that I scarce can tell
Them that created from their creatures fair.
Beings, that in my being make
A change to likeness with their own;
Yea, even in sleep with them I wake,
In solitude am not alone,—
Till through their sweet communion,
In still increasing union,
I seem to share in their diviner life;
And free from the perpetual strife
Of that which is, with that which seems to be,
I doubt no more; enough for me
That what the heart would have to be,
Though what the eye may never see,
    The heart may surely know:
And hence it fears not lest it love
Or in the Earth or Heaven above,
    What Earth nor Heaven can show.

How oft the first-born poet of thy soil
Comes with his antique rhyme and pilgrim's stole,
To charm my weary heart from thoughts of toil,—
Sweet Chaucer! that makes morning in the soul,
And floods with silver light its firmament,
From clouds, like rubious beakers, lipped with gold:
Then, while the heart feeds on the dewy scent
Of new-waked flowers, sings the poet old
    Tales as the breath of April sweet,
        And fresh in their antiquity;
        Or, with 'difference discreet,'

Chaunts his pious legendry,
That at its warbled melody, the notes
Of listening birds die noiseless in their throats,—
The winds in eager silence swoon around,
And all the green leaves tremble without sound.

And, Spenser, like the sunset sky when bright
With golden isles, and silent seas of light,
  That spread along the shore-like blue,
Laving some snow-piled mountain hoary,
  Or stretching far, then lost to view
Behind some cloud-cliffed promontory,—
  While spires and battlements that rise,
  And baseless turrets in the skies,
  And silver swans and dragons there
  Suspended in the enchanted air,
    With half-believing eyes I see—
    Great Edmund! when thine inward glory
    Lights up the cloudy allegory!
    Such my soul is made by thee.

    Milton! with thee it is the sky
      Of naked blue, through which the sun,
    In cloud-compelling majesty,
      And steady splendor, journeys on;
    While from his disk the sunbeams rain
      So thick upon the upward eye,
    That scarce his brightness, without pain,
      Suffers weak mortality!

Shakspeare! with thee it is the sky of stars
  Innumerable!—the lordly Jupiter
Now fills the sight—now red and dusky Mars,
  And now sweet Venus charms the eye to her;
And now the virgin Moon shines out,—
  As she, so pure her look divine,
  In heaven's fountain crystalline
Had bathed her limbs,—and looks about

Upon the fading fires above;—
The while, upon the earth below
The streams her trembling image show;
And from the darkness break, like smiles,
Daisied banks and leafy piles
  Of silver umbrage, field and grove:—
And 'sweetest Shakspeare!' by that name
If one may call thee without shame,
Whose tongue, to praise, must do thee wrong,
So much thy praise exceeds his song,—
'Sweet Swan of Avon!' on the tide
  Thou dost move thy mates among,
Though moving all with conscious pride,
  As when in heaven the ample moon
  Coasting the clouds at night's clear noon,
Through all the trembly region wide,
The stars look wan and guilty-eyed
  Before her gentle aspect clear;
    And all the brightest pale their hue,
Even they that seemed more bright than she,—
Till Dian moves without a peer,
  Sailing in a silver sea,
    Across a sea of blue.

Nor yet do these alone,—nor of their time
  Others less great, but into utterance blest
By the auspicious genius of thy clime,
  Though chief, and of my earlier love possessed,—
But *others,* in the peopled solitude,
  The vocal quiet of my heart—
Where neither sounds nor shapes intrude,
  Nor feelings sway, nor thoughts have part,
  Except of beauty and of love,—
  Dwell glorified,—as dwell above,
  Freed from low care and all distractions rude,
  Their conscious spirits in beatitude;
  And deathless in my soul as there,
Though elsewhere perished, they should still survive,

With me the gift of being share,
And in my life, made twice immortal, live.

Oh gold Hyperion, love-lorn Porphyro,
 Ill-fated! from thine orbed fire struck back
Just as the parting clouds began to glow,
 And stars, like sparks, to bicker in thy track!
Alas! throw down, throw down, ye mighty dead,
 The leaves of oak and asphodel
That ye were weaving for that honored head,—
 In vain, in vain, your lips would seek a spell
In the few charmed words the poet sung,
 To lure him upward in your seats to dwell,—
As vain your grief! Oh! why should one so young
 Sit crowned midst hoary heads with wreaths divine?
Though to his lips Hymettus' bees had clung,
 His lips shall never taste the immortal wine,
Who sought to drain the glowing cup too soon,
For he hath perished, and the moon
Hath lost Endymion—but too well
 The shaft that pierced him in her arms was sped:—
 Into that gulf of dark and nameless dread,
 Star-like he fell, but a wide splendor shed
Through its deep night, that kindled as he fell.

Thou too hast gone, though crowned with silver age,
 Oh, master of the sad and fitful lyre!—
Thou deepest reader of the mystic page,—
 Thou whose pure spirit madest the attire
Of thy most common life a vestment bright;
 Like to the sun, that in his own bright rays
Is always clothed,—or saints, in raiment dight,
 Self-woven of the spirit's effluent light,
That floats around them like a luminous haze:—
 Thou too departedst, while yet incomplete
Thine orb of glory, like the moon
 That, while 'tis but a crescent yet,
 Within her bended arms doth show,

As if she clasped Endymion,
　　An unenlightened orb, whose rim,
　　Though seen but like a vapor dim,
　　Marks a full circle for the spreading glow;—
Yet it hath risen, ne'er to set again.
What though thou didst not urge nor heed the rein
　　　The winged steeds obeyed;—
　　They heeded not the shout nor thong
　　With which the envy-frighted throng
　　Sought to stay them in their course;—
Apollo's gift,—they knew thy song,
　　　And with ethereal force,
　　　In swift and errant course,
Upward they bore thee to the empyrean;—
　　　There mounted, ne'er to stoop again,
　　　They, albeit with inward pain,
　　Who thought to sing thy dirge, must sing thy Pæan!

　　Still mourn for Orpheus; mourn for him whose strain,
Too early mute, had well nigh charmed again
　　Into our cold, degenerate time
　　　The lost Eurydice, that dwelt,
　　　And still by simple hearts is felt,
　　In the antique and deftly-structured rhyme:
Mourn for our Orpheus! What though Heaven finds
　　What earth has lost, 'tis lost to earth no less:
Wail from your thousand, thousand harps, ye Winds!
　　Ye Fields, put on a look of wilderness!
　　　For nature mourns a poet dead,
　　　And men a mighty genius fled,
　　Who sought in golden chains to lead
　　Science with reverence, liberty with law,
　　And free the universal creed
　　　From old idolatries of fear and awe.
Oh! for a poet that a poet's knell
　　Might ring, like him who youthful Adon's rang;—
　　Then with such loud and piercing clang
Of musical vibrations, he should swell

The sound of sorrow, till it fell
  Even on the cold and sullen ear of death,
    And him enforced, whose famine fed,
    Half soothed, on his melodious breath,
      Repenting to give back the dead.

And Thou! whom earth still holds, and will not yield
  To join the mighty brotherhood of ghosts,—
Who, when their lips upon the earth are sealed,
  Sing in the presence of the Lord of Hosts:—
Thou that, when first my quickened ear
Thy deeper harmonies might hear,
I imaged to myself as old and blind,
  For so were Milton and Mæonides!
And worthy art thou—whether like the wind
  Rousing its might among the forest trees,
  Thou sing of mountain and of flood,
    The voiceful thunder of the seas,
    With all their inland symphonies,
      Their thousand brooks and rills,—
  The vale's deep voice, the roaring wood,
    The ancient silence of the hills,
    Sublimer still than these;—
Or in devotion's loftier mood,
  Like a solemn organ tone
  In some vast minster heard alone,
  Feelings that are thoughts inspire;—
  Or, with thy hand upon the lyre
High victories to celebrate,
  Summon from its strings the throng
Of stately numbers intricate
  That swell the impetuous tide of song.
O Bard, of soul assured and high,
  And god-like calm! we look on thee
With like serene and awful eye,
  As when,—of such divinity
Still credulous,—the multitude
  One in the concourse might behold,

Whose statue in his life-time stood
  Among the gods. O Poet, old
    In all the years of future time!
But young in the perpetual youth
And bloom of love, and might of truth,—
  To these thy least ambitious rhyme
    Is faithful, and partakes their worth;
  Yea, true as is the starry chime
    To the great strains the sun gives forth;—
Bard of our Time! thy name we see,
By golden-haired Mnemosyne,
First graved upon its full-writ page,—
Thee—last relinquished, whom the Age
  Doth yield to Immortality.

England! as with Italia, so with thee,
  Thy subject lands shall cease to own thy sway,
The pomp and vast dominion of the sea
  From thine unsceptered hand shall pass away;
Still thou shalt reign—nor *thee* shall loss of these
Ensepulchre with earth's dead sovereignties:
Not these thine empire, but the human soul,
And they thy kings, thy nobles, who control
In that dread realm, where bend no servile knees,
Its hopes, its passions, joys and sympathies,—
No armed host, no thunder-bearing fleet,
Can bring such homage to thy kingly feet;
Lords of the Reason! Monarchs of the Will!
  None from their golden empery would be free:—
Through them e'en young Atlantis yields thee still
  Spiritual homage and heart-loyalty.
These reign, and still shall reign in every clime,
  Where thoughtful hearts and gentle natures be,
Live with the life of Time, and dying Time
  Their names shall whisper to Eternity.

HYMN TO NIAGARA

PROCLAIM, my soul, where thou,—though not unused
To high communion with the powers that hold
The secrets of the ocean, and the earth,
And the blue fields of air,—hast nearest been
To the Invisible, and thyself *most* felt,
Thine earthly garment, *least*. Niagara!
At thy base, uplooking through the cloud
That in its depths of vapor shrouds thy feet,—
There, where the mighty river in mid-stream
Plunges beneath, as if to seek the heart
That sent it forth,—the heart of earth and sea!

Proclaim, my soul, proclaim it to the sky!
And tell the stars, and tell the hills, whose feet
Are in the depths of earth, their peaks in heaven,
And tell the Ocean's old familiar face,
Beheld by day and night, in calm and storm,—
That they, nor aught beside in earth or heaven,
Like thee, tremendous torrent, have so filled
Its thought of beauty, and so awed with might.

Niagara! from thy heights above, when first,
Half fearful, my expectant eyes beheld
Thy inland sea, with its embosomed isles,
Far-stretching and commingling with the sky,—
And nearer, its swift lapse and whitening speed,
And the green slide of waters, that around
The abyss, and 'round the rising clouds,
Which heaven with rainbows painted as they rose,
Stretched, sky-like, in a broad and whelming curve;—
Not then did I behold thee,—and I felt
Even in that moment that I saw thee not!
But still without the veil, before the shrine—
The home of an eternal splendor—stood,
And of thy glory but beheld the skirts.

But when I heard thy thunder from above,
And knew myself within thy misty shroud,
And felt thee in the earth beneath, I looked
Then to behold thee, and that moment broke
Upon my soul a sight unspeakable!
As if I had beheld God face to face.

And then I only felt a rush, a weight
Of waters, a blind sense of power that crushed,
Confounded, and o'erwhelmed me. Like a soul
All bodiless and naked suddenly
Launched forth into another world, before
It had adapted to itself the forms
Strange to its faculties—so did I grasp,
So struggle for my half-lost consciousness.
Chaos was come again.

                    But soon, as rose
The first creation, built upon the form
Of that divine idea whose beauty took
The soul of chaos prisoner, and to law
Subdued his tumult,—so from that dread swoon
When first again my soul drew conscious breath,
Oh! thou didst rise before me, and above,
Majestical, harmonious as heaven,
Unutterably beautiful! Thy voice
I heard like my heart's whisper to itself,—
And not distinguished from my soul, thy form,—
A feeling and a vision, and at once
With inward and external sight beheld:
And thee and God alone I saw and felt;—
Earth, heaven, and all things vanished, but alone
One central stay, and all-pervading soul
Of love, and beauty, and eternal calm,
In which I rested, as upon the heart
Of universal life, and in its depths
Breathed immortality.

From that deep trance
At length my soul awaked,—waked not again
To be oppressed, o'ermastered, and engulphed,
And in the tempest's blind delirium lost,—
Confounded beyond knowledge of itself,—
But of itself possessed, o'er all without
Felt conscious mastery! nor feared adown
The steady column whose perpetual shock
Makes there the thunder of the heavens mute,
To send its thought into thy yawning gulf,
By mists forever mantled from the sight,—
Nor with thy storm to tumult, nor to rise
In thy ascending cloud to heaven.

And then
Retired within, and self-withdrawn, I stood
The two-fold centre and informing soul
Of one vast harmony of sights and sounds:
And from that deep abyss, that rock-built shrine,
Though mute my own frail voice, I poured a hymn
"Of praise and gratulation," like the noise
Of banded angels when they shout to wake
Empyreal echoes.

In myself so strong
And calm, and yet beyond myself so rapt,
I stood, and made that glorious that me
More highly glorified, and to that height
To which its power had uplifted me,
Itself, in praise, exalted. And my cheek
Was wet with tears unwept by that white cloud,
And joy was in my heart, as of a god
At birth of a new world. And earth and sky
Came back and blended with my thought.

So high,
So glorious never seemed the sky:—till then
I never felt the earth itself to be

An awful presence. The stern rocks around,
From whose high-piled and adamantine fronts
Ages have fallen like shadows, without power
To crumble or deface them,—they to me
Seemed as if conscious that they were the shrine
Of God's peculiar presence, in the cloud
And bow beheld, as in the cloud that dwelt
Between the cherubim within those walls
Built for His glory by the hands of men,
As this unpillared temple by His own.

  Eternal symbol of a higher power
And greater beauty than makes earth its home!
Bride of my soul! Oh, thou art not to me
A thing seen only in the fitful light,
And by the weak and oft relaxing grasp
Of memory held,—but like the earth and sea
And all-involving heaven, with the thought
Itself of Being present as its forms;—
So thou art with me; and when these shall fail,
And earth, and sea, and sky have passed away,
And here thy voice is silent, and these rocks,
Unyielding but to thee, have worn through time
Into eternity, and at its touch
Have crumbled and fallen,—Oh, give me then,
Although of heaven's bright habiliments,
Haply than thine more gorgeous, disarrayed,
Give me thy sea-green robe, and these white mists,
These veiling glories painted by the sun,
Give me thy thunder!—and amongst the throng
Of loftiest Archangels let me move
Nearer the cloudy throne, and in His ear
Who gave to thee thy terror, and thy joy,
Thy dreadful beauty and resistless might,
Forever and forever utter praise.

THE SKY

Whoso a wondrous sight would see,—
  Sight perchance thou ne'er hast seen—
Come, and on the sky with me
  Upward look; and let no tree,
No spire, nor hill-top intervene
  To check the thought, that clear and free
Should seek the cope—forgetting e'en
  The distant hills, on which to thee
The bending heavens did seem to lean.

Still upward look,—no sun in view
  Quells with his fiercer gaze the sight;
But, spread through all the spreading blue,
  Quenched and diffused, a sky more bright,
A softer light, hue blent with hue,
  Seems that which late a dazzling night
Of sight-beclouding brightness threw
  From one fierce eye of central light:—
Look upward still;—yon cloud of white,
  A vapor of the purest dew,
That to the azure's utmost height
  Seemed close as if thereon it grew,
Heaven lifts and spreads beyond it quite,
  In grandeur to thy vision new.

Thou hast seen Ocean, in the hour
  When whirlwinds rouse its sluggish might
To wrestle with their viewless power;—
  And more, hast felt, too vast for sight,
How far it stretched beyond the lower
  Of that rude storm and scowling night
In which the headlands seemed to cower,
  Into calm realms and tranquil light.
But what was that to yon blue sea,
  Yon steadfast ocean, spreading o'er

Both sea and land, vast, bright and free,
  Without a sound, or wave, or shore,
    There stretching everlastingly.
And thou on mountain heights hast been
  With heights above, that skyward rear
Their snowy summits, clear and keen,
  Through clouds that in the calmest mood
Of heaven, like the wings of Fear,
  Restless and dark, the tempest brood,
—Ice-rifted summits, keen and clear,
  Not even by weeping night bedewed;—
    Lifted above the changing year,
Naked of flower, or stream, or wood,
  Or scantiest moss—so high that there
Not even the eagle tears his food:
  So high, it seems in that still air
As they, while earth's lone watch they keep,
  Could list each heavenly marinére
That singing stems the azure deep,
  And circling his predestined sphere,
With us around the sun doth sweep;
  And aye in that still solitude,
So high above the stormy jars
  Of Earth and Ocean's voices rude,
Might hear faint whispers from the stars
  That stand in stirless multitude:
—But what was that, to Heaven's blue floor,
  Earth's skiey roof, air's steadfast sea,
That lifts and spreads, and evermore
  Doth spread and lift in majesty
Unseen, unheard, undreamed before—
  And *is*, as now it seems to be,
As high those towering mountains o'er,
  And stretched alike o'er them, as thee!

Thou hast no words, nor could be found
  Words to express that boundless sky,
Though thou the thought of Demons owned,

And given to speak the vision by
A voice like wakeful Ocean's sound
  Or Wind's eternal harmony:—
All sound hath measure, and each tone
  Is linked in thought to things that die:
In the unfathomed depth alone
  And power of silence doth it lie
To speak the sight, that to thine eye,
  (To eye or thought before unknown,
Or known but as Divinity,)
  Seems, as it spreads, vast, boundless, one,—
The shadow of Infinity
  Over the trembling finite thrown.

It lifts, it spreads no more,—but lo!
  'Tis thine own thought, that wondrous thought,—
The thought of which we nothing know,
  But know we cannot deem it nought:
As reeds that ever to and fro
  Wave and whisper, still untaught
The mystery of the winds that blow,—
  Or river-lilies that are caught
In every stir of waves below,
  Yet know not of their motion aught,
And list and list their endless flow,
  But know not whence their stream is brought,
Or why they ever murmur so;—
  It is the thought of *Being*—nay,
'Tis *Being's* self that fills thy gaze;
  And thought, which is a conscious ray
In being's omnipresent blaze,
  Beams back upon the source of day:—
And lost all sense of nights and days,
  (Shadows of *that* and glimpses they)
And form and motion's endless maze,—
  Feels that *to be*, is still *to be*,
And there as on its centre stays;
  And, time and self forgot, doth see

In that blue sea of boundless haze
  A visible Eternity.

Ay, close thine eyes, and from the whole,
  Seek thy lost being to regain,—
Close them, and the wearied soul
  Shut back upon itself again;—
For never hath thy thought before
  Into the soul of Being past;
To life might be revealed no more
  With life, it might no longer last.
Thy sight returns,—and shadows gray
  Fall from the brooding wings of even,
But where that sky stretched wide as day,
  And high as is the thought of heaven,
Even with thy turning eyes it rushed
  Back on the hills and closed around,
Just as the world's first murmur gushed
  Back on thine ear awaked to sound:
'Tis the same sky thy childhood saw
  When heaven did lie above the blue,
And thou beheldst it half in awe;
  For aye his searching eye looked through.
And see, the Angel of the night
  Stands glittering on yon hill,—but why
Gleams his pale eye so strangely bright,
  Then trembles back into the sky?
It conscious looks and jealous seems
  Of secrets seen in day's clear deep,
More wondrous than the thousand gleams
  He heralds on yon dusky steep:—
And thou, in vision past revealing,
  Hast seen without a sense of seeing,
And felt without a thought of feeling,
  The power, the mystery of Being.

TO A DEAF MUTE

On seeing a Song interpreted to her by Signs

Poor Girl! I said, hapless thy fate, to whom
Forever silent is the voice of song;
To whom the viol sings not, nor the sweet soul
Imprisoned in the flute:—to whom we all,
As thou to us, are deaf, and still, and mute,
And even nature moves in a dumb show.
Yet why to thee may not the effect of sound,
Which is the soul of motion, and hence thought,
With high constraint of harmony to move
The throng of worlds symphonious to the sun,—
(And who within himself has never felt
The power of sound control him by this law
To cadent movement of the hand or foot,
Or stirred by swifter impulse, to enact
Its promptings intricate?) why may not the effect
Of sounds melodious be felt by thee
In *motion,* if that sound itself be naught
But motion given to a subtler sense?
If this may be,—and pity for thy state,
Though with less proof, might make me think it so,—
Then, may this dumb discourse to thee be song,
Our looks be music, and a soothing sign
Or glance affectionate, a sweet-spoken tone,—
To thee, the rising sun be a great strain
Majestical, and his departing pomp
An anthem like the evening psalm of heaven,
Sung by responsive choirs angelical
To harp and trumpet,—and the rising moon
May be, what almost it has seemed to me,
A prelude soft to the full hymn which Night
Pours forth with the appearing stars, that fill
The trembling heaven with innumerous sounds—
The streams to thee be music, as to us,

The birds in their winged flight be harmonies,
The tyrannous winds, that rock the earth-fast wood
Beneath its perilous weight of swinging boughs,
Sing thee a song of might; or when from sleep
They rouse with slight continuous stir that sets
The leaves a-tremble, and along the fields
Steal whisperingly, and move the seas of grain
Into slight silvery waves, may seem a tune,
Like those we chaunt in snatches to ourselves,—
A song made in the silent soul, and sung
To the unuttered music of its own sweet thoughts.[1]

ODE

ON THE PRESENT CRISIS

MY COUNTRY! never to that hallowed name
    My soul refused the tribute of deep love;
    Though not to thee the Academic grove,
Nor on thy hills the temples, nor the fame
    Of haunted spring and grot, and hill-tops blest
    With feet of wandering god or angel-guest,
That with high memories fed devotion's flame
    To steadfast brightness in the Locrians' breast;
        Though not to thee the lyre
    That with the theft of sweet and potent strains
    From heaven for a nation gains
        Promethean fire,
    And makes a people conscious of itself;—
Though thee, I saw, no eagle that in flight
Looks with fixed eye against the arrowy light,
    But like a Gryphon over glittering pelf,
        Against the Arimaspian set;—
    Saw vaunted freedom stalk in chains,

And bondsmen toiling on the plains
　　With freemen's life-blood wet,—
Yet, O my country, on whose wooded hills
　　The earth first gave its beauty to my eye,
My ear first heard the music of its rills,
　　My soul received the vision of the sky,—
　　Thy blue and wood-embosomed lakes
In which the sky and headlands sleep,
　　The river's avalanche that breaks,
Far-thundering, from the steep,
　　Thy thousand "headlong streams" which pour
Stern and solemn strains, that make
　　Our inland valley's ocean-roar,—
　　The earth's perpetual thunder bland,—
A sound, as from its craggy caverns deep,
　　Forever to its children spake
　　The voices of the Father land;—
The woods where oft my feet have strayed,
Dim forests vast with memories haunted
Of old heroic tribes that chaunted
　　Their death songs in the shade,—
　　My boyhood's memories of the past,
　　That more exalted than a blast
　　Of trumpets from a pageant gay
　　Of marching men,—the ancient day,
　　The pilgrims in the wood and glen,
　　The Council speech, the midnight fray,
　　The death-yells of the dark red men,—
The time when men for Freedom spoke
Great words like thunder, and like lightning broke
Their deeds refulgent,—Oh my native land!
For these I loved thee, nor too closely scanned
　　Thy deeds, nor with suspicious eye;
And reddened more with pride than shame
To hear the injurious scoffs that came
　　From the lie-faltering lips of tyranny;—
And soon I said for sacred truths avowed,
And ancient oaths to freedom sworn aloud,

Soon from her shameful sleep awaking,
Regifted with her early strength divine,
   They shall behold her each link'd fetter breaking
Like fire-touched flax, or threads of silken twine:—
As when a giant for a moment bowed
   To earth by sleep, or by the might
      Of god-controlling wine,
While scoffs around the base, detracting crowd,
   Instant, among them, at his perfect height,
   Stands godlike-fair and terrible in sight.

For still I deemed thee guiltless in intent,
   Though oft my soul for violated law,
And needless favor to oppression lent,
   Mourned silently—nor less for the dark tribes
From their old graves and shattered forests sent—
   Yet ever against foreign tyrants saw
Thy threatening bow in Pythian anger bent;
   But when I saw thee drink the cup of bribes,
And drain the poisoned draught with eager lips,
   Proffered by lustful slaves of power and gain—
Then first I saw thy brightness in eclipse,
   Then first my heart like death pangs felt its pain!
With quickened ear my boding spirit then
Heard the deep wailing of unnumbered men—
   A groan—as from their graves in all the earth
Who fell for freedom, and a low
Deep utterance of Nature for the woe,
The unrepented wrongs, without relief,
   Of them, who for their sorrows, from their birth
She habits in the sable hue of grief.

Then long my spirit, hushed within the lair
Of silence, listened for a voice to speak,
   And with that Ancient Word of truth and might
Make a deep thunder of the noiseless air:
From grey New-England's hill-tops bleak,
   Where in the furrow, hastening to the fight,

The plumeless hero left the plough and steer—
From the free spirit of the mountaineer,
From green Vermont, from Holyoke's wintry peak,
  Listened my soul the mighty voice to hear;—
  Until—for Freedom—with the pain
  Of that deep silence anguished long,
  Fired to the utterance of her strain,
I seized my harp and poured the impetuous song:

    Sons of the Sons of Might!
      Who sleep beneath the soil,
    Who fell for Freedom in the fight—
      For Freedom lived to toil—
Speak Brothers! shall a race of slaves
Leave our foot prints on their graves?
Shall we whose souls unawed and free
  Upon our bleak and storm swept hills
  With pathless winds, by winding rills,
From youth have walked with Liberty,
Here in her birth-place, in the wintry North,
  Crouch, and speak with stinted breath
  The name for which our fathers bled?
Freedom! Ho, shout it to the mountains forth!
  Speak Freemen! though to speak were death,
  Speak! or you shame the dead.

I KNOW AN ISLE

I KNOW an isle, an island fair and pleasant,
  A fairer than this island never blossomed in the sea;
And ever to my eye is that green island present,
  Ever present as a thing in clearest sight might be,
With its flowers, with its rills, with its clear and living
    fountain;
O ne'er so fair as this, did sea-embosomed mountain
  Flower in its island-top above the sapphire sea.

And with the wind my spirit round it, round it hovers,
  With the wind that dare not touch it for its beauty,
And we sigh evermore, and evermore like lovers,
    And my spirit dare not touch it, for the sacred spell
      of duty—
Though it hovers near and nearer and around that
     island sweet,
For its awe of holy breathings, dare not touch it with
    its feet,
  And the wind it dare not touch it for its beauty.

For if my spirit stoop to touch it with its feet,
  Rise solemn voices with sighs and plaining,
And they shriek beware! and my ears with threaten-
    ings greet,
  With the words beware, beware, my affrighted
    spirit paining:
Touch that island say these voices—voices sad, dis-
    consolate,
And lo an island-desert, a desert black and desolate;
  Thus shriek the voices, and disturb my soul with
    plaining.

So with the wind my spirit round it, round it hovers,
  Swinging in the wind and still clinging to the shore,
And we sigh evermore, and evermore like lovers,
    Though my spirit it may touch it with its feet never-
     more,
Or in the sea below if it seek the isle to lave,
'Tis withheld by the spell that works in wind and
     wave;
  Only sometimes with its strivings it throws pearls
    upon the shore.

THE NEW CASTALIA

On the old and haunted mountain,
(There in dreams I dare to climb,)
Where the clear Castalian fountain,—
(Silver fountain,)—ever tinkling,
All the green around it sprinkling,
    Makes perpetual rhyme,—
To my dream, enchanted, golden,
Came a vision of the olden
    Long-forgotten time.
In the dream-light sitting there,
    Under dim and whispering trees,
I saw the ever young and fair,
    (Such as one in pictures sees,)
Palm-crowned, ever lovely Maids
That weave imperishable braids
For those sweet lutanists to wear,
Whose music keeps *them* young and fair,—
    Ever fair and ever young,
(Such as one in pictures sees,)
Palm-crowned, young Parnassides!
    And ever as the maidens sung,
At each swooning, swooning fall,
Through the air all musical
    Thousand, thousand echoes rung—
    And the silver fountain flung
Its waters upward, ever tinkling,
All the green around it sprinkling;
    And forever as they sung,
At each louder, louder swell,
To the ground the green leaves fell,
    Fell the leaves, and new leaves sprung;—
In that tempest musical
    Fell the leaves, and ebbed the fountain,
    And the echoes from the mountain—
Thousand echoes answered all.

Changed the scene while I was gazing,
And in soul this music praising;
And my eye with wonder dazing,
And my soul with fear amazing,
   Into cypress changed the wood,
   And the fountain into blood,
While the Maids their dolorous lays sing.

And within the pool lay drifting
Shapes and shadows ever shifting,
Ever shifting, ever lifting,
Like bats and vampyres upon swift wing,
   Struggling in the air to rise
   From a serpent-coil that ties
Their talons, twining, wreathing, twisting.

And the maidens there a-sitting
Changed to withered beldames knitting,
Adder's tongue and knot-grass, fitting
Wreaths for Bards our souls affrighting
   With stone-eyed phantoms of the dark,
   Moon-eclipse, and spectre-bark,
Nightmares, ghosts, and ravens flitting,
Whispering, gibbering, croaking, screaming,
O'er a place with phantoms teeming,
Vasty phantoms! staring, dreaming,
Never known in sight or seeming,
Moonlight from their garments streaming,
   With the look, and with the moan
   Of dead men on the sea alone,
Their frozen eyes with ghost-light gleaming.

And the stream flowed lapping, lapping,
And the leaves stirred tapping, tapping,
And the aged beldames napping,
Dreamed of gently rapping, rapping,
With a hammer gently tapping,
   Tapping on an infant's skull,

And of white throats sweetly jagged,
With a ragged butch-knife dull,
And of night-mares neighing, weighing,
On a sleeper's bosom squatting.

Then a pallid beauteous maiden,
Golden ghastly robes arrayed in,
Her dreamy soul thought-freighted, laden,
Such a wondrous strain displayed in,
   In a wondrous song of Aidenne,
      That all the gods and goddesses
      Shook their golden, yellow tresses,
Parnassus' self made half-affrayed in.

For as the wondrous song she sung,
With a subtle solemn tongue,
Like a pall above them hung,
Seemed the heavens fresh and young;
And the trees their shadows flung
   Like long-stretched ghosts upon their graves,
   Or trembled in the stagnant waves,
To see their pale shapes midway hung.

Mournful yew her forehead bound,
That never smiled nor ever frowned,
And ever at her footfall's sound,
Music rose with solemn stound;
   Like a moaning in the ground,
   Ran the strains beneath her tread,—
   Or, like anthems for the dead,
Crashing upward and around.
The green-clad mountain, forest-crowned,
Seemed a gray and ghastly mound,
Sprites and angels swarmed around,
Vapors had a soul and sound,
Men their ghosts by daylight found,
Flowers seemed blood-spots on the ground.
   The rose a bleeding heart did stand,

The white rose reared a corpse-like hand,
And earth and heaven seemed in a swound.

THE WIDOW'S COMPLAINT

O WHAT is this world to me?
  Sad, lone, and bereft,—
O what is this world to me,
  But the world he has left!

O what the green earth to me,
  And what are the skies,
But the skies o'er his grave,
  But the earth where he lies?

And what are these children
  I once thought my own,
What now do they seem,
  But his orphans alone?

And what is their beauty?
  In their kirk-clothes so brave,
Of what do they mind me
  But flowers on his grave!

A DIRGE

IT falls to one, it falls to all!
He that we bear but goes before,—
Goes from his door beneath the pall,
  And comes no more.

From roof and hearth-stone, one by one,
We bear the neighbors whom we love,—
The bearers are the borne full soon;
  Ah! softly move.

And shrink not from the harmless dead,
For ye hasten to their company;
Loathe not, for in the same low bed
    We all must lie.

SONG OF A DYING MAID

OH why will ye make my bed my bier,
Why make this place my grave to be,
With the tears ye weep, and the looks of fear,
The deathly looks that ye bend on me?

Bring, bring me flowers, fresh and sweet,
For O on my breast I feel the heap,
And I feel the stones at my head and feet,
With such deathly look ye stand and weep.

Weep, and let the bell be tolled,
When no breath the glass shall stain,
But let them not my face behold,
When that I cannot look again.

To the grassy yard I go, where tears
Do water all the flowers that grow;
I go, I haste,—O cease your fears,—
Green is the land to which I go.

Dig my grave, where the church-yard spire
Each day may throw its shade on me;
Plant my grave with the bloomless brier,
To show that I died a maiden free.

But now, of childhood speak, and spring,
Give me thoughts that are sweet as its flowers,
The songs that I loved O sweetly sing!
Give me thoughts of the pleasant hours.

TO CHILDREN

BRIGHT things, blest things, to look on you,
   Eyes that are in their wane
Grow bright, and hearts at ebb of age
   Fill with life's tide again.

And you, not age nor death should touch,
   If human love might save;
But stronger is the love that blights,
   And gathers to the grave.

We know that you the angels love,—
   They love all gentle things—
And often o'er you fondly stoop,
   And spread their viewless wings.

And tenderly their starry eyes
   Watch you by night and day,
And sweetly as they smile on you,
   So you on us alway.

And O, should he who smiles on all,
   And loves both young and old,
Should the dear Shepherd take his lambs,
   And bear them to his fold,—

Should he who gave these buds of love,
   Who gives, and maketh lorn,
Leave us like withered stems till eve,
   And take them in the morn;

We still, O God, would trust his love
   Who once in form like them,
Slept on a woman's yearning breast,
   A babe in Bethlehem.

Who hope hath given to death, as dawn
    To thickest dark he gave,
And caused that still the new year's flowers
    Grow on the old year's grave.

TO MY SISTER

On her expressing an anticipation that we who had
been so long and widely separated in this life
should meet in Heaven.

I.

AND shall we meet in heaven, and know and love?
Do human feelings in that world above
Unchanged survive? blest thought! but ah, I fear
That thou, dear sister, in some other sphere,
Distant from mine, will find a brighter home,
Where I, unworthy found, may never come;—
Or be so high above me glorified,
That I, a meaner angel, undescribed,
Seeking thine eyes, such love alone shall see
As angels give to all bestowed on me;
And when my voice upon thy ear shall fall,
Hear only such reply as angels give to all.

II.

Forgive me, sister, O forgive the love
Whose selfishness would reach the life above,
And even in heaven do its object wrong—
But should I see thee in the heavenly throng,
Bright as the star I love—the night's first star,
If, like that star, thou still must shine afar,
And in thy glory I must never see
A woman's, sister's look of love from thee,—
Must never call thee by a sister's name,

I could but wish thee less, if thus, the same,
My sister still, dear Sarah! thou might'st be,
And I thy brother still, in that blest company.

MAGIAN HYMN

O First, and of all living things the Life,
Of all that is, the Being, and the Power
Of all that acts,—O Fire! and thou, O Light,
That art of fire the garment; and the form,
Knowledge and consciousness of all, O Word!
Where is thy centre? where the point intense,
Where all thy rays converge, or whence depart?
I see the host of stars, I see the sun,
And his pale shadow painted on the night,—
I see the moon—but these are not thy seat:
The wakeful stars roam wonder-eyed through heaven;
Like me they seek their source; they and the sun
Live in the skirts of darkness, and would cease,
In thy unclouded blaze, to be or shine.

Where is thy bound? above all worlds thou art,
Above all heavens; in depth beneath the grave,—
Above, beneath, within, surrounding all,
Heaven's higher heaven, and the abyss of hell.
Where thought sinks tired, or back upon itself,
Returns compelled, thou art; and there, as here,
Conscious of All. Thou only art alone;
Silence, and rest, and solitude, are thine
And only thine. The sun's returnless rays
Are quenched in night, are quenched in thee, O God!
But thou, Sun of the Universe! thy beams,
Viewless and immaterial, spread beyond
Even our thought of thee, our widest thought
And strained conception of thy boundlessness.

All forms and things and images of things
Breathed on the frore of darkness, and congealed,
Are but a vapor by the eternal Soul
 And by the Word revealed.

                        Then what are we,
Who worship thee in Sun, and Moon, and Stars,
And earthly fires unseen of eyes impure?—
Motes in the gleam of all-creating Light!
Thin Shadows, Atoms, conscious of ourselves,
Only as we are less, in kind, than thee;
And yet than thee we only can be less,
While we perceive, O God! and worship thee.

HEBREW HYMN

OH Thou, for whom as in thyself thou art,
And by thyself perceived, we know no name,
Nor dare not seek to express,—but unto us,
Adonai!—who, before the heavens were built,
Or earth's foundations laid—within thyself,
Thine own more glorious habitation, dwelt.
But when within the abyss,
With sudden light illuminated,
Thou, thine image to behold,
Into its quickened depths,
Looked down with brooding eye,—
Earth with its mountains rose,
And seas, and streams;
And o'er them, like a cloud,
Rose the blue firmament;
And the sun burst forth
With wide and sudden blaze,
That made the dazzled night
Know its own darkness—and the stars
Rose glimmering in his skirts;

And nearer to the earth, the moon
Above the mountains' blue and skiey peaks
Rode pale and beautiful.
And man stood up before thee, not as these,
The image of thy wisdom and thy power,
But of Thyself; and in his heart was born
Thy highest name, the unpronounceable,
Adorable I AM, and on his lips,
Adonai! Father! God.—Oh Spirit pure,
Creator increate, the work, how vain
Of them who seek with impious hands to shape
Thee, the Invisible; that within thyself
Sittest with glory covered,
Garmented with light,
To them who at its blaze
Kindle their dazzled eyes,
The cherubim, and flame-winged seraphim,
Insufferable as noon:—
Brightness that, more than night
And thickest darkness, hides Thee from our sight.
Oh thou, our Father, Saviour, Sovereign, God,
Immovably the pillars of thy throne,
With all the structure vast of earth and heaven,
Rest on the dark foundations of thy will.
Thy hand is sceptred with almighty power,
The rod of boundless empire, and the bolt
Of universal ruin, should it leave,
Omnipotent! thy grasp,—Oh God,
Our fathers' God! the earth and seas—
The eternal hills, and undecaying heavens,
Shall vanish at thy breath: and all that *is*
Shall be as it had never been; but we,
Thy children, shall we too be naught, when this
That now supports shall perish and dissolve?—
When earth and heaven shall fade and fall away,
Thine arm, beneath us placed, our God, shall save
And from the dark abyss in which the sun
And stars shall sink, extinguished, from the grave

Of universal life shall lift us up—
Shall lift us to Thyself, and we, above
Our own conception glorified, shall live,
And with the Righteous and the Just of earth
In thee, our everlasting habitation, rest.

TO A LADY ABOUT TO TAKE
THE VEIL

OH Lady, Lady, from a heart in pain
Thou seek'st a song, perchance, to please the ear,
And move, with the sweet tumult of its strain,
The thoughtless smile, and oft as thoughtless tear.

But ah! my heart, unduteous to my will,
Breathes only sadness; like an instrument
From whose quick strings, when hands devoid of skill
Solicit joy, they murmur and lament.

Oh Lady, to a dark and sullen creed
Thou of thy youth hast given the light and bloom;
As if a bird whose wing, in golden mead,
And in the leafy city's cheerful gloom,

Held the wide air—itself should seek the cage,
And from its kindred in the peopled wood
Self-exiled, live with men in hermitage,
Sad récluse of a human solitude.

Dear Lady, by the grief of those whose love
Had birth with thee, and with thy life began,
Who gave thee all of life, save from above
That which descends, the life of God in man;—

By them, who, later born, within thy heart
The place which thou dost hold in theirs possess,

And to thy young and virgin breast impart
Something of mother's love and tenderness;—

Oh by the voice that in the myrtle glade,
Which thou hast left, sings sadly all day long,
With hope to lure thee to the thicket's shade,
Love's green retreats, and leafy haunts of song;

By him who waits with eager step to lead
Thee, like Alcestis, rescued from the tomb,
And from pale thraldom to oblivion freed,
Into the land of love and light and bloom:

Into the land, who waits to lead thee forth
Where never skies grow dark, nor swell the floods,
Nor ever smite the bleak winds of the north,
To kill the tender green of growing buds;

A land of flowers, a land of gentle streams,
The land where thou wast born—though *strange* to thee,
So with their sorcery have those pale dreams
Of sin and penance bound thy spirit free.

Oh, by his love who takes thee by the hand,
Who waits, with eager step, to lead thee forth
Into that land of love, whose heaven bland
Makes summer of the bleak winds of the north;—

Where poor is rich, nor sharp extremest need,
Where grief is sweet and beautiful is pain,—
Ere thou, irrevocable, to that dark creed
Art yielded, think, Oh Lady, think again!

SAINT MARY'S GIFT

"Mark it, Cesario, it is old and plain,
And dallies with the innocence of love,
Like the old age."
TWELFTH NIGHT.

I.

O ARCADY, green Arcady! fair land,
Through which, by others led, I oft have trod,
Tracing their footsteps on the golden sand,
Indelible,—or on the pregnant sod,
From which, when feet, like Jove's swift Herald's, shod
With winged sandals, touch the sacred soil,
Thick spring immortal flowers, but to the hand
Is an unyielding clod, whose sordid toil,
As if for earth-hutched gold, seeks poesy's bright spoil.

II.

If I have deemed thy secret springs and glades
Like real, and more lovely than possess
A place on earth,—if o'er all earthly maids
Loved thy sweet Queen, the Queen and Shepherdess
Of gentle spirits,—in thy wilderness
O let me build a bower, where some may rest,
Who seek thy green and never-withering shades,
And haply praise the simple hand that drest
Its wild of tangled boughs, though rudely at the best.

III.

And what, great Queen, shall be thy poet's theme?
Ah, of what else should youthful poets sing
But that of which young maidens muse and dream?
And while they speak of whatsoever thing,
Of that their hearts will still be whispering:—
Sweet Love—the prisoner and the liege of sense,

Fresh spring of virtue, honor's crystal stream,
Green youth of eld, full store of indigence,
Life of all living things, the might of innocence.

IV.

But now to tell what might in love may be:—
There was a lady in the ancient time,
A lady of great worth and dignity,
And for her worthiness I weave this rhyme,
In a far distant age and different clime,
And bind these simple posies in a wreath,
To show her faith and sweet benignity;
The priest had shrived her only son for death,
Prayers for his life no more, but for his soul he saith.

V.

But she before our Lady's shrine to kneel
Went forth at midnight, when no eye could see,
And to that mother pure did make appeal,
That she for mothers' love would piteous be.
And in her need and great extremity
She vowed, if Christ might yield his help divine
Through her petition, and her son would heal,
That he should wed the maid that at her shrine
Knelt earliest at morn, befal him joy or tine.

VI.

And he, so piteous is heaven's Queen,
All suddenly grew well of his disease,—
Such cure could ne'er by mortal help have been,
From death itself as well might it release;
And still the sacred marvel to increase,
They heard him in his sleep an Ave raise,
And on awaking, tell that he had seen
One like the Virgin Mother, clothed in rays,
Whose smile had thrilled his heart into that song of praise.

VII.

The chapel then, in great beatitude
The lady sought; and in her heart, she spelt
Words as she went of silent gratitude;
With such deep joy her gentle heart did melt,
To think that heavenly saints her grief had felt;
And with her vow her heart kept strict accord,
When lo! she sees in humblest attitude
Before the shrine a maiden that adored,
With meek uplifted eyes, the Mother of the Lord.

VIII.

The sun still stood upon the skiey shore
Of the blue east, and through the glistering air
Threw his slant beams, that in the open door
Pencilled with golden light her flowing hair,
And all her form; that she so meekly fair,
And still, and rapt as pictured saint might be,
Like saint-like seemed as her she did adore:
Ah wherefore looked the dame that sight to see,
As one that wakes through fear and sees his fantasy.

IX.

Young hearts forgive her if, one moment, she
Looked on that lovely maid with half-disdain,
When, mindful of her heir's great dignity,
She marked her tattered mantle, coarse and plain—
Beggars or peasants seen with equal pain—
But soon, for she was kind, she took the maid,
Who in her face looked sad and wonderingly,
And kissed her cheek, and gentle speeches said,
And in her castle soon like high-born dames arrayed.

X.

With wonder did the youth her beauty see,
But he was one that oft in musings deep

Of what he deemed his own high destiny,
With books and stars would nightly vigil keep,
While all his fellows were amort with sleep.
So in his heart rank grew the weeds of pride,
Though with some flowers of worth and piety,
And made him loathe the thought that through his bride
His race with beggars base, and hinds should be allied.

XI.

But he was young, and young was then romance,
And oft in thought did cruel pagans fall,
And faitours vile went down before his lance,
And lovely maids he freed from wicked thrall,
Yet for one loveliest maid he did it all;
And what if she, so fair but poorly dight,
So strangely brought, should be a maid perchance
Of noble lineage, but disguised to sight,
And sent, in high adventure, to approve his might.

XII.

But when he said, as to his fancied bride,
That he must leave her sight to seek her praise,
Nearer in soul because apart so wide,
And peril life in lists and bloody frays,
To make her name be heard in minstrels' lays,
And o'er all hearts maintain her empery;
Mutely she gazed, and heard him vacant-eyed:
And when he sought reply,—I would with me
That thou should'st stay, she said, that I may look on thee.

XIII.

So he forsook the mansion, though with pain,
Both for her beauty and the vow that brought
For her dear sake his dying breath again;
And in his sovereign's court advancement sought,
Yet never peace might find, nor quiet thought;

Nor ever could he see that sweetest head,
With its soft ring of light in niche or pane,
But with a thought of her from whom he fled,
And whom he loved, yet loathed, and almost wished were
    dead.

XIV.

And years passed on, but he would not return,
And still the lady to the maid was kind,
And sought by love to recompense his scorn;
And for his absence though she inly pined,
She never sought her promise to unbind,
For in his stead had blissful Mary's dower,
A dearer daughter, of her heart been born:
But she, ah! pale, and like a lily-flower,
Became the cottage rose in that high-fashioned bower.

XV.

At length unto the lady spoke the maid,
With eyes that shunned to raise their glance aloft,
And words that seemed at their own sound affrayed,
So tremblingly she spoke, and low, and soft,
In slow and measured tone, as if full oft
She to herself the pondered speech had said,—
"Than he should longer from thy arms be stayed,
O dearest lady, who from mine has fled,
'Twere better I were gone, and well if I were dead.

XVI.

"So let me seem to die; a flower I know
That grows with innocent look upon the heath,
And yet whose virtue can make sleep to show
A nearer semblance to resemblant death—
Can freeze the eye, and still the pulse and breath;
And he shall hear, nor long will linger hence,
And I, a time, into the tomb will go;

Back to my native humbleness from thence,
And still thy hapless vow be held in reverence."

XVII.

At length the lady yielded her consent,
Though with great sorrow and compunction deep,
And toward the maiden with a true intent
A mother's care for her no less to keep:
And to an abbey near, when waked from sleep,
She thought to take her, with great secrecy,
So like a jewel for a season lent,
To her that gave, the maid returned should be,
The lustre all undimmed of her virginity.

XVIII.

But when the tidings to his ears were brought,
And how without complaint she pined and died,
And of her sad and gentle looks he thought,
And how the frost of his ingrateful pride
Had killed that fairest flower by love espied,—
Love, that revenges still his broken hest,
His grief to its own height of passion wrought,
And late remorse, the heart's unbidden guest,
With self-disdainful shame his guilty mind possessed.

XIX.

Homeward he hasted, but along the way
Heard not the birds, though they sung loudly too,
Nor did the greenness of the fields in May
Make his heart fresh as wont with youth to do;
He heard no song, he saw no pleasant hue,
In nothing dared his heart to take delight,
Ne in the springing leaves, nor glistering day;
And when the moon rose fair and silver bright,
And pale-looked stars peered out,—he knew that it was
        night.

XX.

Unto the tomb wherein he deemed she lay,
All unperceived of any eye he went,
And while they still misdeemed him far away,
He stood before that ancient monument;
He knew not in himself with what intent.
Beneath the portal's crevice, from within,
Into the moonlight crept a golden ray
That made it seem more ghastly-pale and thin;
He wrenched the door ajar, and wonderingly stepped in.

XXI.

And there within an open tomb was laid,
With lighted tapers at her head and feet,
That flickered in the blast, a lovely maid,
Whose youthful innocence and beauty sweet
Kept the flowers fresh upon her winding-sheet:
And as the gusty wind did rise and fall,
From old armorial tombs with knights displayed,
Armed shadows seemed to threat upon the wall,
As if to guard from harm her slumbers virginal.

XXII.

He on his knees sank awed and tremblingly
Before that image of fair maidenhed,
While life and death changed looks dissemblingly;
For such a paleness in his features spread,
That she the live might seem, and he the dead;
And all around the shadows toward the maid
And flamy tapers bended semblably,
While he, with arms upon his sword-hilt stayed,
And fixed and marble look bent forward half-affrayed.

XXIII.

Is it the wind-gust through the creviced door?
Is it the light that flickers on her shroud?

Is it the wind that sighs?—half from the floor
Upstarting to his feet, he gasps aloud,
And stares with eyes all-wide and wonder-brow'd,
To see her slowly from the tomb arise,
And on her loosened arm half-leaning o'er
Look in his face with wild and dreamy eyes,
Like one that wakes from sleep disturbed with fantasies.

XXIV.

And each unto the other was a dream;
And so they gazed, without a stir or breath,
Until her head into the golden stream
Of her wide tresses, loosened from their wreath,
Sunk back, as she did yield again to death:—
Then rose the youth, and freed from his amaze
At what a thing so strange as this should seem,
Sought from its dreamy couch her head to raise;
The other trembling hand upon her heart he lays.

XXV.

And still it beat, at which his own grew mute,
And then beat loudly, as with quick low cries
And soft as breathings of a love-touched lute,—
Sweet maid, he said, my love, my bride, arise!
And kissed awake her drowsy-lidded eyes;
This place is dreary-cold, and full of fears,
Come hence with me;—nor long he urged his suit,
But bore her forth, who only with her tears
And heart that throbbed tumultuous, tells him that she
        hears.

XXVI.

What ails old Hubert at the castle gate,
That, like a sick-brained girl, he screams aloud,
Tale-witched upon the hour of midnight late?—
Pale looked the boldest in the gathering crowd

To see one bear a maiden in a shroud;
Only the lady blanched not to behold.—
Next morn the sun arose with look elate,
And for a bridal tricked himself with gold,
And early waked the birds, numbed in the moonlight
    cold.

XXVII.

And sweetest flowers made open into sight,
For posied garlands with green holly blent;
And never to the church his beams did light
A maid like her so fair and innocent:
Men could not stint to view her as they went,
And whisper of the marvels that befel.
And there her love with blushes did she plight,
And clamored of the thing the village bell;
At length the sun went down—I have no more to tell.

BALLAD FANTASIES

"But God forbede, but men shulde leue
Well more thyng tha they hau sene with eye,
Men shal nat wenen euery thyng a lye
But if himselfe it seeth, or els it dothe
For, God wote, thynge is neuer the lesse sothe
Though euery wight ne may it no ysee."
        CHAUCER, *Legend of Good Women.*

THE COTTAGE

"My eyes make pictures when they are shut."
        COLERIDGE.

—A LITTLE cottage stands
   Half hid in climbing green;
Spreading along the jagged eaves
   And o'er the roof 'tis seen.

Before it are a few meek flowers,
　　Yet garden there is none;
But grass with flowers,—as Art at first
　　His toil had there begun;

Then shamed by Nature, fled, and left
　　These flowrets to her hand,
That hence to wild flowers changing seem,
　　Where 'mid the grass they stand.

A grandame at the open door
　　Sits knitting in the sun;
Who looks at her, need not be told
Of friends and kindred, young and old,
　　That vanished one by one.

Bloom to her cheek returns no more,
　　And soon her smiles depart;
But he that sees no beauty there,—
　　He hath none in his heart.

A little child is sitting near,
　　A white lamb by the child,—
And surely it must be sweet lore
Its eyes and lips are spelling o'er,
　　To read that grandame mild.

———

. . . . A ruined cottage stands
　　Covered with climbing green;
Thatching with leaves the broken roof,
　　Then creeping back 'tis seen.

An old man sits within the door;
　　His hair is white and thin,
But his mild and winning eye is bright;
If not the fire it hath the light
　　Of early youth therein.

Close by his head the little birds
    Carol their morning hymn;
Above the door, on the old woodbine,
They sing at every morning's shine,
    They have no fear of him.

He is getting deaf, but hears them well;
    They sing close at his ear:
Each day he blesses God in heart
    That he the birds can hear.

And they say of that old lonely man,
    That he could tell strange things,
And sometimes speaks of things beheld
    In world-wide wanderings.

And if it now were eventide,
    The children you might see
Turn hither on their way from school
    To sit upon his knee,

And hear from him such counsel sweet,
    As makes them wish to hear;
And better tales, they all aver,
    Than they in books can speare.

THE FOREST

—A FOREST sad and dark,
    A forest still and lone,—
So still, our hearts throb low, and hark
    As if to hear a moan.

A night of thick, dark boughs and leaves,
    A night amidst the day,
Which the scared day-light from its haunt
    Doth never drive away.

And deep within that haunted wood,
  Whose very hush alarms,
Broad gnarled knots like heads look out,
And on the darkness peer about,
  'Neath branches crooked like arms.

And mossy stones lie black along
  A brook which gurgles there,
As if its low incessant sound
  Part of the silence were.

There are two who have lost their way,—
  Mother and child are they,
Who think they see the growing night,
  While yet 'tis mid of day.

Tearless the mother is, and pale,
  And almost stern, through fear;
But in that dark and lonely wild
Nothing affrights the little child—
  Is not its mother near?

And but for her strange look t'would shout,
  As oft as turning back
She stops to listen, or to seek
  The long-deserted track.

And still she struggles to recall
  Each spot where'er they are,
And stops, and looks, though well she knows
  She never hath been there.

And she would call, but that the sound
  Upon her lips doth die;—
How if some evil thing should hear?
  Who knows what thing is nigh!

And what is that, oh help her heaven!
  That stands before her there,—
A tattered, gaunt and wretched man,
  His limbs o'ergrown with hair;

A broken chain upon his leg,
  A gnarled branch in his hand,
A madman, sure, whose rage hath burst
  The dungeon and the band.

All mute and motionless she stands,
  Yet marks his eye is mild;
And mute and motionless stands he,
  And gazes on the child.

Alone she would have swooned through fear,
  But now no fear hath she,
Save for the child, on which his eyes
  He bends so wistfully.

And lest he snatch and bear it off
  Into that forest drear,
She takes it in her arms, and flies,
While backward still its wide blue eyes
  Over her shoulder peer.

With short and hurried step she flies,
  The wild-man follows slow,
With long unhurried strides, but still
  More fast than she can go.

And though she neither sees nor hears,
  She feels that he is near;
And shorter grow her steps—when lo!
  A woodman's axe rings clear.

And then a whistle sweet and loud,
  Which breaks into a song,

And a sturdy voice rings cheerly out,
   The silent woods among.

And the weary mother gasps with joy,
   And sobs, and feels again
The thick hot throbbings of her heart,
   And brings her breath with pain.

And tears fall bright and fast, as rain
   Falls from a flying cloud,
Forwearied by the sobbing wind,
   That breathes and sobs aloud.

She turns to look, and fixed he stands,
   Stopped by the woodman's sound,
All still and motionless, as one
   By wizard's whisper bound.

And mournfully he looks at them,
   And tears are on his cheek;
How for a moment could she fear
   That man so sad and meek?

And she will turn and speak to him,
   In soothing words and kind;
And striving is her gentle heart
   The fitting words to find.

And her lips they move as if to speak,
   But ere they utter tone
She only sees the dark green leaves—
   That strange sad man is gone.

THE BROOK

A LITTLE blind girl wandering,
   While daylight pales beneath the moon,

And with a brook meandering,
　　To hear its gentle tune.

The little blind girl by the brook,
　　It told her something—you might guess,
To see her smile, to see her look
　　Of listening eagerness.

Though blind, a never silent guide
　　Flowed with her timid feet along;
And down she wandered by its side
　　To hear the running song.

And sometimes it was soft and low,
　　A creeping music in the ground;
And then, if something checked its flow,
　　A gurgling swell of sound.

And now, upon the other side,
　　She seeks her mother's cot;
And still the noise shall be her guide,
　　And lead her to the spot.

For to the blind, so little free
　　To move about beneath the sun,
Small things like this seem liberty—
　　Something from darkness won.

But soon she heard a meeting stream,
　　And on the bank she followed still,
It murmured on, nor could she tell
　　It was another rill.

Ah! whither, whither, my little maid?
　　And wherefore dost thou wander here?
I seek my mother's cot, she said,
　　And surely it is near.

There is no cot upon this brook,
   In yonder mountains dark and drear,
Where sinks the sun, its source it took,
   Ah, wherefore art thou here?

O! sir, thou art not true nor kind,
   It is the brook, I know its sound,
Ah! why would you deceive the blind?
   I hear it in the ground.

And on she stepped, but grew more sad,
   And weary were her tender feet,
The brook's small voice seemed not so glad,
   Its song was not so sweet.

Ah! whither, whither, my little maid?
   And wherefore dost thou wander here?
I seek my mother's cot, she said,
   And surely it is near.

There is no cot upon this brook;
   I hear its sound, the maid replied,
With dreamlike and bewildered look,
   I have not left its side.

O go with me, the darkness nears,
   The first pale stars begin to gleam;
The maid replied with bursting tears,
   It is the stream! it is the stream!

THE GOLDEN ISLE

. . A PEAK, that from the sea
   Shoots upward like a spire,—
The clouds far down around it lie,
And ever as the sun climbs high,
   Glow like a belt of fire.

And where, upon the sands below,
    The waters come and fleet,
A youth lies stretched, so near the waves
    They almost kiss his feet.

A boat stands beached upon the sand;
    'Tis calm, and yet her sail
Is wet and torn, as if but now
    In struggle with the gale.

He sleeps—and in his sleep he smiles,
    But 'tis a troubled smile,
As if he dreamed of guilty things,
    And joyed, yet feared the while.

Higher and higher climbs the sun;—
    The clouds around the peak
Show softer hues, then fade to white,
    Edged with a faint blue streak;—

Its beams upon the sleeper's eyes
    Shot from a kindled cliff,
Dispel the dream in which he lives,
    Stretched death-like, stark and stiff.

And is that gold, which in the boat
    He marks with eyes that glow—
That yellow sand, bestowed to keep
An upright keel when mad waves leap,
    And the winds that mad them blow?

He eyes the gold, and then the sun,
    The mountain, and the sea;—
If 'twas a dream, he seems to say,
    Then these a dream must be.

He sits and laughs, to hear afar
    The mingled voice and bleat

Of men and flocks, and far away
Of a boat that toils at sea to-day,
　The faintly flapping sheet.

And now he hath forgot the gold,
　The sea, and mountain nigh;
And one may read, as in a book,
　The musings of his eye.

Returning from his toil, at sea,
　Ever as came the night
He lowered his sail and dragged his skiff
　High on the tide-marked white.

But with sail all loose and wet,
　Drenched to the top with brine,
Hath found it now these six days past
　At early morning's shine.

And where his boat may go at night,
　And wherefore, he would know;
And crept beneath, so bold his heart,
　The short deck on her prow.

And there he waited long dark hours,
　Till—when the stars were gone—
A sudden light, all-dazzling white,
　Whiter than moonlight, shone.

And yet so blinding bright, it quenched
　The watcher's falcon eyes,—
That long he nought could see, or know,
Save that the boat, like a bolt let go,
　Cleaving the water flies.

And then he saw the boat's swift wake,
　Her wake in sea and air;

In sea, 'twas flame, and in the air,
  It was the flame's white glare.

A broad swift light—it shaped the gloom,
  So steep on either side,
It cleft the solid darkness sheer,
And shone astern a river clear,
  So far it burned and wide.

And o'er and aft the driving boat,
  High as the eye could see,
Each side the light, the parted night
  Towered upward threatningly.

A damsel sat upon the helm,
  Loose was her robe and slight,
Thin as a vapor on the moon,
  Through it her limbs shone white.

Another clung with one fair arm
  A-top the bending mast,
Her other reared a torch, that shone
Pale as the wisp of a weird crone,
  At her mumbled spells aghast.

Beneath it streamed her long black hair,
  That, in its backward flight,
Flickered, and darted above, about,
Like tongues of gloom by night thrust out
  To cleave the flying light.

A third was there, and death-like fair
  That lady's neck and cheek;
Binding her hair, a serpent braid
A crown upon her forehead made,
  Each serpent's head a peak.

Their tongues shot forth like ruby lemes,
  Their eyes like jewels glowed,
Their bodies flecked with gold and red,
Brightened and paled, no monarch's head
  Such crown hath ever showed.

A yellow robe flowed to her feet,
  It was her golden hair;
She of the boat was mariner,
She guided, and they sang for her,
  Those voices in the air.

First Voice.

Whither hast been? what thing of sin
Made seem a thing of beauty?

Second Voice.

A heart that had no love therein,
Ha! ha! in hope it heaven should win,
  Gave alms through sense of duty.

Third Voice.

I with a priest, at a secret feast,
  Sat, while the poor did fast;
When next in church he banned and blest,
He spoke with faint and fasting breast,
  And his eyes were upward cast.

Fourth Voice.

I saw a man, who, under ban,
  Dangled till life was sped;
The judge was calm; but had his hand
Touched its breast at the gallows stand,
  The corse had stirred and bled.

Fifth Voice.

I saw an eagle gasping lie,
  His flights for aye were done;

But still the bird of glory turned
  His bright eye on the sun.

The peak which in his pride he sought,
  A serpent thither clomb;
No wings had he, and save to hiss,
  His poisoned mouth was dumb.

The eagle rose, and towered, and screamed,
  The serpent hissed and clung,
He stooped to touch the peak—when lo!
The reptile beat the winged one low,
  It struck him with its tongue.

    First Voice.
I saw a sleeping maid at night,
  The moon was in her wane,
I gazed, but ever when in a dream
  To approach her slumbers fain,
Her limbs shot forth a sudden light
  That drove me back in pain.

But I found another and—

    (All the Voices.)   Why
  Our spirits still torment?
All night we wander like the wind,
All night we seek but never find,—
  The watchful stars prevent.

On sped the boat; the strains did float,
  Now low and then aloft,
Now loud and shrill, and then did fall,
Like sounds from those who songs recall
  In whispered music soft.

On sped the boat; the torch-light paled,
  Flitted, and died away;

Like thought they crossed the thin grey dawn,
  And drove into the day.

Into the day, under the moon,
  From mirk of night they shot,
Then shook the man, whose heart till then
  Wondered, but trembled not.

A ghostly thing, by gloom or moon,
  Whoso to view it dare
Sees but his thought before the sight,—
But what have things so wan and bright
  To do in day's broad glare?

A moment, and 'twas dark again,
  As through a black ravine
Glinted the sail, the keel just kissed
  The roaring tide between.

When lo! a bay, and rocks that rise
  Crag upon crag around,
Like smouldering fire their edges burned,
And glowing streams that cleft and turned,
  Leaped down without a sound.

It was the sun, that o'er the chasm
  Which opened to the sky,
Through jagged peaks and branching trees,
  Looked with a moon-like eye.

Through limbs that branched and crossed
      looked down
  That rayless sun o'er-head,
As in a wood he looks at eve,
  Through leafless trees, blood-red.

The boat shot round an islet small,
  And grated on the sand;

But ere it touched, those ladies wan
   Had flitted to the land.

A flickering shade fell on the sail;
   He looked, and on the trees
The branches waved, the leaves all stirred,
   And shook without a breeze.

He looked;—the trunks did seem to live,
   To breathe;—he saw the rings
Move up and down their barky skin,
And the branches twisting out and in,
   They all were living things.

The leaves, like heads, did gently threat
   And turn, in serpent-wise,
And from among them gleamed like gems
   A thousand little eyes.

Amidst,—a serpent, glossy black,
   Ascended fold in fold,
And, rising from its wreathed spire,
   Bent down a neck of gold.

One shuddering thought of fear; and then
   He only felt a sense
Of deep and mournful eyes, that bent
   On him their influence.

Nearer they came; swift colors played,
   Like those that come and go
On eye-balls pressed, then all was clear:
What then he saw of joy or fear,
   Only his heart can know.

Nor well knows that,—but something knows
   Of one so passing fair,

That to the bower in which she lay,
She seemed to flatter from its way
　　The gently winging air.

That turning caught her hair, and tossed
　　Her slight robe at its whim,
And in her heaving breast her sighs,
Unheard, he saw,—and in her eyes
　　Wild light and sparkles swim,
And wishes soft, that kindled these,
　　And still she gazed on him.

And something of a heap of gold,
　　An old blind wretch thereby,
Who still kept strained upon the heap
　　A bleared and sightless eye.

And by that old and sightless man,
　　All helpless and alone,
A deep dark pit, that tells no tales,—
　　What ear would hear his groan?

And something of a stately pile,
　　A palace, past the might
Of man to rear, or of his thought,
In sleep, or day-dream wonder-fraught,
　　To conjure to the sight.

And of an ebon throne, that blazed
　　With some strange, dazzling stone;—
Something of skulls, which flecked the steps
　　That mounted to the throne.

And something clearer of a maid,
　　The queenliest of three,
Who all were queenly in their look,
　　And beautiful to see.

The first wore sable plumes with white,
   Her robe was crimson-dyed;
Who saw—need not her empire see
To know that she held sovereignty,
   That lady haughty-eyed.

And bright her eyes with glancing light
   Of thoughts that from the wing
Did never rest, but in the sight
Of things most sought, and deemed most
      bright,
   Dreamed of a brighter thing.

The one least fair was clad in garb
   That seemed with gems to live,
Some beaming as they eyes had been,
And some that seemed, from a pulse within,
   A throbbing light to give.

The third was she he saw at first,
   And still she breathed in sighs,
And all her robe—her flowing hair,
   Her only gems her eyes.

The proud-looked maiden seemed to say
   Who wins must dare and toil—
She, with the gems so richly dight,
   Who wins—must cark and moil.

And I will win them both, he thought,
   My heart shall teach me how;
But this soft maiden speaks as plain,
   Who wins—must win me now.

Just at his thought she forward stept,
   With motion loose and free;
Then turned to fly, then turned again,

And then, as less ashamed than fain,
   Stept towards him suddenly.

With arms just raised, on tip-toe stepped,
   As still half-bent to fly,
Then dropped her eyes, as if grown meek,
   Through shame of coming nigh.

So low their lashes drooped, through shame
   That would not let them rise,
The pencilled blushes on her cheek
   Seemed painted by her eyes.

Again she stopped,—on trembling foot
   Just poised, as if for flight;
But he, like thought, would seize her fast,
   So quick he leaped upright.

So quick he leaped,—as quickly fell,
   And she and all were fled,
And there before him, on the boat,
   Rested the serpent's head.

Again he saw those large bright eyes
   Bent mournfully on him;
But all that he had seen therein
   Seemed like a vision dim.

And then the serpent seemed to know
   Of all that he had seen;
And somehow in those eyes it seemed
   His thoughts with hers had been.

And can'st thou give? he sighed; when lo!
   No serpent's head is there,
They are the damsel's eyes that peer
   Half-laughing through her hair.

His heart throbbed quick—his eyes suffused,
　He stretched his arms and sighed;
She came and o'er him stooped, and shed
Her glossy hair about his head,
　In ringlets falling wide.

He felt her breath,—he sought to clasp,
　When, with a sudden pain,
The life rushed back in giddy whirl
　Upon his heart and brain.

And after that he nothing knew,
　Till waking on the strand,
In morning's broad and dreamless eye,
　He saw the golden sand.

SONNET

TO W. B. K.

FRIEND of a lifetime! for while yet unknown
I was thy friend, and knew, though all unseen,
That thou must be,—else why should I have been,
And why that eloquent and gentle one
Brow'd like an antique god, with eye of fire,
But chastened soul too strong and calm for ire.
Yes! we were ever friends,—nor strained the thought,
Fantastical or wild, howe'er it seems
To thoughtful fools. Two once united streams
In the far mountains whence their flow is brought,
Are confluent floods, no less than at the place
Where first they hear each other's voices deep,
Lift their white crests, along their channels leap,
And rush together in a glad embrace.

SONNET

Oh, 'tis a night,—on such a night as this
Methinks the earth itself must feel such bliss,
Such deep and quiet-breathing joy as we:
Loved one, come near, and look! nay, not on me,
Look upward—and yet turn not, love,—one kiss!
For nature for our love more beauteous is:
The heavens are all tremulous like a sea;—
Mark yon slow cloud that moves voluptuously
Across the moon and lags upon its face,
And drinks its light;—even as that vapor base
And born of earth, is made all silver-white,
So low and earth-born sense in love's pure light,
Turns to love's essence, and from thoughts of blame
Is innocent made, and purified from shame.

SONNET

My heart built up a palace, and approved
The gorgeous work in all its parts to be
Stablished in beauty, love's true mansionry;
And thou didst dwell therein so truly loved
As none have been, nor shall be loved again,
And yet perceived not how all structures vain
Of human artifice it did excel:
Thy heart built not, nor yet of mine might know
The work how real, would'st thou deem it so:
But thou didst doubt its glory, and it fell—
Fell, never to be built again by me;
For Love is dead, and Hope no longer lives:
Only amongst the ruins still survives
The image sad and pale of one like thee.

SONNET
BIRDS IN WINTER

How still the air within this forest brown;
So still, you hear the snow fall through the trees,
And on the yellow leaves beneath them strown;
And thick it falls, unwavered by the breeze,
As if the white clouds piecemeal should come down;
And mark these little birds that sit and freeze,
With half-closed eyes, and ruffled feathers, known
As them that fly not with the changing year.
O birds! had I your wings would I be here?
And yet why not? the winter has its flowers
Varied and wondrous,—crystals, stalactites,
Nor undelightful these soft fleecy showers;
And why not birds?—whom love of these invites
More than the summer with its green delights.

ON THE DEFEAT OF A GREAT MAN

FALLEN? How fallen? States and empires fall;
    O'er towers and rock-built walls,
And perished nations, floods to tempests call
With hollow sound along the sea of time:
    The great man never falls.
He lives, he towers aloft, he stands sublime—
    They fall who give him not
The honor here that suits his future name—
    They die and are forgot.

O Giant loud and blind! the great man's fame
    Is his own shadow, and not cast by thee—
    A shadow that shall grow
As down the heaven of time the sun descends,
    And on the world shall throw
His god-like image, till it sinks where blends
    Time's dim horizon with Eternity.

SONG

O soft is the ringdove's eye of love
When her mate returns from a weary flight;
And brightest of all the stars above
Is the one bright star that leads the night.

But softer thine eye than the dove's by far,
When of friendship and pity thou speakest to me;
And brighter, O brighter, than eve's one star,
When of love, sweet maid, I speak to thee.

SONG

I.

The rosebud that you gave me, love,
   Beneath the lintel vine,
Although it fades in other's eyes,
   Unfaded seems in mine;
No common flower it seems to me,
   On sunshine fed and dew,
By others reared, by others viewed,
   Then plucked at last by you.

II.

But, 'tis linked in thought with you, love,
   With you, and only you,
As if it in your bosom chaste,
   Among the lilies grew;
As if it in your bosom grew,
   O gentle maid and fair,
Grew close upon your nursing heart,
   And fed its beauty there.

III.

And you pressed it to your lips, love,
　　The night you gave it me,
And thence I deem, its life, its sweets,
　　Its deathless bloom must be:
It drew its vermeil from your lips,
　　'Tis fragrant with your breath,
It lives upon that balmy kiss,
　　That gives it life in death.

IV.

But if *they* see best who deem, love,
　　It sere and yellow grows,
I'll tell you why the life and bloom
　　Have left the withered rose:
The flower upon my heart has lain,
　　And my heart has drawn away
The life, the sweets it drew from yours
　　What time on yours it lay.

SONG

Oh! a heart it loves, it loves thee,
　　That never loved before,
Oh! a heart it loves, it loves thee,
　　That heart can love no more.

As the rose was in the bud, love,
　　Ere it opened into sight,
As yon star, in drumlie daylight,
　　Behind the blue was bright,—

So thine image in my heart, love,
　　As pure, as bright, as fair,
Thyself unseen, unheeded,
　　I saw and loved it there.

Oh! a heart it loves, it loves thee,
   As heart ne'er loved before;
Oh! a heart it loves, loves, loves thee,
   That heart can love no more.

TO ROSINA PICO

REGENT of Song! who bringest to our shore
   Strains from the passionate land, where shapes of Art
Make music of the wind that passes o'er,
   Thou even here hast found the human heart;
And in a thousand hearts thy songs repeat
Their echoes, like remembered Poesy sweet,
Witching the soul to warble evermore.

First seen, it seemed as if thy sweetest strain
   Had taken shape, and stood before our sight;
Thy aspect filled the silence with sweet pain
   That made it long for death. O creature bright!
Or ere the trembling silence had ta'en flight
We *listened to thy looks,* in hushed delight,
And from thy motions sought a sound to gain.

Then on all hearts at once did pour a flood
   Of golden sound, in many an eddying tone,
As pours the wind into a breathless wood,
   Awakening in it music not its own;
Thy voice controlled all spirits to one mood,
Before all eyes one breathing image stood,
Beheld, as if to thee all eyes had grown.

Yet did I seem to be with thee alone,
   With thee to stand upon enchanted ground,
And gazed on thee, as if the sculptured stone
   Should live before me, (so thy magic bound
My soul, bewildered) while a cloud of sound
Rising in wreaths, upon the air around
Lingered like incense from a censer thrown.

A RIME

*Which is yet Reason, and teacheth, in a light manner,
a grave matter in the lere of Love.*

I.

As Love sat idling beneath a tree,
A Knight rode by on his charger free,
Stalwart and fair and tall was he,
With his plume and his mantle, a sight to see!
And proud of his scars, right loftily,
He cried, Young boy will you go with me?
   But Love he pouted and shook his head,
    And along fared the Warrior, ill-bested:
Love is not won by chivalry.

II.

Then came a Minstrel bright of blee,
Blue were his eyes as the heavens be,
And sweet as a song-bird's throat sung he,
Of smiles and tears and ladie's eé,
Soft love and glorious chivalry,
Then cried, Sweet boy will you go with me?
   Love wept and smiled, but shook his head,
    And along fared the Minstrel ill-bested:
Love is not won by minstrelsy.

III.

Then came a Bookman, wise as three,
Darker a scholar you shall not see
In Jewrie, Rome, or Araby.
But list fair dames what I rede to ye,
In love's sweet lere untaught was he,
For when he cried, Come, love, with me,
   Tired of the parle he was nodding his head,
    And along fared the Scholar ill-bested:
Love is not won by pedantry.

IV.

Then came a Courtier wearing the key
Of council and chambers high privity;
He could dispute yet seem to agree,
And soft as dew was his flatterie.
And with honied voice and low congeé,
Fair youth, he said, will you honor me?
  In courteous wise Love shook his head,
    And along fared the Courtier ill-bested:
Love is not won by courtesy.

V.

Then came a Miser blinking his eé,
To view the bright boy beneath the tree;
His purse, which hung to his cringing knee,
The ransom held of a king's countreé;
And a handful of jewels and gold showed he,
And cried, Sweet child, will you go with me?
  Then loud laughed Love as he shook his head,
    And along fared the Monger ill-bested:
Love is not won by merchandry.

VI.

O then to young Love beneath the tree,
Came one as young and as fair as he,
And as like to him as like can be,
And clapping his little wings for glee,
With nods and smiles and kisses free,
He whispered, Come, O come with me:
  Love pouted and flouted and shook his head,
    But along with that winsome youth he sped,
And love wins love, loud shouted he!

PASTORAL

Lo! Summer, half waking,
Her long slumber breaking,
Smiles all the clouds away,
   Then seems to sleep again:
    Over her frozen bed,
Hark! the sighing winds say,
   While fast the cold tears they rain,
    She is dead, she is dead!

II.

Trees stand weeping,
Flowers all sleeping,
Cold mists creeping,
   Drearily:—
When, to assert his reign,
Lo! over hill and plain,
Shines forth the sun again
   Cheerily.
Never were hill-tops green
Bathed in so deep a blue;
Never the green leaves seen
   Springing so fresh anew:
   The sun at his noon,
   But bland as the moon,
Sleeps on the open plain,
   Sleeps on the meadows;
Back to the woods again
   Glide the black shadows;
Wild flowers are peeping
   In beauty forth
    Fearfully;
Winter back creeping
   Toward the north
    Tearfully.

III.

The ploughshare is clinking,
The oxen are swinking,
  And the ploughboy's rude voice,
Though he sings without art,
  Makes the listener rejoice,
For 'tis spring in the heart.

IV.

The birds are all singing,
And chirping, and winging
  Their way through the boughs;
The snowy flocks bleating,—
The grassy year greeting
  The glad heifer lows:
And sweetly these noises all,
And soft, on the hearing fall:
  Even the husky crows
Seem to grow musical.

V.

And, where in the brook
  Their shadows are sleeping,
The green willows look
  To see themselves weeping:
  For here it is still,
  But under the mill,
  Although but a rill,
  Like a torrent 'tis falling:
And children come forth to-day
On the green banks to play,
And hark! to the woods away!
  Voices are calling.

CALLIOPE

LATE as I sat beneath the kissing boughs
Of a dark wood, within whose shadow deep
My soul bathed, naked of the fretting vest
Of human care—in the green seat of gloom
Half-lost and grown oblivious to change,—
I mused upon the time when not as now
Men from the cities and close-girded fields,
From drowsy hearths and roof-cast shadows came,
Led by a feeble longing of the soul,
To drink the breath of forests, and explore
The realm of wonder and dim haunt of dreams;
But dwelt or wandered there the early race,
Men lion-limb'd, and like the eagle eyed,
And met with frequent gods and piping fauns,
And white-limb'd nymphs, and dryads; for the trees
Not then were deemed unconscious, in each other's sight
Who grew through centuries of age; nor then
Was there no soul within the singing brook
To prompt its music, and each hollow cave
Had its blind nymph aye pining for a sound,
To feed the dark and silence-hungered void.

O golden time, when life was poesy!
And he who sought the forest's sombre depths,
With a fresh child-like longing for the life
Natural and sweet, prefigured in his heart,
The life of gods, and nymphs, and early men,
Was not awed back by dire portents of fear,
And sharp necessity, and famished want,
Time-meting foresight, and forecasting doubt
Of place and limit, but their green labyrinths
Pierced, nor guided his interfluous feet
With other thought than, in some deeper heart
Of forest gloom, to see rough-footed Pan
With budding forehead and wood-witching pipe,

Or the white bosom through a parting mist
Of oriad, or goddess, or with limbs
That shamed the foam, the naiad, or, less happy, she
Born with the oak to perish with its age.

So long my soul, numbered with a drowsy grief
In thinking of these old divinities,
Gave ear unto the whisperings of the Past,—
Into the labyrinths of my dream so deep
It wandered 'midst dark figures bronzed by time
Into a look of sadness that makes yearn
The mortal heart with more than mortal love,—
That longer the dark hush and torpor deep
Of that unpeopled wood it might not bear;
And I, so rapt, as I had been Apollo's self
Awakening from a sleep of centuries, rose
And bound my head with laurels, and aloud
Shouted Awake! unto the woods and caves,
And Echo from the woods and caves unto the air
Re-syllabled my shouts. Then from my hand
Upon the thrilling strings arose a strain,
Beyond my power, from impulse not my own,
Which with my voice made deep and passionate wail,
That with its longings almost might create
The thing it sought; so deep and loud it swelled
As it had caught all sounds into itself,
And left an aching silence in the air,—
Piercing the hollow and wide-listening void,
Like lightning the else deep unlightened night.

And still I cried, Awake! sometimes in tone
So musically plaintive as might wake
Oblivious wonder in the ear of death,
And all his realm unpeople with its might;
And sometimes in a fiery transport of swift strains
My invocation rose, Awake! Awake!
By the old trees whose fresh young hearts, each spring,
Load all their branches with sweet-scented buds,

By flowers, of young poets the first words,—
The lovers, that first press young maidens' breasts,—
By mossy grots, by all the singing brooks
That teach the wood-birds songs, Awake! Awake!
By trees none love, by echoes unawaked,
By brooks unheard, by flowers—when at my ear
I heard a voice that said, Apollo, turn!
Turn, O Apollo! A voice? it was a soul
That breathed its audible thought upon the air
In music: On swift foot I turned, and lo,
Beauty that awed the sense like fear! a form
Majestical and lovely as a shape
Born of the slumbers of a dreaming god,
And bright as she begotten of the Sun
On his own splendor; yet were her dark eyes
Sad as the evening: My unprompted lips
Breathed forth Calliope! Scarce was the air
Made music by the word, when from my sight
She faded, and her eyes alone from the pale air
Looked sadly forth, then waned,—with them my life
Seemed to dissolve—my anguished soul grew dim,
And falling there where should have been her feet,
I shrieked, Return, return, Calliope!
And Echo, that re-syllabled my shouts
When to the woods I cried Awake! Awake!
Shouted, Return, return, Calliope!

TO AN AMERICAN
STATESMAN

I.

UNTITLED Hero! what though war
   Swells not for thee her loud acclaim
Of voice and trumpet sounding far;
   Nor shows the heaven of thy fame
The star to form whose halo bright
Must rob unnumbered eyes of light;

Nor burn as to a Hero's name
The altar fires whose baleful flame
Must ever be (that fear and pride
May see their Moloch deified)
Kindled by the expiring breath
Of thousands on the field of death.
Oh! dearer far to freeborn men
   Hath ever been the simple style,
The home-borne title, citizen!
   Nor fear we that their hearts the while
Will deem that less a Hero thou,
Than if the laurels on thy brow,
   Won by the toil of patient thought,
Green trophies of the might of mind,
   Were plucked where purple conquest fought,
And by her blood-stained fingers twined.
   Brighter the leaves that crown thee now,
Than those, though bright, by Valor torn
   From danger's dragon guarded bough,—
Brighter,—yea, and proudlier worn
   Than those which, wreathed by Fortune blind,
As if in toiling Virtue's scorn,
   The temples of her minions bind.

II.

When Freedom, for her sons oppressed,
   Rose with defiance in her look,
And from her locks and threatening crest
   Thick beams of dazzling lustre shook,
To other hands than thine she gave
To wield in fight her deadly glaive,—
She had a nobler task for thee,
A higher fate than e'en to be
The chosen leader of a band,
      Who to her aid,
      Each on his blade,
Half leaping to the ready hand,

Had sworn such oaths as martyrs swear,
 Who for the faith their lives contemn,
That they for her should laurels wear,
 Or she the cypress wreath for them.

III.

And when around her throbbing star
Darkened like night the clouds of war,
And millions watched the struggling light,
And cowards gazed in faint affright,
And in each other's eyes the fear
Which none might speak, and none might hear,
A secret spirit-mastering awe
The strongest and the boldest saw—
Thy voice, in words as pure and high
And deathless as thy name shall be,
Called back, like some old battle-cry,
The parting soul of chivalry!
From backwoods wild to where the sea
Beats on a shore as bleak and free,
Men kindled at that word of might,
  As they had heard
  Our forest bird,
Rising from fierce and doubtful fight
And perched on Freedom's lifted beam,
 With bloody beak and dripping wing,
Aloud, in wild exulting scream,
The death note of a tyrant sing.

IV.

And when from her long pilgrimage,
Far wandering, through many an age,
Back to her birth-place Freedom came,—
And in their own faint hearts her flame
Kindling, they felt who deemed her fires
Slept with the ashes of their sires,—
And tyrant-slaves who had no care

For Freedom's ancient presence there
Turned pale, as on Platea's plain
She set her war-shod foot again,—
While Salamis! thy conscious wave,
   Which in its hallowed depths received
The blood of the immortal brave,
   With wild tumultuous motion heaved,—
And greener grew a thousand graves
   Where Freedom's bards and heroes slept,
As, less for them than living slaves,
   The stern-eyed Goddess o'er them wept:—
What voice was that which even then,
Heard from afar, could cause again
Her half-dejected soul to rise
Like morning to her drooping eyes!
Ah! well she knew its fervid tone,
Like her own thought that voice was known;—
The voice so lately heard before,
   When her fierce eaglet, southward flown,
Was left upon a distant shore
   To wing the hurtling storm alone;—
The voice, that in a darker hour,
When under northern skies her car
Turned back before the threatening lour
And thunder of approaching war,
Broke forth in tones as loud and dread
   As if her dead in conflicts past,
Starting from honor's gory bed,
   Had poured their voices on the blast.

v.

Our hope! Our pride! not thine the fate,
Unwounded by the hand of hate,
Unworried by the soulless pack
   That bay at rising honor's name,
To follow on the open track
   Of greatness to the goal of fame;—

But yet it may not, cannot be,
   That thou at length hath sunk to rest;
Still, still thy tranquil light we see
   As they who long by storms distrest
And driven outward see, returning,
And hail with shouts the ever burning,
Rock-lifted tower, whose quenchless light
   Untroubled, on a starless sky
And restless sea, and louring night,
   Looks forth like an unsleeping eye.

L'ENVOI

TO E. C. K.

AH, once I little thought the rill of song
   That gushed within my heart, would other be
Than that deep stream that flowed unseen along
   To far Sicilia, dark and silently.

An Arethusa of the heart, a stream
   That only for a moment into sight,
In some still grot where Hamadryad's dream,
   Should murmur up, then vanish into night.

But thou, while listening at its secret spring,
   Did'st hear, or seem to hear, a sound divine;
Was it thine own heart's river, murmuring
   With full deep flow, mistook by thee for mine?

Howe'er it be—I have assumed the part
   Of one who in the heart of Nature lives,
And, in the tuneful oracles of Art,
   Unto her secret thoughts their utterance gives.

And if my Muse for pinions have mistook
   The up-buoyant sense and wild desire to fly,

Felt by untutored spirits, as they look
    On some strong bird that seems to cleave the sky,—

And though like him to light's eternal springs
    It ne'er may rise,—'twill joy that others may,
And hear the sound of height-controlling wings,
    With eye of worship upward turned for aye.

Or if, with callow wings, too soon it seek
    The mount of song, and ill-assured in flight,
Be backward struck from its attempted peak
    By jealous gods that dwell upon the height;

So thou dost hope it shall not yet despair,
    But nestling to thy heart, more joy receive
From thy indignant plaint and soothing care,
    Than their neglect can wound, or scorn can grieve.

CHRIST
IN
HADES

CHRIST IN HADES:

A Poem.

BY

WILLIAM W. LORD.

Κατέβη εἰς τὸν ᾅδην.
SYMBOLUM ATHANASIANUM.

He descended into Hell.
THE APOSTLES' CREED.

Mortem suscepisse et vicisse, intrasse inferos et redisse, venisse in
jura Tartari, et Tartari jura solvisse, non est fragilitas, sed potestas.
PET. CHRYSOLOGUS.

NEW-YORK.
D. APPLETON & CO., 200 BROADWAY.
PHILADELPHIA:
GEO. S. APPLETON, 164 CHESNUT-ST.
M.DCCCLI.

PREFACE

"Of those which did believe the name of Hades to belong
unto that general place which comprehended all the souls of
men, some of them thought that Christ descended to that place
of Hades, where the souls of all the faithful, from the death of
the righteous Abel to the death of Christ, were detained, and
there, dissolving all the power by which they were detained
below, translated them into a far more glorious place, and
estated them in a condition far more happy in the heavens
above. * * * Another opinion hath obtained, especially in our
Church, that the end for which our Saviour descended into
hell was to triumph over Satan and all the powers below, within their own dominions. And this hath been received as
grounded on the Scriptures and consent of Fathers."—*Pearson
on the Creed*.

IT was my purpose, in undertaking this work, to give
poetic form, design, and history to the descent of Christ
into hell; a fact that has for so many ages attracted the
curiosity of the human mind, as to furnish occasion for
surprise that the attempt has not hitherto been made. As
regards the end for which He descended, I have adhered
to the Christian tradition that it was to free the souls of
the ancient saints confined in the temporal paradise of
the Under-world, embracing also in my design the less
general opinion, that it was to demonstrate His universal
supremacy by appearing among the damned.

A source of additional human interest was suggested
by the relation which men, as a distinct order of beings,
might be supposed to sustain to demons in the place of
their common doom, and under new conditions of existence; such, I conceived, as would make it possible in
some degree to realize even the divine fictions of the
Greek mythology, under the forms and with the attributes accorded them by ancient religions, and by the
poetry of all time. This could not fail to suggest the
further conception of introducing the divinities of our
forefathers, and of other great families of mankind, thus
bringing together in action and contrast the deified men,
or various representatives of an heroic humanity, among

different races: nor did it seem too great a stretch of imaginative probability to conceive that their general characteristics might be adopted and imitated by beings already invested by the human mind with an indefinite power, and inhabiting a world in which the wonderful becomes the probable.

But it is, after all, the general purpose of exhibiting the triumph of moral power over all physical and inferior spiritual force, in the descent of Christ into hell, which gives my design the complex character of a mythic, heroic, and Christian poem, and, at the same time, constitutes the unity of its parts. The ancients, whose representative types I introduce, knew and appreciated but two kinds of power, brute or physical, and spiritual, including all occult and supernatural efficacy, and strength of intellect and will. Virtue, triumphant by the aid of adventitious force, or relying upon unconquerable pride and disdain to resist it, was the highest reach of their dynamic conceptions. Moral power is properly a Christian idea. It is not, therefore, without what I conceive to be a true as well as a poetic apprehension of the design of the Descent into Hell, that the heroes of profane, and the not fabulous Titans of sacred antiquity, by their rivalries and contentions, brought together in arms for a trial of their comparative strength, are suddenly confronted with a common and dissimilar antagonist, and "all strength, all terror, single or in bands, that ever was put forth" opposed to that novel, and, save in the Temptation, hitherto untested power, represented by Christ, the author of the theory and master of the example.

He is not supposed to appear among them "grasping in his hand ten thousand thunders," but endued with an equal power, the result and expression of perfect virtue and rightful authority. His triumph is attributed neither to natural, nor to supernatural power; but to moral superiority, evincing itself in His aspect, and exercising its omnipotence upon the soul and conscience. That in the conception of a great Christian poet, His appearance among the rebel angels in heaven was distinguished by the former attributes, is due, perhaps, to the heroic prejudice of a mind thoroughly imbued with the spirit of pagan writers, and of the Hebrew Scriptures.

As to invention and art, if a poem does not commend itself by the interest it excites, the author, except in writing it, could not worse bestow his tediousness than in its defence and exposition. I may be permitted to say, however, that while a conviction that the character of my own performance must necessarily bring it into comparison with greater works, could not deter me from undertaking what seemed of sufficient promise to justify some degree of daring, I am well aware that, compared with these, it is but a symphony to a strain—an urn to a temple; and as such let it be judged. The reverence for great poets which, after them, would give no hearing to one using what we may call, for convenience' sake, the Christian mythology, is a prejudice as fatal to creative art, and as certainly tending to the poverty of letters, as would have been a similar notion among the Greeks and Romans with respect to the mythology to which Homer in like manner, and to a still greater degree, gave form and expression. The question in such cases is not whether the later poet uses associations established in the minds of men by earlier poets,—if it were, even Milton, and perhaps Homer, would stand convicted of obligation to greater inventive genius,—but whether he combines, for an original purpose, newly discovered with existing materials; whether the impression produced is that of invention and novelty;—not whether he originated the entire mass of materials, some of which, at least, are, with all writers who endure the test of time, as old as history and nature:—in a word, it is whether character and incident are taken from existing works, or are the result of new combinations, which flow naturally from an original design, working itself out in intelligible poetic forms.

EASTRIDGE, DEC. 8, 1850.

ARGUMENT

BOOK I.

DISCOVERS Satan seated in despair among the infernal powers, upon his return to hell after his defeat in the Temptation
of Christ.

Baal, an angel and one of the ethnic deities, rising in his
place among the dejected fiends, denounces Satan; accusing
him of imbecility, on account of his defeat in his recent trial of
the divine pretentions of Christ, and the despair into which he
is thrown by his failure. He advises that some other take the
throne,—which Satan, not ascending, seems voluntarily to
have abdicated, as the former intimates, in view of the predicted descent of his Victor into that world. He complains
that they have been disappointed in their hopes of relief from
the pains of their present condition through the agency of
Satan, and inveighs against the human race in hell, and their
elevation by Satan to equal dignity and power.

Astarte, a female angel and one of the Sidonian divinities,
replies; accusing Baal of disloyalty to his natural sovereign,
and defending Satan from his imputations. She is followed by
Cain, who, as the oldest of his race in hell, and as their natural
head, has been elevated by Satan to the place next himself. He
retorts the taunts of Baal, on behalf of himself and his kind,
defies and denounces him and his faction. In consequence, the
human and the angelic powers separate, and draw off under
their respective leaders, leaving Satan, where the opening of
the book discovers him, buried in apathy and despair.

BOOK II.

The inferior paradise and its inhabitants described.

Abel narrates to Adam and the Saints a vision, in which the
death of his Antitype, Christ, is revealed, and its relation to
them, and to mankind in general, indicated. At the conclusion
of the narration, the Saints break forth into a hymn, in which
they adore the Word in His threefold aspect of Creator, En-
lightener, and Redeemer of the world, and implore His
immediate presence and revelation among them, in their world
of banishment and privation—banishment from Him, and
privation of His light. Christ descends. The meeting of Christ
with Adam, and His reception by the Saints.

BOOK III.

In the infernal Hades the human and the angelic powers meet in the field to test their comparative strength, and decide the dominion of hell. The conflict, yet undecided, is terminated, through divine interference, by a tempest that overwhelms both.

BOOK IV.

Christ in Paradise declares to the Saints the purpose of His descent; explains why it has been so long delayed; announces His intention of passing over into the Tartarean Hades; and informs them of what is there performing, viz., the convening, through their contentions and rivalries, of the infernal powers, by their own act, but in the divine intention, in anticipation of His appearance among them.

BOOK V.

In Tartarus the angelic forces, withdrawn from the field, take counsel how to retrieve the disaster suffered in their first conflict with the human powers. Baal accuses the tyranny of fate, and advises another trial of their fortune, but unavailingly. Asmod rises and refutes the doctrine of fate, and denies that their defeat is to be attributed to its influence—concedes the equal power of the human spirits, and advises a secret and sudden assault; which they prepare to put in execution.

The human powers, convened upon similar occasion, are addressed by Cecrops: he congratulates them upon their partial success, but argues the necessity of strengthening themselves by alliance with all the races in hell of a common origin —intimates that the Titans, conceived to be the Antediluvian or Archaic race of men, and also the Asar, the Northern heroes and deified men, or those who enacted their parts, should be sought in the several and distinct regions of hell which they chose to inhabit, and their alliance and aid solicited. They approve the project, and send ambassadors to the Titans and the Asar.

BOOK VI.

The Ambassador to the Asar, after a difficult access to the region, enters the imitated Valhalla. His reception by the Asar.

The Ambassador to the Titans discovers and addresses them. His reception by them; their rising.

BOOK VII.

The Asar, seized with the Berserker fury (see note 2, Book VI.) at the sight of armed strangers, fall upon them to whose aid they had been summoned. While the Northern powers are thus engaged in contest with their kind, the angelic enemy make their attack from the air.

At a sound, supposed by them to be a manifestation of the divine power for their overthrow as in the former conflict, the angelic host retire. The Titans approach. The meeting of the Titans and the later races of mankind. The angelic powers return and renew the assault, and the whole human race in hell become engaged with them in a general conflict.

BOOK VIII.

A light appears on the side of hell next paradise, and Christ, followed by the unarmed host of saints, approaches the embattled fiends and infernal powers. Terror-struck, they retreat for aid to Satan (who has hitherto remained, as the First Book describes him, seated apart, and indifferent to what was passing in his domain). Satan rises and advances to meet Christ. Their meeting. The triumph of Christ, and His ascent from Hades with the Saints.

INVOCATION

THOU of the darkness and the fire, and fame
Avenged by misery and the Orphic doom,
Bard of the tyrant-lay! whom dreadless wrongs,
Impatient, and pale thirst for justice drove,
A visionary exile, from the earth,
To seek it in its iron reign—O stern!
And not accepting sympathy, accept
A not presumptuous offering, that joins
That region with a greater name: And thou,
Of my own native language, O dread bard!
Who, amid heaven's unshadowed light, by thee
Supremely sung, abidest—shouldst thou know
Who on the earth with thoughts of thee erects
And purifies his mind, and, but by thee,
Awed by no fame, boldened by thee, and awed—
Not with thy breadth of wing, yet with the power
To breathe the region air—attempts the height
Where never Scio's singing eagle towered,
Nor that high-soaring Theban moulted plume,
Hear thou my song! hear, or be deaf, who may.

And if not rashly, or too soon, I heed
The impulse, but have waited on my heart
With patience, and its utterance stilled with awe
Of what inspired it, till I felt it beat
True cadence to unconquerable strains;
Oh, then may she first wooed from heaven by prayer
From thy pure lips, and sympathy austere
With suffering, and the sight of solemn age,
And thy gray Homer's head, with darkness bound,
To me descend, more near, as I am far
Beneath thee, and more need her aiding wing.

Oh, not again invoked in vain, descend,
Urania! and eyes with common light
More blinded than were his by Heaven's hand
Imposed to intercept distracting rays,

Bathe in the vision of transcendent day;
And of the human senses (the dark veil
Before the world of spirit drawn) remove
The dim material hindrance, and illume;
That human thought again may dare behold
The shape and port of spirits, and once more
Hear voices in that distant, shadowy world,
To which ourselves, and this, are shadows, they
The substance, immaterial essence pure—
Souls that have freed their slave, and given back
Its force unto the elements, the dread
Manes, or the more dread Archetypes of men:
Like whom in featured reason's shape—like whom
Created in the mould of God—they fell,
And, mixed with them in common ruin, made
One vast and many-realmèd world, and shared
Their deep abodes—their endless exile, some,—
Some to return to the ethereous light
When one of human form, a Saviour-Man
Almighty, not in deity alone,
But mightier than all angels in the might
And guard of human innocence preserved,
Should freely enter their dark empire—these
To loose, o'er those to triumph; this the theme,
The adventure, and the triumph of my song.

BOOK I

CAME on the starless age of the uncheered
Dark night, that in the shadow of the earth
Hid the dead Saviour of the world, and gleamed
Upon the warrior-watched and virgin tomb
Which held the mortal of that man foredoomed
To visit the deep region of the dead,
And thence to reascend both earth and heaven,
The first pale day; and more mean-time the gloom

Deepened in hell—where, motionless, reclined
The sad immortals, chief among the powers
Of earth and air, giants and fallen gods,
And looked upon each other without word.
Nor might the grief that bowed supremest shapes,
Nor the dumb trouble in their eyes, find voice
While he before them sat who with a word
Had made them voiceless, and spake not again,
And looked not up, since when his looked despair
Had darkened hell, and like a black eclipse
Covered the hope that was its only day.

   Half to his throne ascended, on the steep
Sole-touched by his proud feet, as if dethroned
By his own act, and into ruin fallen
Self-hurled, sat Aïdoneus,[2] discrowned,
With foot upon a broken sceptre set,
And head stooped forward to his hands, and seemed,
But for the rising and the slow decline
Of his wide-lifting shoulders, like one dead.
And dread his aspect, even to their eyes
Used to all sights of grandeur and despair,
All tragic posture and the pomp of woe;
Not only for his immemorial state
Abandoned, and the rightful awe that still
Sat on his unkinged head and vacant hand,
But him most capable of grief they deemed
Whose strength was greatest to endure or dare,
And deepest his despair whose hope was first.

   So there before him, each upon his throne,
Sat as if throne and shape were but one stone;
And, for that space, more like their idols seemed
In regions orient, sitting, hushed and dark,
Within a woody cloister of close palms,
Or, old with lifeless years, in some forgot,
Rare-pilgrimed temple, or dim cavern, ranged,—
Unseen by all the stars. At length to break
The latent chain that bound the force of limb
And faculty in each fierce spirit, rose

Barbarian Baal; in his depth of shade,
Save by their gloomy and familiar eyes,
Not from the dark discerned; in shape conjoined
Angel and brute, in temper brute, but strong,
And third from Satan; whom with unfixed glance,
Under low-dropped and sternly neighboring brows,
He now regarded, as a frenzied beast
On his still dreaded master rolls his fierce,
Inconstant orbs. Him, ages now, unfed
With blood of slaughtered bulls and fragrant smoke,
Sharp hunger seized, and lion-pangs, to taste
Again such offerings, and repossess
The dark and secret land, whence fled of late
His desperate chief; not now from the armed voice
Of his great plaintiff, summoning its bands
Of vassal evils; not from thunder piled
On the crushed air, and titan-lightnings hurled
From his black solitary heaven, high
Above all reach; but from his far-stretched hand
Disguised as human, and the all-pure force
Of virtue, clad in human voice and shape.

   Thus hindered of that hope, and chafed, and what
Was godlike in him fired with shame, to think
How one by one the ethnic gods had fallen,
Disarmed, before the constant powers of heaven,
Met in the battle-region of the earth—
How many forced by slight antagonists,
Of puny frame and seeming, from their old
Usurped domain,—himself, on Carmel's top
Amid his howling prophets, by a man,
Defeated, and their prowest, in the wide
And wild arena where he met the last
And wondrous apparition marked with signs
Of Heaven and hostile purpose;—by such scorns
Panged and enraged, and long made pale with hate
Of gods terrestrial-born, but equal made
With the celestial, and to like domain
By Satan raised—the mighty bulk stood up,

Strong but irresolute, and sought to throw
The weight of that stern presence from his soul,
And from its ward unlock imprisoned sound.

But scarce they heard the first hoarse breath, that died
Ere his dumb lips had shaped it to a word
Of any import, when throughout the throng
They stirred, and grasped their arms, as if some ill,
Long pondered and expected, from the heights
Of ether suddenly had fallen; he,
Around and upward, looked with listening stare;
Then, like a cloud arming in heaven, grew
More black and dreadful, and his giant peers,
With copied brow, frowned back dread sympathy,
Published revolt and general discontent:
Yet unprepared they heard, when words like these,
Forth poured like shaped, articulate thunder, shook
The wide Infern, that from its shadowy sides,
Of deepest region, ruined back the sound,
As when one shouts within a hollow cave.

"Abjects—once gods! befits it now that he,
Sole cause of this despair, and for whose sake
We suffer, that his pride may play at Jove,[3]
God of this subterraneous world—with us,
His toys, for subjects—should here sit infirm,
Like his Memnonian image, blind and deaf
To evils that can add to grief that seemed,
Ere this, at greatest, and where all was lost
Bring ruin, and make woe in hell? 'Tis fit,
And time, methinks some monarch should ascend
The abdicated throne, which he perchance
Leaves to his recent victor, hitherward
Pursuing him, with unfamiliar feet
In the blind access hindered, if aright
The babbling lips of oracle have told
Of such a one's descent to these abodes."

He paused, checked by no voice, by none assured:
As when a ship, that on the world's great sides
Climbs the wave-ribbed Pacific, 'gainst the weight

Of tempests from the skiey Andes pressed
Upon the barriered continent of air,
Resistless back, and leaning on the sea,
Is hit by thunder, and intestine fire
Breaks forth, and lights the inexorable face
Of her wild doom; the stark, bewildered crew
Give her to wind and sea, and as she swings,
Helmless, from wave to wave, with crashing spars,
Sit idle,—so sat these who manned the torn
And struggling wreck of heaven, in this abyss
Storm-tossed; so startled, yet infirmly sad
With such surmises as could make gods pale:—
When Satan reared his head, on which no crown
Might plainer have writ king, nor horrent plumes
Shadowed more terror: His immane right hand,
Armed with a gesture of supreme command,
Rose with deific grace to herald speech,
Then, from changed purpose or disdain of words,
Convulsively reached forth, and, as it seemed,
Grasped at the shade of an imagined power
To wield the elemental arms that hung
Gleaming and tremulous in the storm-lit air;
And muttered thunder bayed the ear: At once
A thousand hands upon the broad defence
Tightened their grasp, and half uprose the throng,
Or in their places stirred with ringing sound,
Like the faint threat of war: But Baal, prompt
To seize the imperial moment that controls
The after time, though not without some sign
Of effort in his mien, wrenched forth these words.
    "Think not, twice-conquered, from thy sovran place
To awe us with a look, who see crowned Fate
Frown from a greater height on thee and us—
Thee quelled—and us, who far above all fear
Raised, as below all hope dejected, dare
The eternal Tyrant: the malignant star
Of thy dominion rose before our eyes,
Within our own horizon rose, and burned,

And fell toward the darkness, and, like thee,
A creature of the finite time—finds here
Its temporal limit and for ever sets.
Thy strength we know is great, but equals not
The combined strength it governs, the great force
And title of so many worshipped gods;
Which, if it be that might is proof of right,
May rightly govern thee, and henceforth shall."
   No answer Heaven's great traverser returned
To these bold taunts, though loud, he marked them not,
Nor heard; as showed his sinking head and arm,
And all his gestureless bowed form, collapsed,
As from a blow by an invisible hand.
And the infernal tribune poured amain
His turbulent speech, with words that swept like storms
Across the souls, celestial still, though fallen,
Of those high-thoughted gloomy deities;—
Words of just right and freedom, tyranny
And usurpation, lore their king himself
And tyrant taught them, when of old it served
'Gainst the All-Ruler: Nor did he forget,
But with the music of some sadness now
In his harsh tones, subdued, and smoothed, to speak
Of hoped deliverance, and the Babel-dreams
With which high-building fancy whiled their pain,
As of things real, merged in this despair,
And whelmed in this last ruin whose full wave
Broke high above them; and with wilful grief,
Over their drowned magnificence his soul
Still wandered and lamented, as the sea
Wails through a city sunk with all its towers.
   Nor spared his insolence the highest names
To whom heroic deeds had given praise
Among earth's deities, and so place in hell;
Or those for fortitude as high advanced
By its great regent; Cain and Nimrod first,
Alcides, Theseus, Orion, blind
Bellerophontes, and the names, long since
Dead to the human ear, of Anakim,

Titan, and Demigod, the infant words
Of fame, forgotten in her age, but here
Retained, and honored as became the great
And first-born offspring of the virgin earth,
The giant nurslings of her mighty youth.
　"Easy for you," he said, with voice and look
As when the aerial storm-maned lion roars
Against the earth, and glares upon the doomed,—
"Easy for you to king and lord it here,
High-seated 'mid the tyrannies of hell,
Who know no greater state, nor ever felt
Contrast of hell and heaven, nor proved his might
Whose lightning strikes high tops, but such as ye
Leaves safe in weakness, fable what they may
Of wars on Jove. No dizzy height ye fell,
From climbed Olympus or towered Babel hurled,
Here in these depths to find far higher place
Than, though presumptuous, your low thoughts aspired
Above the cloud-spread air; whose blackness scared,
And casual fire—not frighted Jove—deterred
Wingless invaders, heavenward, step by step,
Ascending; know, proud reptiles, mated ill
With children of the air, that from this hour
We recognize no monarch but our fate,—
No peers but are our equals, thus at first
Created, or approved by might." He ceased,
And his defiant foot and planted spear
Brought up an echo from the heart of hell.
　Astarte, then, whose anger, scarce restrained
To hear these words from her Sidonian mate,
Burned like the glow of fire through binding smoke,
Blazed upward suddenly, and all her moons
And deep tiaras of stars flashed rosy ire,
Virgin disdain tempered with grief divine.
Like her own planet rising in the east,
So large and fair the beauteous giant stood,
To them who gazed, more lovely for her wrath.
To none was she unknown, to angels there
A woman-angel, from her faith seduced

By bright Abaddon, and to them of earth
Regent of moonèd skies; but in the west[4]
The elect infernal queen, to whom far-strayed
In Nysa's flowery field, from out the earth,
Naked and grisly, came the king of night,
And shamed the modest day of her fair eyes,
And chased the clear Aurora from her cheeks,
Displaced with evening red, and dewy tears.
And thus she spake, with voice as when at night
One hears afar the instant birth of sound
In brazen tubes melodious, mixed with touch
Of stringèd sympathies, that with their tide
Of human feeling fill the hollow air,
Up to the dreaming moon, that stoops to hear.
  "More than defeat, oh worse than this despair!
Oh shame, twice shamed with worse defeat, that thou,
An ancient god, his fated feodary,
Who knew him in his greatness, when we all
Could not perceive in what he seemed, who took
The star-bright name of Lucifer, less great
Than stern Jehovah, or in what his state
Shone less magnificent,—that one who sat
High-throned beneath his feet, supremely placed,
And him adored, his creature, he thy God,
His pliant hand, his foot, his smile, his frown,
His friend, and favorite, till ruin came
Like night upon his radiance, and he fell—
A falling sun that after him drew down,
What could he less? his firmament of stars,
And left mid-heaven dark an equal space,
Here in this cavern with his troubled light
To glorify perdition; oh worse fall,
And death to our divinity!—that they
Should faithful stand who only know him fallen,
And thou shouldst be the first, while thus he sits,
His soul striving its death, to launch these shafts,
Making the wounds trenched by the bolts of Heaven
The mark of thy more dire though feeble aim.
What did I hear thee urge, deedless declaimer,

Against his faith and conduct, from the hopes
Fallen in his defeat? Who gave us hope
Whereon to build these hopes that we lament?
Who gave us from this den unhoped reprieve?
Gave yonder flowery world and sapphire sky
In the celestial ether, and, to soothe
This pain, gifts, incense, ritual dance and song,
With clashing cymbals jubilant, awed looks
And smiles and supplicating tears? Who raised
Our prostrate deity, in this abyss
Half-buried in its ruins, where it lay
Spurned by the brute and unintelligent
Wild powers of nature, storm, and flaming fire,
And loud, insulting thunder,—its whole force,
And almost life, extinguished, and its light
Nigh trodden out by darkness,—who restored,
Reared, and enthroned it on the heart of man?
And thou, who gave thee thy high-altared hills
And woody temples? whose pale rites my soul
Not more abhorred, above the cedarn tops
Of Syria gliding nightly, than to hear
These blasphemies that more pollute thy lips.
And what though from green fields and azure air,
In that fair heaven of our exile, sent;
Thou for thy vulturous thirst indeed long since,
And we by this defeat? What can be said
But that our enemy, and his, is God,
The eternal elder of all spirits, sire
Of all control and power, over all
High head omnipotent; with whom he now
Strives inwardly, and not with such as thou,
Nor thy reproaches feels, nor hears these words
I speak in his defence, who little thought
He ever would need word from any tongue!"

 Thus spake the queen of night, nor deigned to know
If well or ill regarded were her words;
But as when Judah's daughters mourned defeat
And desolation from the foe, she shook

The cloud of her dark tresses to her feet,
And sat beneath them, like a veil; dark, vast,
And stone-like motionless, like the great shape
Of their despair and grief before them set,
By the wan star above her stooping head
Silvered with light. Then high-placed Cain stood up,
A king in semblance, but whose head superb,
Gray with the downfall of afflicting years,
Suborned no greatness of its golden tire;
Nor among kings less than the first might seem,
Nor less than equal among angels stood
Hell's human premier, pale and sternly fair,
Of arch-angelic stature, like a god.
For spirit freed from bodily restraint,
Forced circumscription, if in essence great,
Of its true greatness then puts on the form:
If feeble and irresolute, though of bulk
Typhöean, adequate shape assumes,
Lopped of its huge proportions: And thus spake
The Homicide, whose hand first gave to death
The taste of blood; the lion of that pit
Where fallen he lay, unhumbled fierce and loud,
The first and eldest of his race in hell,
And by its older spirits, though heaven-born,
Feared for a youth accursed above their age.
    "Princes, since I, it seems, must prove my right
To call you peers, I stand not here to speak
In his defence who needs none, and whose soul
Would deem such words dishonor, did he hear.
But this I say, that of necessity
Ye fell with him, who fell; his satellites;
Who, had ye then been left, as now ye would,
In that metropolis of all worlds, (by me
Unseen and undesired,) without your head,
Had fallen to ruins, and been darker left
In heaven, deprived his light, than in deep hell.
Fatal dependency, and if unjust,
Let Fate be blamed, not him: But I, who stood

Probationary heir to those bright seats
Whence ye were hurled, I, of free will, joined cause
With you against your tyrant, and alone
Among you came, not with these scoffings hailed,
The first ally of your new founded state;
Nor heard their omen in the infinite cry
That killed the silence when your monarch gave
To this red hand, with that permissive shout,
Hell's second sceptre, as by natural right
King of the new-confederated race."

    Thus far, he spake with low but rising sound,
As when, uprousing in his shadowy lair,
The storm-hound of the north begins to bay,—
Thenceforth,—as when into the sky he pours
From his distended breast prolonged stern tones,
And, leaping forth, breaks through the crashing pines
With one wide roar, that swallows up the air.

    "Baal, thy airy vaunt of ancient state,
That overtops our new-raised deity,
Must be perforce the scorn of him who deems
Lost honors a disgrace, and sees not yet
What glory comes of station forfeited,
And while retained, ingloriously held
By sufferance, not by might: Not to be great,
Hear it ye pining factions twice the slaves
Of Him ye hate, slaves of his power—and pride,
And Thou, great egotist of heaven, pleased
With fair-shaped breath of muses that accord
Praise to demands for praise—not to be great
I deem it, in the summits of the world
To sit with worshippers in loud-hymned state,
Pomp blazing back on pomp, and voice to voice,
In swelled antiphony and chorus bland,
Returning echo up the wearied air:
Nor is it from an armèd hand of cloud
To cast the thunder-darkness that dismays
Affronting men, nor to their dreadful aim
To guide the whirlwinds that upkindle here

These black and smoke-enveloped lakes to flame:
This to be strong and greatly cruel—that
Is to be weakly glorious;—to be great,
Lies in the soul that on itself retires
For strength; this, serviles! I deem great,
Not to possess, but to contend with force;
By strength of will to dispossess our Hate
Of his chance sovereignty, who, spite his boast,
Is not almighty while the will defies,
And heart dethrones him. Be it yours to wage,
Who know no victory but success in arms
Or treachery, base quarrel with your chief:
I will assume the war; this arm shall lead
The earth's divinities, when Fate permits,
'Gainst your victorious kindred of the air,
By you more dreaded than ere you by men;—
But first, untimely scoffer, mean to prove
That other stroke than Michael's can smite down
Thy vain pretentions, who, with all thy host,
In second rout, hurled down these yawning gulfs
May find a greater depth than hell from heaven."

    He ceased, and with a sound as of the sea,
When some fierce wind that in the tropic sky
Hung black and dreadful, from its continent loosed,
Roars down upon the flood, the throng uprose;
And sea-like swayed unto its outmost verge
His audience, as the stormy impulse rolled
Onward, beyond his ken, its helmèd waves,
Up thundering far and wide, with crash of arms,
And spray of flashing spears, and plumy foam.
And far beyond his voice, as, where the wind
As yet fills not the air, wave urges wave—
Thousands on thousands rose in glimmering ranks,
Apparent through the gloom: At once, the broad
And rival standards of the earth and heaven,
This azure and that emerald, unfurled,
And opening, shadowed battle on the air,
Filled with armorial horrors, as beneath

Stood the deep space replete with armèd shape;
Then, soon, diverse, like clouds athwart the sky
Diversely driven, moved to form the war:
Whose dawn in their display the hosts beheld,
And, as when swift Achilles cleft the power
Of Ilion betwixt Xanthus and the gate,
They parted; these with Baal to the south,
Those north with Cain: But Satan where he sat
Like a huge tower half sunk upon its height,
Rose not, nor stirred, and starred Astarte there
Sat motionless before him in her light.

BOOK II

In the same world, of demons and damned men
The endless-fixed abode, the same deep world
Of pale, unbreathing realms, but in a clime
Where horror became awe, and darkness shade,
Lay Paradise;⁵ divided from the dark
And punished region by a gulf, so wide
That scarce a level arrow, launched across
By stronger than a mortal archer's arm,
Would plumb the centre; and so deep, the thought,
Though swift and patient, that should track its flight,
Must deem the abysm's bed had stayed at last
The fast descending arrow—falling still.
And here, as on the gulf's Tartarean shore,
Of wild and abrupt aspect was the soil,
Shaped by creation's storm, and unadorned
By the six artist days of after calm;
But full of wilful grandeur, and rich gleams
In rocks of carbuncle and all ores, and like
The floor of heaven in rough gold unwrought,
And idle wealth; and for a living realm,
In this bright desert set, as in the sun,
And like a dim and vast oasis, stood

The Paradise of God; of earthly saints,
Born ere their Saviour,—till that Saviour's arm
Should break its shadowy door and make them free,—
The sad Elysium.[6] Still the place as sleep,
And as dreams—beautiful; along the plains,
Swept by no wind and withered by no star,
With fixed, wan shadow, stirless aspens stood,
Dark myrtles, and gaunt poplars still and pale,
With cypress mixed: and many a frowning brow
And melancholy look in crag and steep,
Was smoothed by climbing vines and flowery weeds
That built themselves on high, with all their gay
Thick-tangled blooms, and on the barren rock
Hung odors; soft and subtle next to heaven
The clime, and, fit for spiritual breathing, pure:
Nor did it want some glimmerings like day,
But oh! how different from the dewy clear
Of open heaven; nor could it want, if fair,
The mirror, that by hand-clasped mountains raised,
Or set in emerald vales, earth's sceneries hold
To their own beauties; from the hills around,
Browed with black firs and cedars, with thick boughs,
That mingled with the darkness cast from peaks
O'er peaks uprising in the skyless air,
A thousand sinuous or precipitous streams
Lapsed with dim-heard decadence, and from sight
Fled, in devouring clefts, or slept in pools,
That deep within their bosom, held a dream
Of rocks and falling streams and prospects still.
    Nor did the place adornment lack from art
Of towers and temples, that a rugged clime,
Of hilly aspects, best befits for show.
For the pale meditative shades that here
Waited release to heaven, had not forgot
The beautifying skill of men, nor lost
The nature that impels them to indue
The nobler moods and unessential forms
Of spirit with material ornament

And visible being,—giving thus to sense,
And so by sensuous reflection to itself,
The pure immortal part. And hence as where
A stranger, in the opening flower of day,
Approaching far Ægina on the sea,
Or Corinth o'er the isthmus, sees in air
The snowy edifice of temples old,
That sleep upon the hills, like clouds of Jove,
And paint the fronted sky, but which the sun
Dispels not, to his wonder,—here the hills
At every spot of vantage, bore on high
Fanes with white statues set in shining frieze
And spacious pediment: such shapes as seemed,—
So airy light they stood, or large reclined,—
As they had down descended on the vast
Columnar pedestal, rising from beneath
To meet and give fit resting-place to gods:
And, though but human, not less grand the groups
That all the famed heroic story told
Of Jephtha and of Samson, regal Saul,
And David, sweeter Orpheus than harped
At hell's deep portals, with prolonged, wild sound,
Down the abysses wailing on the ear
Of the infernal Fate; but this, inspired,
Sang at the gates of heaven, and his strain
Bade the eternal doors of glory move.
  Upon a height by that dividing gulf
Once measured by the eye of Dives, fixed
On the cool extreme,—to the abhorred abyss
More near than the blest people used to roam,
Sat Adam, doomed, sad penance self-imposed,
His offspring to behold, who fell from earth,
Struck with mortality for his sake, like leaves
Cut by the noiseless frost from some full tree,
In yellow autumn. None escaped his sight,
Of them, who from the region of the day
Alighting, brightened the Elysian peaks,
Or those, more numerous, who, along the brink

That shored eternal night, discerned, afar,
Like dusky shadows driven athwart the clear,
Into the darkness fell, unnoised how deep.
   This without grief his nature might not bear,
Though nerved to patience by the strength sublime
Which he who views his crime with steadfast eye,
Finds in the stern regard. What could he seem,
Although but shade by grief more dimmed with shade,
But sire and head of an immortal line?
And now there was a splendor in his look,
And conscious strength in his large-limbed repose,
As in a man whom destiny inspires
To assume in soul the greatness which her hands
Invisibly prepare; or as they feign
Of the swart Brahmin, who beneath the sun
Sits without time or change, till death thinks scorn
To touch his withered life,—his penance done,
His eyes grow terrible with light, his limbs
Put on their youth, and his impatient feet
Already feel the steps of Indra's throne.
Eve on his right hand sat, with head declined,
From recollected shame, or weaker mind
Than to endure, with Adam, sight more sad
Than haunts the wide and ever frighted eyes
Of Niobe, for tears compassioned into stone;
And opposite reclined his second born,
First wept, and Moses at his feet, with fixed
Unalterable brow and eye severe;
And in his hands the tables of the law.
These solitary sat, and lower stood
Gray seers, and warriors, in old times revered.
For here came not the general crowd, though free,
Familiarly, nor lightly dared obtrude,
Nor but with awe approach the unborn man.
   But now intenser awe pervaded all,
For Adam's voice upon their wonder fell,
With shadowy, but so vast and solemn sound,
That silence not displaced but deeper seemed

In the deep listening of the dead around—
As thus the Sire to Abel—"Whence, oh son,
Was that sad look, the unforgotten sight
Of death, in thee first given to my eyes,
Again upon thy face, and in thy limbs,
But chased by smiles more bright than that was dark,
And such a glory in thine eyes and brow
That scarce I knew thee?   So on earth the sun,
When first I saw him darkened by a cloud,
And thought him gone forever,—like some grand,
High fronted, glorious angel sometimes seen
In-looking on our bower, then seen no more,—
Bursting again imprisoning cold or dark,
Rolled from his vapory cave, like noon on night."

　"Adam and Sire," the favorite replied,
"Unconsciously thy speech has touched the cause:
For to my eyes methought the sun appeared,
As often to my thoughts, a golden round,
That turned too soon its darker side to earth;
Or by the intervention of a shade
Stood ruined of its splendor: as it seemed
To my last-looking glance when sudden death
Fell on these darkened eyes, and like a blow
Bore me to earth, unstayed by foot or hand.
Nay, Adam, thou and Eve,—why does that look
Still haunt your downcast eyes at words like these,
As if I only of my kind had died?
And soon a flight of angels I described,
Together driving, in that dim eclipse,
From the four sides of heaven, so thick as yet
Came never, in an orb of cloudy wings,
Hitherward wafting the insphered souls of saints.
And that way looking whither they all held
Their mid-air voyage, I perceived at length
Why utmost heaven, through its golden ports,
Emptied itself of glory, and its state
Dissolved; while powers pre-eminent, confused
With meaner angels, filled the inferior sphere.

For Him, oh Adam! who on earth oft came
As from no higher power, and spake mild words
But awful, which we spake not and yet knew;—
Him I beheld, uplifted in the air,
Upon a bleeding tree that struck no root
Into the earth, but by the evil hands
Seemed fixed, which on a branch transverse had stretched
Him bound and naked, who still seemed, though worn,
By mortal-haunting sorrow and great pain,
To the gaunt spectacle and hue of death,
The same we called Jehovah, and no less—
To me a wonder—than Almighty God.
And, as I looked, it lifted up its head
And cried, so loud as never thou and Eve
Made lamentation erst in Gihon's vale,
On the returning day of sin and doom.
And darkness fell upon me with the sound,
And mortal fear.—But when unclosed my eyes,
To utter dark near wounded by that sight,
With orb restored, the like affronted sun
Stood large and glorious; and methought I knew
Havilah's cedarn shade, but dreamy dark
It fell around; and on an altar near
A lamb sent up its snowy wreath to heaven."
    Here stood a while the stream of strange discourse:
But none with stir or speech the wonder loosed,
Mute in all tongues and fixed in all their eyes;
But wider browed, intelligent, and intent
Beyond all picture, in the aspect old
Of bards and prophets and the mighty shades
Contemplative, that sat before the mount,
Themselves like hills unmoved. But now their heads,
Each head marked regal by the silver crown
Of millenary years, great Elders leaned
Involuntary forward, and their harps
Touched with preludings to intended song;
As when a breeze breaks from its crystal cave
In the all-tranquil air, and at deep noon

Sweeps through a grove on momentary wings.

But soon the silent seer from revery raised
His eyes, re-lumined with the vision's close,
Most difficult in memory for thought
To unperplex; where wake begins with sleep
To mingle rays, as oft the sun and moon
Shine in the uncertain dawn: and thus resumed.

"Then in the sun where, beamless, in the air
With sacrificial vapor filled, it stood,
I of a human shape became aware,
That me more glorious seemed; my bright
Celestial counterpart; that nearer came
Until the sun its circle wide enlarged
Around us both, and me invested fair,
Within its rosy atmosphere, with bloom
And splendor like the other, more and more
Transfiguring to his brightness all of earth
And gloom that lingered with me, till—too near
Or bright—I lost the image, and awaked
Here in this dusky light to see you sit
Familiar as before, with sunless looks."

Here ceased, but not in silence ended, that
Which to their shadowy senses seemed a sound:
As when one instrument, to tell its tale
Of wondrous motions in a human spirit,
Sounds in an orchestra, and all the throng,
In solemn trance, like lively sculpture sit
With open eyes, and mark not what they see,
Or through its unapparent forms look out
Into the world from which these sounds are sent—
Or with closed orbs, but sight attentive still
And subtly present in the hearing sense,—
Then, like immediate thunder heard, at once
From the long calm of all the powers of sound,
That slumbered in the banded tubes of brass,
The sea of music breaks, with wave on wave,
Rolled high, and driven by the storm of soul
Forth poured in human breath;—like swimmers they

Amid the sounding billows sink and gasp;—
So on the voice of Abel when it ceased,
A thousand voices burst the gates of song,
And on a thousand and ten thousand souls
Of the redeemed, through all that region deep,
Poured like a wind upon the sea. The sound
Even to the Earth went up; from voice and hand
Rushed mingled song and strain, like fire and flame.
And heard again were Israel's solemn strings
And Judah's singers, and the alien harps
That on the willows hung by Ulai's banks,
Voiceless above the murmuring stream. And Thou,
Celestial Light! thy praises filled the ear,
Abysmal, of immeasurable night.
Sun of all stars, star of all heavens, Thou
Wast by their song adored—resplendent Word,
"Let there be Light!"—and Thou, creative Hand,
That on its flying beams the image laid
Of all the flaming world, tremendous Power,
That gather'dst in thy wide-exploring grasp
The dark, diffused materials, and framed
The earth, and reared it; by thy mystic skill
Untaught, and force omnipotent, it rose
From gloomy waste, and bore the mountains up,
And hung their peaks in heaven;—Hand of might,
Wisdom, and mastery, that pour'dst the sea
Around the earth, the air around the sea,
And light round all; that weavedst the blue sky
Throughout the starry space, and held'st the entire
And rounded universe like an ornament
Before the infinite Reason's raptured Eye—
Thee glorious in day and night they hymned,
In hell and heaven; but Thou, of human spirit
And reason the light, redeemer of the soul
From darkness of worse night, eternal Word,
Begot without beginning, without end
Existing, thee, as the Messiah, sung,
As Saviour far more glorified. And break,

Thus rose the invocation of All Saints,
Break wide, bright Word, upon these sunless realms,
Prime fiat of creation, Word of power;
Light of all vision, glory of the light,
Lightning of glory! and on us whose eyes
Turn ever on the darkness a blind prayer,
On us, who, sunk below the living world,
See not earth, ocean, air, nor the vast wheel
Of heaven, swift-turning with all-circling flame—
On us, thou, milder than the lunar dawn!
Thou, brighter than the towering orb of day!
Sun of all suns and worlds, beyond the reach
Of night and earthly shadows, riding high
Above all heavens in eternal noon,
Descend—or to our eyes transmit thy beam.
        Scarce yet the strain could from its echoes deep,
With fourfold repetition from all sides
Of the wide subterranean cavern beat
In higher concord implicate, be told,
When from above they heard a louder strain
Responsive; and immediate light afar,
As from the disk of an appearing sun
In their dark sphere, shone o'er them, and in gold
Clad all that stood thereunder, gloriously
Revealing the assembly on the mount.
The splendor on their upturned faces fell,
And shone in each, as when the morning beams,
From the high east, number the ocean sands.
Yet blinded not, so clear and soft it fell,
And like a cloud of light, athwart the deep
And painful gloom: And distant, in the midst,
Girt by an orb of seraphs—on the immense
Circumference hovering, each with pinions twain
Erect, twain prone, and twain that clasped the air,
And spreading sunny locks o'er-streamed with gold
From open heaven—stood a shape like man,
With bleeding hands and feet, but joyful mien;
Wan, but with recent triumph in his look,

And calm, as one with victory not elate:[7]
And through the central glory drawn transverse,
As if upon his shoulders borne whose death
Redeemed its shame, behold the accursed beam,
Intelligible to their wonder through the dream
Of Abel, soon confirmed. Not swift the sphere
Descended; like a hovering cloud it came,
Toward them compelled, as if descent, opposed
To its unprompted motion, and against
The upbuoyant strains from all sides blown beneath
By trumping angels, were more difficult
Than, from the instant impulse, to obey
The stress of harmony, and mount to heaven.
  At length it rested, like a radiant crown,
On that sole awful peak, where sat apart
The Sire of men; who to their Saviour rose,
And for a space the First and Second Man
Confronted stood, each father, and each son;
The heavenly Father and his earthly Son,
The earthly Father and his Seed divine;
And Moses rose, his head unantlered now
Of the bright beams that made it dreadful, quenched
Before their brighter far; and from his hands,
Not passionate as once, with solemn act,
Cast down and brake the tables at his feet.
Then patriarch and prophet bowed at once,
Nor thought it shame that their large fronts sublime
Should touch the ground; and Abel bowed, and Eve
Clasping his feet, and all the multitude
Toward the transfigured mountain where he stood,
As on that Galilean hill beheld
In raiment clear, (yet rather, on this peak,
He glorified Calvary and the tree of shame,)
Throughout the utmost region, bowed the head,
Bending one way like plants before the wind.
  And oh! hereafter, thou whom this dark strain
Scarce dares to mention, for the deeper awe
That sinks its numbers, may my soul indeed

Join in that worship that it renders now
With visionary effort, or, more blest,
With tears, behold thee, though afar, in heaven.

BOOK III.

BACK into Tartarus from that bright peak
Resting celestial feet, and made the immense
High pedestal of a god indeed, my muse
Compels the wing; intent to sing, and me,
Her earnest listener, teach the fiery war
Of those intractable despairing spirits,
Demoniac and human, blown into a heat
And sevenfold rage of fire, that made the hell
Which outward burned and flamed against the shore
Of their assaulted being, a septentrion sea
O'er-glassed with cold in winter's dark extreme.
  Now like as day, struck with the mortal dint
Of cold and gloom, when rises from the earth
Black night, floods out his glorious life, and stains
With flaming or and gules the argent field
Wherein, upon his sinking orb, he leans
In haggard splendor, and, athwart the world,
Throws back his mighty image on the east,
And makes it seem two suns or set or rise,—
So with a sicklied glory from the blaze
Of martial pomp the region shone,—appeared
Like these the hosts opposed, as far apart,
In radiant gold and brass and pallid steel,
Glimmering athwart the intervening gloom
In either side of hell; but not like these
They faded, leaving night: in order set
For battle, and in thought prepared as erst
In will, at once with caution armed and rage,
Their mutual motions and swift steps o'ercame
The interval of darkness deep with space,

Till now into each other's gleam they fell,
Contiguous; though from each other still
So far remote in space as from the east
To the west cape, that shut the Atlantic gulf;
Then swifter rushed to meet, and swift, behind,
Wide-following darkness like a storm came down.
And high above them, in the air disturbed
By moving armaments, grim lightnings broke
In wavering lines, and seamed the opaque far dark
With rivers of fire, and hairy meteors streamed
Along the immense, or in the skyless height
Wheeled, and around them with swift motion wrapped
Vast lengths of sounding flame; or bursting shone
Like shattered suns, and either army dazed
And far-illumined; nor beneath their feet
Less glowed the iron path, and frequent flamed
The smouldering base under their dread advance.
    So many warrior-shapes then moved beneath
As never on the surface roused at peal
Of clarion, or in cadence beat the ground
To the loud hand of war upon the drum,
Or pale lips pressed upon the thrilling reed,
When moving nations armed flashed back the sun:
Nor had it been a field so full, or vast,
Though of all fields and battles were made one,
So thick the clime-bronzed race of demons swarmed,
So numerous the fairer flock of men;
The field so spacious that they trod, who not
For burning sea, or torrent rolling fire
Under its cloud-white veil, or vacuous gulf,
Or marsh of pale-spread flames, made turn or stay.
    So on they came, revealing and revealed,
And imminent with light, in what it showed,
More dreadful than the deep accustomed gloom
That partially concealed them each from each.
Nor were they undismayed, but high-enraged
Above a doubt of the event, they strode
With undiminished steps the lessening space:

Black and precipitous battle on each brow
Hung threatening; and each eye with victory blazed,
And saw the foe already by their feet
Down-trodden. First, and far-seen Baal loomed,
Swift-nearing, like the highest peak of lands
Half hid in mists, that moving seems to one
Whirled by it on the sea at morning-tide.
Asmod the right, and Ammon led the left,
The orient Jove though this usurped the name,
Nor less that Grecian god. To these opposed,
Towered adamantine Cain, both doomed and writ
Unconquered in his brow sedate and stern;
Naked as erst on earth, and yet than none
Less terrible, and armed with that dire plant,
Torn by the gnarled roots, whose stroke accursed
First burst the gates of war. Upon his right
Athenian Theseus marched, nor other seemed
Than when at Marathon his mighty shade
Paced giant-like before the patriot Greeks
Awe-thrilled and joyful, and his armèd foot
Broke through the Asian line. In look like Cain,
Alcides stalked upon the foremost left,
Thus naked and without armor, better armed
With strength and courage; the Nemean's hide
Thrown idly backward, showed his queller's hand
Laid on its knotty engine, with a mien
Lightly secure. On each part they appeared
As once in earth they did or ether; these
Like themselves,—those like the hero-gods,
They were or imitated there; but all,
Although in look still human and distinct,
Of spiritual stature, and with arms
Proportioned; like hill-crowning cedars waved
Their plumy helms, and, at each forward step,
Shook nodding ruin down and dark defeat.
    The other side, supreme, as they who feel
Superior worth innate, or time-faced right,
Meet rebels, with superb presumption came,

And port omnipotent; by which dismayed
And awe-struck as it seemed, the adverse front,
When now so near the tread of each to each
Like echoes came, made halt, and through their lines,
Suddenly retrograde, disorder fell.

 Then Baal, prompt to scoff, made hoarse the air
With triumphings like these: "Warriors in peace,
Peaceful in war! not overweeningly ye scorn
I see, and see in time for peace, wise thoughts
To entertain, though late; better resolved,
Doubt not, ye mockeries of our state, ye mimes
And shadows of our grandeur, pigmies swelled
And puffed beyond proportion—better willed
You seem in act to fly, than when, too bold,
You thought to meet the substance of your shade,
And try what strength might lie in real gods.
But thou, first parasite of hell, remain,
And fly not, as becomes their leader, first,—
That in the rear of rout this arm may reach
To drag thee by the false-crowned head reverse,
And strangle thy new godhead in my gripe."

 Wide-eyed retort with lightning filled the face
Of Cain, but thunder from Alcides broke.
"Weak head and arm, but warlike frown and sound,
And gesture dread, thee, and thy vaunting mates,
What dumb hierophant could doubt divine,
Since ye sustain so many dire defeats,
And live, yet only know defeat? And this
To us you threat, whose fame has made the stars
Still shine in our renown, and tell our deeds
To mortal eyes—such deeds as fill not heaven
Without faint glory even in this pit,—
To me!—who never knew defeat or shame,
But mean to add a labor to my twelve,
And from thy impious mouth tear out that tongue,
Engine of blasphemy and faction still,
And to this leonine trophy add the fell
From thy brute-browed and far less godlike head."

Thus, pillared Hercules,—and Baal replied,
But more disturbed, as more like his own boast
The harsh refrain, shook like a tower, that sapped
By secret mine, though full of war and means
Against assault and siege, threats instant fall.
"Dismay of thieves and brutes! learn from a god
Defeat, honored too much should I say shame,
Who honor thee to chastise: but know, that loss
In such a warfare as we waged, I deem
More great and glorious, than such as thou
To quell with easy victory, as we shall."
  He ended, and no time for further vaunt,
Or deeds, when lo—the cause of the delay:
On right and left, between the open ranks
Of footmen in deep files withdrawn, afar,
Through the dispersed smoke, chariots and horse,
In size and action to the gods they bore
Not disproportioned, nor unwieldy, showed
Tremendous through the gloom: of all-pure fire
Their subtle essence, into shapes like these
By orient or Argive warriors wrought,
At the quick hint of ancient use afield.
For spirit from the bonds of matter freed
Over the baser substance has more power,
To mould it into shapes diverse, and life
Infuse, impulse, and energy divine,
With swiftest operation of a thought.
  Ere word might fill the pause, upon the foe,
For such encounter unprepared with like
Or other means, rushed down the ethereous steeds,
Winged, swift, far-bounding, thunder-hoofed, and each
With lightning maned; and from their nostrils wide,
Breathed pestilence and flame. Themselves in look
And motion irresistible, 'neath the flight
They ran of spears and javelins, thrown behind,
Innumerous, from the chariots, that from far
Rained wounds and wide confusion on the foe,
Dismayed and broken; and the gulfing wheels

Trenched their deep way through ranks on ranks
        o'erthrown,
While in the swarth of their armed axles fell
Whole groves of legionary spears, like reeds
Cut by the sickle, but more quickly strowed
That living meadow by swift reapers mowed,
And iron harvest—stunned. But not by all
Was the fierce onset unwithstood: and chief,
And full of strength and stature, Baal stood,
As when in some great deluge, bearing trees,
Ships from their anchors loosed, and fabric huge
From its foundation raised, with clinging life
Upon the wreck, and all the human wealth
Of promontories from the mainland torn—
Or in the steep flood of Vesuvius poured
Adown its vine-clad sides—some hill untouched,
With its green top and plumy forest stands,
With promise to the world of future life,
And safety possible to men:—So stood
The Toparch strong: On whom drove Tubal-Cain,
Thence Vulcan 'clept, whose hands, upon the forge,
First shaped the warlike soil to sword and spear,
And chariots framed, and bade the trumpet neigh,
And gave a tongue to war. But in the field,
Too late, the fear of his great baron smote
The armed mechanic: by one impulse swayed,
The conscious coursers swerved, and where the head,
From the strong spine, stooped o'er his guiding hand,
A blow from Baal's sequent blade, reversed,
And sheer descending, fell; and into wreck
Sunk his wheeled pomp, together fiery horse
And chariot into smoking ruins fade.

  But him Alcides met, as through the field
He sought whatever had withstood the shock
Of hippogriff, and centaur, and armed wheel,
With courage still for conflict: whom, unarmed,
Fierce Baal thought, with one sure stroke, to cleave
Miserably twain: a moment his huge sword,

Uplifted, adding terror to its sway,
Hung like a bladed comet in the air;
Then fell, unmeasured, dreadful, from its poise
Thrown forward with resistless force and weight.
Back swift Alcides leaped, nor fled too soon;
His right foot stained the adamantine point,
That trenched the rock beneath, as where a stream
Breaks fissured way. Ere Baal from the blow
Retrieved his height, the hydra-quelling mace
Fell through the air, with horrible descent:
The stroke roared like a wind, and on his casque
Struck thunder, and his linkèd armor burst
From his huge trunk, as lightning from an oak
Breaks shattered rind and limbs; crushed acres groaned
At his decay, and o'er the din of war
High rose the iron rumor of his fall.

   Nor did less tumult swell the late defeat
Of monstrous Dagon, from whom, worse deformed
With hippodame and kraken, self-assumed,
So spirits can, turned infantry and steed,
Nor chose the ambush of his doubtful shape.
On him Orion clear, came undismayed,
And as a dusky dragon, in close shade
Of horrible thicket, sees, from his deep lair,
With sleepy orbs amazed, a silver knight
Shine toward him like the sun, with like blind look
He saw Orion; who, while thus he stood,
And unresolved to fight as god or brute,
Upon his many shapes discharged a stroke
More ruinous, than when, rising from the ark,
Angered Jehovah, in the secret night
Of his dark house, the biformed Triton struck
Invisibly, and both his shapes deformed.

   And they no better fared at human hands,
Who, vain of human empire, chose to seem
Their own invented fictions, in the wild
And wasteful riot of imagining mind,
By high, angelic genius poesied

In vedas and puranas, full of gods,
By accident or penance, raised to heavens
That on the blue Sumeru's summits lie,
Above the sun, in the unmoving light
Of Brahm;—but their romancers pined beneath,
In the immovable darkness, by no day
Alternated: Who yet, this day, would be
The awaking of their dream, the living gods
Of their stone idols, and together marched—
Bi-headed, many-membered, monstrous shapes;
That more by their complexity of parts
Encumbered than assisted, fell and writhed
Beneath the single, flashing hand that held
One sword, directed by a dual eye,
And by swift motion multiplied to meet
Their many-weaponed, idly striking hands;
Too late, in the dread imminence, to change
Back to angelic shape and wieldy limbs.

  Before all others terrible, advanced
Eight-handed Shiva, and, with insult stern,
Demanded Magog and great Madai old,[8]
Whose filial nations peopled the world's east,
That to their children's deities they, too,
Should worship render; but the answer felt
On his crushed brain, so swift—more lion-like
Than like dead stone—the fragment of a rock
Leaped from gray Madai's hand; unstayed,
Huge Shiva's head sunk on his rear-ward breast;
Then, one by one, relaxed his threatening arms,
Hand after hand its clanging weapon dropped,
And clutched the air, or sought with outstretched palms
To upstay his reeling trunk: Then Vishnu forth
Sprang warrior-like, and stood in guise and shape
More human, but, in stature, vast as when
To Shiva and to Brahma, claiming each
To be the oldest of the gods, he said—
"He that ascending shall behold my head,
Or that descending shall descry my feet,

Is oldest:" Weary years swift Brahma climbed,
And Shiva dived, but neither what he sought
Discovered, although Brahma's lie prevailed.
    All stood amazed, by wonder more than fear
Disabled, and no champion to assail
The armed and living mountain dared a thought;
Till Indian Dionysus, reckless, drove
His leaping chariot, whirled by tawny pards,
Toward the colossus; and a javelin hurled
High in the air where seemed to be his head,
But vainly, and another at his breast
As vainly threw; both through the phantasm passed
As through the air; then at his feet—where stood,
Beneath the mighty umbrage, the true form—
A third, and suddenly the towering shape
Fell into shadowy ruin, as a cloud,
By lightning rent, bursts, and descends in rain.
    But there the greatest imminence of the field
Hung doubtful, and the noon of battle stood,
Where Cain met Asrael.[9] He from heaven held
Commission still, executor of the word—
Fatal to all, in Adam—"Thou shalt die."
Task to fulfil by no damned angel sought,
But, eagerly, by him; less through desire
Of the carnivorous glut, than from the strange,
Inventive pleasure that he took to try
Each different means of death, and power in each,
And task the last capacity of pain:
To men invisible, yet by many names,
White Leprosy, and pined Consumption, known,
Hot Fever, and immedicable Plague.
But now, in his own shape, more ghastly stood
The mighty Ethiop: from his caverned head,
With hiding basilisks terrible, and browed
With night, down to his noiseless feet
Two sable wings fell wide; on which he sails,
Each day, o'er all earth's region, and which oft,
When he o'er some full capital, forewrit

For desolation, hovers with the Night,
Rain pestilence. And thus spake the fiend
Polluted most and deadliest of all powers
In earth or hell. "First rival, and my first,
But too reluctant victim,—who this hand
Preventedst of its right to the first death,
Thyself to feel it first; and found'st the charm
Sought of thy God against my dreaded power,
Less potent; seek'st thou again to prove
The miserable hour, the fear, the pain?
Or wouldst thou, for my victim not again
Fate yields thee, as thou deem'st, become my slave
By second conquest, and with torpid chain
Lie fever-bound in hell, or, at my choice,
Sit leprous at my feet, or ague-struck,
Unnerved, and palsied in my presence live?"
  To whom hell's premier answered, with close brows:
"Sick-haunting raven, pleased with carnal taste
Of carcasses, and stench of monuments;
Queller of babes, fierce troubler of the old
Bed-rid humanity, night-dismal kite
Earth's scavenger! dost thou thy service deck
With name of conquest?—for thy office erst
On me performed, of which thy boast is framed,
Take late requital now." Swift, at the word,
The felon plant that armed his hand, propulsed,
Swung circling to its aim: down Asrael sunk,
Like a hurt vulture, on his ample wings
Recumbent; but immediate rose—as she,
Sick with the peaceful prospect and pure air,
Aloft, springs from her rock against the wind
That brings the taint of death—and with that sword
Unseen, beneath whose wound the host
Of Sennachèrib without battle fell,
Or in dark duel, touched triumphant Cain:
No wound, nor perforate nor trenched gash appeared,
Ichor or blood diffusing; pale he stood,
A breathing time, but breathless; forward then,

As when that tropic wind that comes unseen
In sea or sky, a tall mast, cordage-knit,
With all its drawing clouds, snaps short—it falls
Sea-ward, and circling half the sky—he fell,
Without a sound till fallen, and felt death
So as the spirit can, and as the parting soul
Perhaps may feel it, when with mortal pangs
Struck through the bodily sense, but not destroyed.
    But courage now, from the first shock o'erpast,
Encouraged more, to see the fall indign
Of one so potent, in the heavenly powers
Revived, with furious shame; and, by their foes
Taught horror, armed with flames they fought,
And fire opposed to fire: flash lighted flash,
And lightning against lightning streamed adverse,
An on their helmets blazed, and round their shields
Rolled in terrific circles. Each a Jove,
Ethereal-armed, seemed, fighting; and the crash
Of simulated thunder wanted not
From fall of heroes armed, and din of shields.
Earth shook, and universal silence roared
With sudden dissolution. Nor withstood
The fiery cavalry the assault of arms
Of their own substance forged; down sunk
The snorting team, or into formless flame
Their speed scaped: when lo—a stranger change!
Below heroic dignity debased,
Gods, by demoniac instincts and wild rage
Excited, leaving form and port divine,
Took shape of lion, pard, or serpent fanged,
As bold or treacherous nature prompted each
With horrible suggestion. On each side,
With shapes of heaven, and human features, mixed,
Huge tigers crouched, and glared, or the scared field
Circled with threatening yell and fiery spang;
And unicorn and centaur to the clang
Of trumpets neighed. But such a sight not long,
God, from his all-surveying height, might leave

In heavenly prospect. Suddenly a storm—
Blown periodic from the wastes of hell—
Fresh fuelled with the wrath of fire, came down,
Involved with thunderous roar and dismal shade.
Like mountain peaks above the mist, the flames,
Through pitchy clouds, rolled their advancing spires
To heights unmeasured, and the sulphurous air
Kindled with quick combustion: wide around,
Linked lightnings fell, and thunder denounced wreck
To all that stood before. Not sooner fall,
When, in the desert, 'gainst a caravan,
Of merchant-camels Bedouin horsemen ride,
If the fierce saymel redden the blind air,
Robber and spoil, than these, of men or gods
Embattled, first, and in most dreadful field,
Fell miserably, with all their useless arms
And puissance, defeated, at the breath
Of their great Arbiter, unmoved, in heaven.

BOOK IV.

JUST then, as on the night that with veiled stars,
And brows with deeper folds of darkness bound,
Attended Christ's great burial, Titan-morn,
From out the east horizon's fiery gulf,
Upheaved his flaming orb,—just then, and near
Where, sunk below its farthest published beam,
Abaddon sat dethroned before his throne,
Amid the stern and darkness-deepening frown
Of mutinous gods,—the silent throng of saints,
Before the mountain-altar on which stood
Their sacrifice and Saviour, from the floor
Of paradise uprising, to the day
Of his refulgent look, unveiled their eyes—
Splendrous with unaccustomed light, and bathed
In the translucent dew from their great joy

Distilled, in unrepressed, calm tears, that each
Insphered a smile, as dew-born drops, a sun;
And made fresh flowers spring wher'er they fell.
    He, from his eminence, discerning all
His rescued flock, as, with the rising sun,
A shepherd, from his height, o'erlooks a field
White with his peaceful feudatories, smiled
Manifest love, which that far-banished realm
Than sapphire heaven more brightened; and these words
Spake,[10] far and near heard equally distinct.
"Loved and elect of Heaven, loved by me,
From everlasting, with fraternal love;
For whom I left the Godhead's high repose,
And clear and tranquil sway, and, in this form,
Have sought, and in this place—from earth
Descending, through the gate of death—
Meet you, with joy like yours; and greater joy
Preparing, shall soon lead you where with me,
They whose sole rest has been in sleep and death,
Shall rest from death in life, from sleep awake,
To rest in waking, where no night, nor sleep,
Falls on the eyes, nor dimness of the soul
Beclouds them, or from weariness or tears.
    But first, I hither come to win the keys
Of heavenly access from the sovran foe,
And your accuser; yielded to his hand,
Till one of human kind shall wrest them thence:
Nor does he doubt, who put to test the strength
Of military heaven, and dared to cite
His thronèd liege to duel, these to keep
In his propriety, 'gainst a foe so weak.
Now, first, shall your dark janitor suspect
That not for his strict hate, and your fixed doom,
He holds that office, but for his defeat
And your advantage, in the distant scope
Of Heaven's purpose, that debars your right
To heavenly station with the pure unfallen
Deities, and yet creatures, (who, because

Created, use their gift of narrow thought
More to be just than merciful, and great
More than magnanimous,) until a man,
Never polluted, and with glory more
Than they adorned, and with the Father's love,
Lead up his erring race, and in their shape,
Before the bosom-seraphim, and great
Angelic elders, high above all place
Throned, and advanced at the right hand of Power,
Authenticate their title to a seat
Above their origin or merit; and pride,
Heaven's sole temptation, and through which alone
Angels are fallible, to worship turn
And meet humility. My coming long deferred
You deemed, and, in this banishment, complained
Yourselves Heaven's orphans, if indeed his sons.
I came not in the green and sunless time
Of patriarchal writ, the shepherd age,
When on the sparsely tented Asian fields
Still hung creation's early dawn and mist,
Lest legendary soon, forgot, or mixed
With fable, should become the act whose fame,
Though harsh to untuned ears the hymn of death,
Shall henceforth be the music of the world:
But on the plenary and highest noon
Of human wisdom, though at brightest dark,
I rose with light, and to the greatest height
Of man's ascent descended. Now begins,
Far stretching o'er all empire to the end,
My reign on earth: Jerusalem no more,
But all the earth is holy. Sion still
Bears on her hills a temple, fashioned high,
And full of glorious office, but devoid
His presence who from human lips loves truth
More than his praise; and soon her Holiest Place
Beneath the feet of nations shall be stamped,
And bruised with iron dint: To-day is laid
With deep and sure foundation in my death,

Soon, in my resurrection, to be raised
With heavenly superstructure fair, the new
Jerusalem; the undecaying pile
Of glory spiritual, whose most pure walls
Shall be the illimitable air, her gates
The East and West,—but Sion is no more."
At this, not spoken by their heavenly Guest
Without some touch of sorrow, not a few
Among the dwellers on that pallid shore,
Wept irrepressibly; and hoary heads
Desponded patiently upon the breast
Of king and prophet; and a sound was heard,
As of the golden strings of many a harp
Broken by hasty hands, and sighs were breathed,
And sobs tumultuous; as when a band
Of exiles, on a foreign coast, to hear
The ruin of their city, while for wrongs
And injuries they should smile, break out and weep.
    But thus his interrupted speech pursued
The orator divine, seer self-inspired:
"The earth is mine, my empire over all
Imperial; and now to the defeat
Of hell, and of the last infernal hope,
I lead you forth; not for the unarmed aid
That ye can render, who, at rest, shall see
Victory from armies wrested, without arms.
And to this end, through recent quarrel, sprung
From the unnatural league of fiends and men,
Innumerous hell is gathering to one field
Her legions; and, in realms of heat and cold,
All the remotest lurkings of despair
Yield their dark tenants, in one confluent host
Assembled, to receive me with my saints.
    He ceased, and to the earth once more they bowed,
Thanks giving and adoring: low, at once,
Bowed saint and airy minister: but one
There was who nearer clung, and at his feet
Bewildered wept; no citizen more old

Of this fair region than that hour, with Christ,
The only human shape besides, he came,
And proved so soon the promise, "Thou this day
Shalt be with me in paradise." Then all
The ethereous host, inspiring mighty breath,
For conceived anthemings of vaster tone,
With noise as of the calm sea thundering, stirred,
And sunk and rose in sounding depths and heights;
And to that dark profound, from highest heaven,
Their harps drew echoes; and the solemn crowd,
Beneath and distant, whitening hill and plain
Far stretched without horizon, hymning in
With apt and instant hallelujahs, poured
Doxology and thanksgiving, highest praise,
And glory highest; while, through all the air,
Upon the multitude around fell flowers,
By seen and unseen hovering angels showered,
Profusely, from their hands and loosened locks;
Fresh roses, lilies, and violets, like morn
With evening blended: as if flowery heaven
Had shaken down its blossoms to the wind,
And all its thick, ambrosial branches loosed
Their bloom and fragrance; or the under sky
Its stars had snowed down, noiseless, from the blue
Serene of night. That moment, where, beneath,
The dread, transfigured peak leaned from the verge
Of the ingulfed, unfathomable void,
A shadow fell along the airy steep,
And vanished, like a just appearing cloud
Below the horizon driven by the wind—
A shadow, but with lineaments and shape
Like human, that grew pale almost to air,
And cast a look behind, that had made dumb
Deep groaning pain, or hollow-shrieked despair;
For Judas knew his Lord, and stretched his arms,
With that last look, reverse to his descent,
And, headlong, disappeared in the deep gulf.

BOOK V.

WITHDRAWN from that dire field, and far remote
Each from the other in the unbounded waste,
The hostile powers took counsel for their state
What farther, on each part, might be devised
To end the war, and in their vexed domain
Fix the disputed sceptre. And not long
The place to which the angelic tribes retired
To build again the wreck of war, remained
Without intelligent sound amidst the roar
Of elements dismayed, and guttural dash
And low-lisped threatenings of the sinking storm.
First, Baal lingered up, and cast around
A sullen eye, as if to seek a foe
Or challenge accusation; but none stirred.
Some sat with head bowed low, some lay supine
At monstrous length, and others, half reclined,
Looked up into the darkness with fixed eye.
But by their apathy not less enraged,
His fury dashed itself against despair,
In words like these: "Since none who shared with me
This late prodigious fortune, would impeach
My conduct of the war, or cares to hint
It otherwise had fallen had Satan led,
There haply needs not to enforce my words
The rebel-dared decadence of this hand.
Yet why of words speak I? at all why speak!
'Tis not the skill of words can cure these wounds,
Or heal the breach in our strong title up:
It lies not in the flowery epilogue
To an act barren of glory, or the pomp
Of eloquent declaim 'gainst earless fate,
To excuse dishonor, thus dishonored more,
And doubly shamed defeat, from foes so weak.
But this we all have proved long since, that fate,
Who to the strong gave courage, on the weak

Bestowed more cunning, and, for want of power
Found in themselves, the mastery o'er powers
Extrinsic: yet their artifice once known,
What more can it avail? But strength bestowed
Is a perpetual gift, if courage not deserts
The citadel of all power. Rise then, and arm!
Prevent their new devices, and perchance
Their triumph may prove prologue, in the end,
To worse disgrace, and be to our defeat
As when one lifts a foe above his head
To dash him from the height beneath his feet."

   He spake; but none who bowed looked up, and they
Who flooded all the field with disarray,
And loose disordered arms, rose not, nor stirred.

   Then to the moody senate, from his seat,
Composed, nor with defeat in look or mien,
Stood up mercurial Asmod the divine:
His argent shield, thrown back in peaceful guise,
Horizoned, round, his head and shoulders fair;
And on his ebon spear he leaned, with mien
That made it seem for this, not war designed.
And thus, unchecked by Baal's hostile eye,
He spake. "Much have I heard of late, oh friends,
Since the all-golden day of our estate
Gave place to this sad night, in which we dream,
With strange invention—heard and pondered much,
In the celestial argument of gods,
And imitative poesy of men,
Of destiny, necessity, and fate:
But only this have learned thus far, that fate
Is power, and power in us is fate, till met
With greater power, be it of strength, or skill
That makes strength instrumental. Both we find
Abundant in our foe, though of the first
Our leader but complains, with what just cause
Both to accuse ye know. Omniscient craft
I, least, can doubt in them, who me so oft,
Their instigator to device, have taught

Means to the end. The race, in motion warm,
Symposiac and amorous, yet forced
To rear their lives upon an iron soil,
And make their over-peopled rock yield life
Against its nature, every faculty
Of art apply, exhaust; and hither still
The warlike breed descend, and bring to these
Who arm against us each invention strange,
Each artifice and new implement of war—
Huge catapult, or enginery to raze
Walled cities at a blow, or overthrow
Whole armies, at safe distance, and secure.
What can avail blind force, though armed like Jove,
And limbed like Atlas, that bears up the world,
Against high stratagem, that turns its harm
Against itself, and binds it with the chain
Of its own rage, toils in its own attempt,
And makes its arms the armory whence it draws
Means for assault. Sooner shall we, here shut
Under the dark, unyielding doors of earth,
Storm the closed gates of heaven, and repossess
The seats imperial where our ruin sits,
Or, from this gulf of night ascending up,
Hang trophies on the pillars of the sun,
Than found a kingdom, here, upon the forced
Subjection of these less, yet more than gods.
Our utmost flight of hope must perch, this side
Success, on special victory, whose bruit
May clamor 'gainst the fame of this defeat.
But from what stratagem, since even here
Mere force is vain, as this sad field attests,
Shall hope commence? I know of none but this;
They through old instinct, though with choice of state,
Still keep their ancient shape, firm-knit to tread
The earth their limitation. Also we,
Though in this dungeon shut with human gnomes,
Agile and tall remain, with wings to soar,
Or dive, or sweep the air in circles, or extend

The equator, or the horizontal plane,
Or the deep pole. I counsel, then, to ascend
Into the darkness, bearing all our war,
And, coasting near the upper light and air,
Until arrived to where they sit secure,
In loose unharnessed ease, and pæans sing,
On them—whose wave of battle in this deep
Broke highest, and o'erwhelmed us—down descend
In cataract of main war. Which, if approved,
With instant speed perform: lest while we sit
And meditate the voyage, they prevent
Our purpose with the sudden clang of wings
Induced at like suggestion, and rain chains
And fiery missiles from the darkness down;
Or come trailing along the ground some damned
Invention, and strange implement, to throw
Huge fragments, crags, and flaming stones, and turn
Hell's bottom on our heads, who sit thus prone,
Disordered, unresolved, a host disarmed
With arms around, as if, without a foe,
By their own weapons fallen; so dismayed
And lost we seem, without all pride and shame,
Thus miserably escaped their first assault."

  He ceased; and they approved his words as wise,
And fit to become deeds. Straight, from the heap
Of waste confusion Alpine statures tall
Gathered themselves upright, and plucked their arms,
And standards reared, redressed their shattered gear,
And in their threatening limbs, new-armed, their strength
And purpose felt, and poised themselves in air
On their long-idle wings; with not less stir
Than the black cranes in Lithuania's fens
When, from the austral winter overpast,
Rise all the stormy clans, and seek the north.

Meantime, the earth-descended powers convened
In martial diet; and—high-seated Cain
First worshipped with obeisance due—began

Colonial Cecrops, father of the West,
And founder of the famed Athenian pile:
With weighty brow, that frowned high enterprise
Above sagacious eyes that tempered fear,
He stood erect, and crowned with that sole star
Of Hesperus; and these his words, that fell
With sound of weight, that echoed ponderous thought.
"Not less, in this armed council, than the first
To exult, I glory in the event
Of this late trial with the elder powers
Of their celestial vaunt. Yet victory I know
Not certain conquest; and to overthrow
Not always subjugates; nor in one field
Is empire lost or won; nor can one day
Decide the next, when foes so potent join.
They who best know and prize themselves, least fear
To prize their enemies. To us their power
Is neither shame nor loss, to think them weak
No credit to our own; nor shames it strength
To seek for aid, that oft prevents its need:
Which, not delayed, I counsel for our cause,
Against the next encounter, sure to fall.
None here would use a thought to look for help
To mighty Aïdoneus where he sits
With Hecate forlorn. Nor, if unsought,
Perhaps for sullen ages may he rise
From his stern apathy: while these will wage
Eternal war; and as the blue-eyed race
Of Asar, daily, in their own demesne,
On bannered fields, with joyful peal of arms,
Contend in tournament and knightly joust,
Or downright battle soon repaired—so we,
Not with like gentle purpose and stern love,
But fierce unsated hate, the deadly rut
Of unrepairing rage, and pined revenge,
By slaughter unappeased, but fed by strife,
Shall meet a foe as strong and stern; and, each
Unconquerable, to each the endless strife

Shall be defeat. In numbers we exceed,
And this advantage will our party still,
With augmentation, keep; for every death
On earth above, save of the few who pass
To blest Elysium, is to us a birth:
While to their side, the kindred powers of heaven,
Unprocreant, immortal, and ordained
Infallible, yield not the numerous might
Of their addition. But we need not wait
The harvest of our race for multitude,
If not controlling, not to be controlled.
The sons of Cœlus and of Odin sit,
Titans and fierce Einherier, undisturbed,
Each in their toparchy; and have not heard
The larum of loud war, or from the noise
Of elemental conflict in these gulfs
Distinguished it. I counsel that from these,
Ambassadors, on early foot, entreat
Availful aid. Besides the advantage sought,
'Twere to mankind much shame that our bad foes,
Who no relationship sustain or ties,
But of degree or rank, should make one cause,
And we, derived from the same loins, with one
Sole father, and one common spring
Of all our streams, not make one flood, one sea
Of confluent battle, and in one armed wave
Break on their leaguer, or main head of fight.
From Saturn, of the Titans youngest born,
So the Olympian parables unfold,
(Whom the pragmatic Judeans would fain
Demonstrate Noah,) sprang the race of gods.
Him vengeful Earth, we story, armed with steel
And saved from Uranus what time he thrust
His giant offspring from his sight beneath
The floor of day, but whom by Heaven himself
They celebrate preserved. From him, three sons
Shared all the earth we also said, and named
Zeus, Hades, and Poseidon. But the Greeks

To old Iäpetus [11] trace the human stream,
Brother of Saturn, whom these call his son;
From him Iöan, whence the Iönians spread
Westward; and from fair Gomer,[12] eldest born
Of the same sire, the north derives its swarm,
That from the flowery south poured forth, to hive
In frost and cold; from him it takes its name
Cimmeria, thence the Cymri, and from him
The Rome-recoiling German; and his sons,
Guileless and simple, virtuous without lore,
And warlike without pomp, spread from the steep
Sides of hoar Caucasus to the region dark
That neighbors the sea-washed Atlantis vast,
And northward, at the entrance to these shades,
Shores on the cavernous pole. There oft, at night,
The solitary fisher hears upon his door
The hollow summons to his task, and finds
His boat deep-freighted, sinking to the edge
Of the dark flood, and voices hears, yet sees
No substance; but arrived where once again
His skiff floats free, hears friends to friends
Give lamentable welcome: the unseen
Shore resounds, and all the specious air
Weeps forth the names of father, brother, wife.
There the weak commonalty of mankind
Most haunt, reluctant exiles, who their fond
Abode choose regional to earth; the more
Heroic enter the immediate heart
Of most profound perdition, and divide,
In these interior depths, their full-swayed power,
Imperial, with the ancient thrones of night.
    But not the whole of our unhappy race
Make that dark journey: they who erred
Through Heaven's ark counsel, or by high constraint,
Just homicides, and violators bred
To violence, the rash incontinent,
And they who break injurious oaths, at death
Are wafted to deep-realmed Atlantis, o'er

The wide sea unwounded by a keel.
Immense and dark the land; all the remote
Wild region in one solemn shadow lies
Of green contiguous woods, with rivers spanned,
That in their arms wind half the earth, and hills
Dependent, and dividing the blue air,
From arctic to antarctic Cold: and here
Live the new race a timid, twilight life,
Oblivious and expiatory, spent
In feeble war or chase. But soon, (so shows
Our divination dark, a gift no more,
Itself informs us, to suborn the praise
And adoration, as to gods, of men,—
Once yielded to our oracles, on earth
For ever sealed; yet who can cease to feel
A human interest in our common race,
And their dark history, storied or foretold?)—
Soon shall this upper limbo, and in part
Elysium, dissolve; the older breed
Of actual men shall touch the farther shore
Of ocean, and the hybrid race shall fade
Like hyperborean flowers, that in the rear
Of winter spring, and at his bleak regress
Fall, sickled by the steely touch of frost.
West from the gulfèd pillars of the wide,
Victorious Hercules, swift equine ships
Shall ride the unfooted ocean-road, before
O'erpassed but by the chariot of the sun;
Or when his golden cup Alcmena's child
Employed for Erythea, and against
Old Ocean bent his bow, so fable tells.
These, one shall guide, whose greater deeds shall make
Mine, and the more vociferated fame
Of Jason—in the voyage that called gods
To venture, and pressed Theseus to the oar,
The Dioscuri, and the aged might
Of Hercules—an old-time tale, a faint,
Far-listened echo in the ears of men.

Him following, the sons of that stern race,
Here seated by themselves, but whose strong aid,
If I advise with wisdom, should be sought,
Shall there build up a world against the old,
And balance East and West, and wield far-swayed
But liberal empire, and themselves their king.
   But what imports us more than such discourse,
Though what at other times best pleased to hear,
Is now to fortify our assaulted state
With league proposed to their great ancestry,
Already storied in deific runes,
And to our own and theirs, the Titan brood,
Antediluvian; and to this end,
Let speedy heralds to the north and east,
Their early-seized partitions of this realm,
Fly, winged with your commands." Here ceased the
       sound;
And the pleased diet on his proper hand
The peaceful wand imposed, and bade him seek
The Titans with soft words; the other charge
On fleet, aerial Perseus bestowed;
Then rose, and filled the dusky height with shape
And feature, and, for dawn of danger, roused
The hoarse, prophetic thunder of a camp.

BOOK VI.

To punish them, though damned, in whom the light
Of heavenly counsel scarce displaced the dark
Of human ignorance, the rod is slight,
The penalty not extreme. This, to their gain,
Found the gigantic children of the north
In the dim house of Hela entertained
More like death's guests than victims, though at best
With dreary cheer. Their empire, dark and wild,
But not from Pandemonium less remote

Than Paradise, in the uttermost bleak sides
Of that deep region, stands, replete with fear
And howling dangers, but unvexed by fire.
Here pallid heroes act again their deeds
Rehearsed in runes, and emulate the fame
Of the bright Asar,[13] and their state by bards
Imagined, in great Asgard, seat of gods,
Or frozen Utgard, territory wide
Of giants mountain-tall, and strong as winds.
Here Nastrond's snaky marsh, whose waves freeze black,
And thaw in blood, spreads under curdling mists;
Where base and coward lie, forever scared,
For punishment, with terrors ever new.
For the less monstrous, frowning Helheim stands,
Within whose icy halls the dead guests sit,
Unmoved, and mute through noiseless age on age.
But in more temperate air Vingolfa's bower
Shelters the tall blue-eyed, and flowers; both fair,
But without bloom; and Trudvang here in-walls
A space wide for a realm: as high up piled,
Valaskialf rises, roofed with blazing shields,
That spread a golden blush upon the clouds
Hovering on earth's near confines in the north,
And from beneath, like sinking Titan, light
A skiey arc above; so vast it towers
O'er deep Valhalla and its seated throng
Of godlike tenants: and the dome resounds
With fierce festivity and iron din.
    Here, with the Asar and Asynior, sit
The Einherier, and Valkyrior virgin-eyed,
Who each her chosen warrior—wooed a-field—
Binds to her breast, with golden tresses wound,
And pure-lipped kisses, for the only love
Of glory, yields: The Beserker,[14] who scorn
Armor, and armed, contemning coward herds
Hid under shields, and crippling from afar
The fair athletic limb with treacherous dint
Of foreign substance, hardened wood or steel—

Crouch naked and apart, and tear their food
Untouched by fire, and drain the brimfull skulls
Of giants, while their insolent wild scorn
For Odin's self, and for the thunderer Thor,
The danger of his hammer scarce restrains.
Beneath the board huge wolves, like house dogs, slink,
Whose hunger glares, alike, on feast and guests;
And haunting ravens flit above, with song
Dissonant; or the dusky favorites perch,
And wing the foodfull hand imbrued with war.

   Then rise the throng with frowns, who late like friends
Sat side by side, and spoke each other's praise,
And to the field rush stormful; where each day
The Valkyrior choose the brave, and to the rest
Leave widowhood. Yet oft to him that falls
Comes the impartial maid, as when at first
She marked his red cheek in the pallid field:
Who as he fell—stooping with arms dispread
Under her smiling locks of shadowy gold
Down from her checked, ethereal, snowy steed—
Beheld her, and forgot defeat and shame;
Nor heard the taunts of his too numerous foe
The dying warrior, on whom Glory's self,
Incarnate, seemed to smile, and bend her rays.

   Now, on his broad-winged sandals, to this bourne
Of souls heroic, Perseus, from the bow
Of their great purpose sent who ruled his speed,
Came like an arrow; nor once paused in all
His spacious flight, till far pursued, as when
A ship from the equatorial—through half
The heavenly—circle, down the polar sky
Sails till she hits the impenetrable cold.
At length his swift feet stayed upon the edge
Of the steep gulf Gingungagap, that yawns
From shore to shore, as wide as that which laves
Swart Afric's forehead, and the pillared feet
Of Europe, her pale sister, on each hand.
No element, however, that which parts

Bleak Niffelheim from Muspelheim contained,[15]
For oared or wafted way, with transport large,
Like that which from old Carthage to the wall
Of Roman empire, and to Afric back,
Defeating and defeated nations bore;
But in its stead a void and dismal depth,
Whose dumb abyss afflicted more the ear
Than that when roars, with side-redoubled sound,
The inwashing sea 'gainst Calpe's windy stroke.
No other means of passage here appeared,
Than a faint rainbow, that, by what dim light
Strays hither from the earth, upon an arch
Of mist, foundationless, stands built, and spans
The dreadful space. Still he who boldly treads
Will find it firm, but with one fear he sinks
Into the steep vacuity, unstayed
By foot or grasping hand. Let him who knows
What glory is, bethink him if his feet
Have not o'erpassed this bridge, in Sagas called
Bifrost, that leads to the abode of gods.
O'er this, as on a solid arc of rock,
Or mortised timber firm, undaunted strode
The mighty courier; and before him found,
Upon the farther coast, a barrier huge
Of icy mountains, upon either side
Stretched like a sheer precipitous wall, whose top
Rose inaccessible to sight. But he
Like wind or flame, aloft, unbaffled, sprang;
And, like an eagle on a mountain's side,
Upright ascended, with ethereal step
Scaling the dizzy steep: availed him then
The wingèd gift compelled, for their one eye
And single tooth, from Ceto's hoary brood.
　　Now on the breathless peak he stood, and cast
On all sides round his armèd image down,
That from the icy cliffs gleamed out infract.
And far across a plain, and o'er wide seas,
And deep-sunk vales in which the glassy mist

Stood undistinguishable from lake or sea,
In the inferior horizon, he beheld
The top of huge Valaskialf and the tower
Of godlike Odin; that, far-off, appeared
A natural mountain, overshaped by art.
Soon on that side, precipitant, like a star,
Or meteor, he fell from peak to peak
Just touched with winged and scarce alighting feet,
And reached the level vale; through which so swift
Half ran, half flew the wing-dight, glorious child
Of golden Jove, the mist on the cold air
Blown from his nostrils—and that half concealed
His burnished armor, and the nymph's clear gift,
The sun-forged helm whose day-like beams could make
Invisible whoever wore it, at his will—
Behind him shone in the clear ether, stained
By his irradiant voyage, like the wake
Of a swift orient ship when it seems one
With that of the great sun, that sinks astern.
    At length Valaskialf's gates and solemn porch
Stood wide and deep before him, only kept
By Cerbèrean Fenris, who, too late,
Uproused his gaunt and monstrous corpse to bay
The foreign step. Before the snaky head
By the intruding Gorgophont displayed,
Fixed stood the stony glare in his wide eyes,
The huge portcullis of his craggy jaw
Stood open, and the warning howl, unheard,
Still swelled his rigid throat. So on he passed
And in Valhalla at the banquet stood
Unseen, beneath the wondrous helm, by eye
Of any god; who wondered not the less
At the fixed stare, and long, affrighted howl
Of spectral ban-wolf, and the ominous croak
Of wheeling ravens, with the instant scream
Of joyful vultures from their bannered perch
Along the wall. Then runic Bragur, moved
With frenzied portent, loosed his robes and hair,

And to his shrieking harp loud raved the song
Of Ragnarok,[16] oft heard in Odin's hall
With imitative din. Profuse of death
The rune, sung with a battle's sound, and shrill
With desolation, fit to please the ear
Of dreaming horror: and its theme the great
And final war in which all gods and men,
And beasts, and giants join; till in the end
The gloomy Surtur from the heart of night,
To their destruction by Alfader doomed,
Leaps, armed with flames, and burns the day's clear light,
And stars, and sun, and earth and heaven away.

   Came to the fearful strain as fearful pause,
And, at the moment, the all-golden child
Of Danäe from his mystery flashed out
Upon their wonder; fair as Mars he towered,
Thus godlike tall, and terrible in arms.
Amazed the winking giants sat, and scarce
The clear sheen of his complete mail could bear,
And dazzling, sunny crest; each, meantime, drew
The breath through his stretched nostrils back
Into his breast, distended with affright;
Irresolute all, if they at once should fall
And worship, or strike dead the intruding guest:
Who spake—well guarded between sight and sound,
Bright apparition and smooth speech, to leave
No interval. "I come to lead you, gods,
To Ragnarok: no more the mimic war
Ye need to wage; now real danger sounds
To utterance of conflict, and the last
Occasion now of glorious strife, soon past,
Trumpets the universe to arms. The field
Awaits you where the Jötuns join their powers
Against our race, and Surtur sits aloof,
But doubt not shall avenge us, when the blow
Of God Alfader breaks the chain of fate."

   At this, like magic scene, throughout the hall,
At once, the crowded banquet to a host

Of warriors turned. He from his side forth drew
His adamantine sword, a beam of day
Tempered in deepest night, and waved them forth:
And from the towered and ample port, whose height
They threatened with their stature, crowd on crowd,
In thousands on thousands, rolled, as from a bay
Returning, when, at once, the land wind blows
And tide makes out, the many-murmured sea
Gluts through a gulf, pressed by the storm behind.

A smoother way, though in attempt and aim
Of equal enterprise, the wandering chief
Of Saïs found, than tasked the bright and swift
Son of the golden rape; yet passed a wide,
Abrupt, and dismal interval of life
In man, or plant, or reptile, which itself
Had seemed fraternal in that total death,
And solitude without an eremite
To feel it solitary. On he fared
O'er plains like great Sahara, only marked
And measured by the sky, but more immense
And sea-like smooth and drear; and seas o'erpassed
Like that which rots without a breaking wave
Upon its desert shore, and spreads above
Ingulfed Pentapolis, but rolls not out,
Nor in, at all her gates; with patient feet
Ascended mountains self-revealed, whose tops
Burned, from their base, like stars at distant heights
In the immense of gloom; then under earth,
Through caverns within caverns wound his way
In close ravines, across the gloomy roar
Of subterranean waters, and deep gulfs
That yawned immeasurable; his only guide
Down these sunk mountains, and inverted heights,
The star that crowned his forehead, and inwove
His sable locks with gold, and flushed his eyes,
Replete with eager fire. At length emerged
Into an ample region in the main

And common cavern of that lower world,
He sees what distant seemed like hills, and rocks
That fragmentary lie, confusedly heaped
Where left by some great deluge or of sea
Or sliding earth, with thundering glaciers borne
From higher regions, and whose awful shapes
Hint of old worship, fabling to the eye
As if for sacrifice by giants piled.
Instant he lingered,—and breathed, half aloud,
The Titans! but none moved; some on the arm
Leaned far, with head depressed, or raised; some lay
Recumbent, and half buried, where the soil
Had grown around them and the frequent rain
Of fire and ashes strown the unmoving bulk,
Incrusted, that it almost seemed a mound
Grotesque with human shape. With noiseless awe
The ambassador advanced, as if to rouse
Them loth, though for that purpose sought;
And, nearer now, the bright surmounting star,
That lamped his wondering eyes and wary feet,
Bronzed with its light archaic, wondrous shapes,
Things fabulous-vast and rude, that nature seemed
Striving itself to art, in head or group
Of half formed sculpture struggling from the rock,
Or art Memnonian, to nature turned
In gradual process, broken and deformed
Under the noiseless hammer of strong Time:
These, near, with human shadows broke his gleam;
And others, in the distance, half revealed,
Lay undefined, like fragments of the night
With which the path of morning is forewrit.
None looked, or turned, or deigned to mark who came
With unaccustomed light; nor might his look
Have awed them into audience if seen,
Though, as he stood to gaze, his measure seemed
A cedar's shadow in the evening sun.
But soon thus proemed his Egyptian tongue:
"O wonder never raised by gods or men!

And see I then the more than men or gods,
Of that old world the citizens, here doomed
To this inert yet glorious rest of power
Deemed dangerous to Destiny itself?
The creatures of a greater time, and doom
Proportioned! less than your once selves, yet oh,
How greater than the greatest of our world!
I from the later born of our one race,
And common mother, Earth, have hither sped
Ambassador, in their need against the power
Of ruined—not ruling—gods, to seek your aid,
Sought now, rest sure, where Destiny not fears
Your, but for her, omnipotent avail."

    At this Hyperion roused himself, and ope'd
His sunless eyes, assaying sight of whom
He thus bespoke. "Art thou from earth, O voice?
Then tell me if the sun still rolls through heaven:
An age, old with more ages, and I saw him not;
Nor his translucent ray has washed these orbs
With dewy light, and purged their thickening gloom:
And fear has much possessed me that he comes,
'Mid his long journey sunk in age or sleep,
From Ocean's doors no more, nor comes the moon,
That in his shadow walks, nor banded stars."

    "I come not from the earth," the voice returned,
"Yet doubt not that her green demesne is still
The journey of the sun,—but from the heart
Of this Tartarean deep, where gods with men,
Or gods with gods more truly, wage once more
The ancient war: but weaker now the foe,
We stronger far; yet not too strong to ask
The aid of your great potency—for right.
We also for a fallen Saturn fight,
And his old cause, against revolted sons;
Whom, for more shame, he finds in his defeat
Unfaithful; though his first dethronement found,
With that Hesperian Saturn, no sweet isle
Beyond the ocean, where soft nymphs support

His hoary head, loosed from its golden load,
And bed him in their bosoms, in his ear
Whispering the while old tales that make him dream
Himself still master of the earth and air."
    This heard Prometheus, where he lay supreme
Upon his rock, from which a tree, of those
Unsightly roots that rude and sparsely grow,
But never verdurous, in that clime, had forced
Its tough gnarled bole and split the stone;
As if from his indomitable life,
One nature in the rock and him, it grew,
Fed by the excess and bounty of his strength.
And thus he spake, but took no greater heed
Of any presence there, than if the voice
Had fallen from the air, or out of heaven.
    "Who speaks of war to us! who have subdued
All strength in armies lodged, or single arm,
Omnipotence himself have dared, and chained
With his own chain—these bands that bind us fast;
And by existence here in this dark pit
And closet of the earth, still check his power,
Limit his infinite, and imprison Jove
In his imperial domain. To act—
Strong should he be who acts, or weak, advanced,
Or overthrown—is weakness, and shows need.
But he is strong who with Omnipotence
Or wills without constraint, or else defies,—
And I defy. Then let the eternal power
That knits the universe with his strength, and feels
It through, and wields it as one moves his limbs,
Hurl himself on me, I stir not this arm,
Yet in the end shall conquer: let him break
His aggregated thunders, storm on storm,
Through deafened ages, till he lose, at last,
The reckoning of his blows, it is to me
But one concussion, heard, not felt, or felt,
Unpained; for I am all one thought, one will,
And that is to defy." He spake, like one

Silent thenceforth, and all the Titans groaned
A stern response, as at the skiey fall
Of region-thunder neighbored mountains raise
A deep and sullen clamor, long prolonged.
   Yet the sage emissary to despair
Gave not his purpose, but inspired to act,
Unconscious whence the courage came or thought
For such adventure, instantly advanced
To the great atheist, and with his staff
Caducean, charmed, unlinked his chain, and freed
The sleeping force of sinewy neck and limb.
Awhile with the strange motion of free power,
Restored from so long lapse that it seemed given,
And passionate incipience of thought
As to what might proceed of that great gift,
Weak as the unbreathed yeanling of an hour
Fate's aged rebel and Jove's tyrant lay.
Then, as the sea retires and for a space
Leaves where he leaned upon the gulfy coast
His caverns void, and the emerged rocks in air,
Inflowing on his steps,—anon he roars
Up from the dangerous main against the high,
Percussed, resounding, limitary shore,—
So rose the Titan, and his struggling arms
Extended in the air, as if he sought
The power who on his impious strength had fixed
With unrelenting hand the band of law,
Indissolute, though a world grew old the while;
Meantime the ear of Hell ingulfed these words:
"O Jove! and do I feel thee yield at length,
And tempt me to be God? yet tempt in vain!
No! though the universe besides should feel
Unworth and misery, and for that cause
Be seized with instant longing to rush back
Into thy bosom, I remain, and I
Deny thy greatness, greater in myself.
Yet should it be of fate and not of thee
That I am loosed this chain, but for her power

Not worn; O thou, who hast with me so long
Parleyed in thunder, and with lightning fought
'Gainst the impregnable fort of my disdain,
Then shall I see if thou with change of place
Shalt conquer me, as I have thee o'erthrown,
Though with all gods, and earth, and heaven to aid."
    Then old Iäpetus, of his stern son
Impatient, and his long inactive scorn,
Upheaved his gray paternal head and rose,
And cited their despair to answer hope
In words like these. "O breathren bound
In these afflictions, shall we wake, or sleep
For ever? rather should I not say die!
Here stretched until we turn again to earth,
Our mother, as they tell, to whose dark womb,
Meseems, we have returned to find our grave;
Or living, do but live as parts of her,
And she but live in us, as in these rocks.
Not without stern endeavor shall we climb
To heaven, and the stores of thunder reach,
That give us mastery, though, as ye have heard,
Our right at length sinks the fixed beam of fate.
Which way first opens, there success will prove
This change in fortune, or in time prevent
Our worse defeat: therefore this herald star,
Whose human, pleasing voice has filled the ear
Of dateless silence here with sound, whose theme
Is life and strength in arms, and vital stir
Beyond this tideless realm, all they will rise
And follow, who henceforth companion me."
    He spake; and at the sound, as when that famed
And wondering traveller a great city saw
Turned into stone, and all the peopled streets
Made marble, nearer life than pillared groups
In sculptured Memphis or great Athens set,—
Noble and merchant, citizen and slave
Stand statue-like, with rigid hand, that grasps
The stiffened mane, the warrior, prompt to mount

A reined equestrian shapely rock, that shows
The stony foam in his wide nostrils, curved
By his long-parted breath, but uncollapsed,—
What time a disenchanting trumpet blows,
The warrior mounts, the steed with fiery hoof
Resilient starts, the crowd throng in and out,
And all the city thunders with the burst
Of instantaneous motion,—or if where
Great Arthur and his champions around
Sit on their dreaming steeds in warlike muse,
Sage Merlin's wand, unburied to restore
To British chivalry its strength and flower,
Should split their viewless prison, forth they start
With levelled spears, but find no giants now,
Themselves grown giants to their dwindled race,—
Like these, or those—weak figures both to express
Such magnitudes—up from their wearied couch
The ease-tired Titans rose; but with a sound
As when an earthquake, from the centre, tears
'Gainst its circumferent motion through the earth,
And for an instant checks its solid wheel;
That shakes down cities with the sudden pause.

BOOK VII.

O Spirit of sweet Song, and child of Heaven,
Miraculous Music! who upon thy string
Hast caught, and, more subliming, poured the noise
Of bursting thunder, and the ocean's wild,
Vast monotone, and the shriek of hovering winds;
And, of slight instrument dost with a touch
Give to our ears the sempiternal chime
Of heavens through heavens revolving, I full oft
Have heard thee and rejoiced. But thou, stern harp,
Æolian, golden, of heroic fame,
Through which the airy spirits of the dead

Move viewless, and for ever breathe like winds
The Manes of the great! for other sound,
Who, with profaner hand, shall tune thy strings,
Tense with the touch of Homer, and to fame
Revived, his haply listening heroes bid,
Though in a darker state, appear in arms?
Yet thou, deemed dead, immortal-young and fair,
Divine Calliope—where in some cave
By old Scamander, or the yellow wave
Of Tiber, sitting, hushed in marble trance
Of statue pale, or thy own shadow hid—
Shalt hear my early strain, and lest the attempt
Jar on thy golden dream, thyself with touch
Of many-memoried fingers aid the song.
  Might creatures be called happy, the dark stream
Of whose existence from the only source
Of happiness is cut off, such might be deemed
The earth-sprung powers in hell's begun campaign,
Plumed with such desperate fortune, and their state
Of sullen passion into action changed,
And busy hope and fear; the tideless bay,
Their solitary port, that to the main
Of being heaved no wave, uproused once more,
And swelling with the self-same tides of power
And sympathy, that move both earth and heaven.
They all who toiled, or idled in the camp,
Drew from the fresh and glowing breeze of life
A seeming health, and to their aspect pale
Apparent bloom in cheek and lip, and fire
And sparkle in the eye. Some their new powers
Tried on the elements, to invent strange arms,
Missiles that on their object should beget
New weapons, wounding wide, or in the air
Burst horrible, and fall with showers of fire.
Yet here but little used, nigh useless made,
Where swifter means and motion stead, and weights
Thrown irresistible by a living arm.
Others defensive armor wrought, to fit

All movements, welted firm, and closed to search
Of tempered weapons, or the subtle wound
And venom of insinuating fire.

 And beings now of female form appeared,
But haggard beauty, to their former selves
Such as the day-paled moon, by early men
Distinguished from a cloud: and still their eyes
Gave light to their wan beauties, and seemed stars
Wandered from heaven, or such as hear the knell
Of fading night, with twofold service loud,
Rung by the shrilly summoner of morn:
Nor did their womanhood make hell more fair,
Nor its harsh gloom might mitigate for man:
Their sole employ, before this warlike stir,
Seated apart, to mourn, and like unseen,
Transfigured Progne, grieve out all their night
With tales of treacherous love in life long past,
And go through all the story of the world,
And all their scorns and loves, here turned to hate
If lust, indifference if love. But now
Familiar war with pleasing dread subdued,
And glorious lure of famed heroic strength
Attracted these stern dames again to mix
With hated men. Nor did they want some sense
Of old association in their sex
With warlike feats on earth, by them admired,
For them achieved. Mycæna's rugged queen,
Frowned back by stern Ægisthus, turned
To Agamemnon, who turned not, nor met
Her eyes, but with his own, amidst the crowd,
Sought Iphigenia. Helen armed the pale
Priamides, to whom the presence there
Of great Achilles was more sad than hell.
Electra to Orestes half gave heed,
Half to Pylades, and the manly queen
Penthesilea on Achilles gazed,
And marked the hand that wounded, and the eye
That other wounds might make and heal: and midst,

Sat, in a hushed and unintruded space,
Eternal Homer, and his thousand-toned
Continuous harp, to that immortal tale
Of Troy subverted, and the adventured way
Of gray Ulysses, rung with sounds that awed
More than Dictæan thunder; and which drew
To that dim deep the all-illumined shape
Of glory down from heaven: Achilles smiled,
The Atridæ, and grand Ajax, his self-judge
And executioner, smiled each to see
His virtues and the faults, his virtue's best
And best loved flatterers, distinct alike,
In the just mirror of his Jove-like thought
Reflected; and more wondered to perceive
Himself made greater to himself, and deeds
Heroic, and armed fortitude admired
More in rehearsal than in conscious act.

Which to repeat, indeed, full soon they met
An unexpected summons. For the Northern powers,
Advanced far as to the aspect of armed men,
Reckless, and blinded to the swift affront
Of their bright leader, and remonstrance loud
To their mistaken fury, with unchecked,
Headlong proclivity to whatever seemed
To promise their sole joy, upon them fell,
Unsignalled, as a self-loosed weight of snow
Tears down some Alpine summit to the vale.
But like a torrent they, or like a sea,
Received it, and up-foamed, with wasteful roar
Swallowing its ingulfed wrath, and melted soon
The fractured and dissevered mass of power.

Perseus first himself, withstanding, met
The immediate onset, overborne by Thor,
And backward thrown upon his empty hands,
With head and feet bent under, and each link
Of his Hephestian armor rent from each;
That anvil for his stroke he seemed, whose sledge
Stayed not ascent with gain of gathered force;

But ere contrary hurled, it hung in poise,
While Thor glared up and down and saw but air,
So swift his foe escaped. But better matched,
Achilles of the sworded Odin stood
The fierce encounter. Yet they lingered both
Awhile, and gazed, and each admired and praised
The other for a god. So when a bull
That through the wild his vanquished kind pursues,
Or hunts the wide-mouthed bay of wounded dogs,
His hunters erst, by chance a lion sees,
With lowered horn he stares; the bestial king
Struck with his aspect, imitating, glares
With large recumbent head and glowing eyes,
His shaggy strength reposed upon his loins,
Thrown back and bent to spring. And soon uproused
The Achæan lion, but at distance first
Put forth his strength; and from his hand a spear
Sprang effortless, like lightning from the arm
Of alway-tranquil Jove—with aim as sure,—
But from the tempered barrier which the arm
Of Odin raised, glanced downward and struck through
Where joined the ankle his supporting foot;
Who forward fell, but with directed force
Threw all his height into one blow, heaved high,
And far descending, and the steely hand
Cleft from the wielding arm of Thetis' son,
Deemed woundless, but in vain baptized in Styx.
  Amazed Achilles stood with doubt and pain,
While Odin to his Vulcan-mated feet
Restored his stature. But, soon reproduced,
The living from the severed member snatched
The fallen sword; and now his two-edged grasp
Each plies, nor in the dazzled space between
Leaves interval; and shrilling winds rush forth,
With momentary swiftness, from the sway
Of their immense, wide-sweeping falchions, oft
With dreadful shock colliding, and forced light,
That kissed the gloom at every touch of steel.

And what would be the end might almost seem
Doubtful to Fate, where each with so great fame
Stood forth, and ancient laurels now refreshed,
Or withered more and rent, and strength so great
As if the embodied West and glorious East
Full-armed, in single duel met, should try
Their past and future quarrel for the world.
   But, on the instant, now above their heads
The darkness darkened more, and through the hosts
The tongues of wide-loosed fury ceased, at sounds
That ruined ruin, with the horrid stun
Of falling rocks, and swift projectiles hurled,
Resistless, from the height; so, ere the earth,
Their solid roof, unpillared by deep mines,
Down thunders, where, beneath the surface, delve
Gain's swarthy slaves—a shower of loosened ore
Foretells destruction: but still dreadlier fell
War's deadly forgery, spears and darts that rung
Like iron on iron shivered, where they struck
The adamant field, rebounding, or pierced through
Armor and armed, pinned to the fissured rock,
Inextricably, or where crushed between
Nether and upper flint, shield worse than wounds,
They lay afflicted with the dint that fell
Thick as falls hail, when, in the dropping year,
To rocky Sipylus bearded Winter climbs,
And marbles with his look the ceaseless tears
Of the invisible Niobe of the air.
   As when a wind upon the sea descends,
And hurls himself along, and holds his foe
Beneath, who leaps against him in mad waves,
If rain pours down with thunder, they their strife
Both cease with mingled moan and dash, and flood
Drowns flood and wind—these in mid-tempest stood
Becalmed, and suffered storm. But impious Cain
From where he lay, with hands and feet transfixed,
Crucified on a rock, supine, thus loud
Blasphemed. "Jehovah, or whatever power,

Hidden in gloom, exhausts his store of ills—
Armed coward, great in accidents! who vaunts
Of goodness, and the original pretends
Himself of soul and spirit, with discourse
Of holiness and justice, but brute strength
Employs against us still; think not defeat
Follows assault though unresisted found.
Pile earth and heaven upon these fettered limbs,
And me to ruin, thy creation make
One ruin, and thyself thereon sit throned,
And I stretched under; I am still as far
Above thee, and my unimprisoned soul,
Untouched, and free from chains, on all sides space
Smiles out upon thee in disdain. In arms
Strong I believe thee: author of a strength
Greater than found in thee, the will and power
That in himself he finds to be unpraised
Yet just,—good, yet not hourly kneed and sung
By angels, nor reflected in their smiles,
Who, though thus crushed, can deem? or who believe
Thy nature could produce aught to oppose
And hate it, foreign to itself, and doomed
Therefore to punishment? Or, if thy pride
Must claim our origin,—as misbegot
Unnatural offspring, why not then destroy
Thy alien creatures, and the ill-tuned harp
New string, harmonious with perfect praise?
They nought so much desire; and to unmake
At least might prove thee maker, which till then
Whate'er thy power contingent, or by fate,
Or elder birth bestowed, and kept, once gained,
By cunning, and made sacred with the awe
Of forged religion, I shall dare to doubt;
Though with more waste of thunder urged and noise,
Thine ancient dialectics, or enforced
With arguments like these, so apt at hand,
And potent to convince those formed for pain."
    To whom thus scoffing, from the gloom a voice

Responded in like vein: "Great Cain, our foe
And signal dread, but dangerous most to Heaven!
We own the honor great, and not unfelt,
To be mistaken for all-swaying Jove;
Nor does our power proved on thee warrant less,
Nor the deep pain thy speech betrays; but yet,
Sooth to confess, we only use, like Him,
The just prerogative of superior force
To afflict inferior natures, without grant
Of privilege to retort. Of old indeed,
We little thought, at variance ourselves,
His rebels to have punished, and much less
Reasoned his cause: which now I do to show
Thee imbecile in intellect, thy sole boast,
As body, though more obstinate in will,
'Tis granted, than are some; yet less by far
Than many a brute, whose ignorance, the cause
Of his low fortitude, had been also less
Perhaps, had he, like thee, for ages been
Academist in this unfettered school
Of intricate and dark theology.
Learn, sophist, that Jehovah's right obtains
Not from his being this or that, but is,
Because it seems, and has the power
To enforce what it pretends, and punish those
Its claim withstanding. Higher proof who needs?
Or what superior sanction could the fact
(Though proved) of our creation to his deeds
Afford? or what thy arrogated proof
Of genesis by our destruction shown?
Vain argument! for we ourselves unmake
Both what we neither make, nor yet restore.
Or what propounds the imprecated bolt
Annihilating—that but itself leaves nought—
To the annihilated, and of proof
Made unintelligent; or if restored,
After what lapse of time, yet who shall know
Whether by power extrinsic or innate?"

Thus, to the atheist, the libertine,
Dark Asmod, subtlest litigant for ill
In the infernal forum; who his foe
Reviled, and with injurious defence,
Alike derided Heaven. But now in him,
And in the angel-host, and those oppressed
Beneath the advantage that their station gave,
Hearing took sudden captive tongue and hand
And every power, as all a coming sound
Discerned, yet distant, indescribable,
Nor to be told if it was tread or flight,
Or under ground, or both in earth and air;
As when an earthquake, on its march along
The Mediterranean shore, or o'er the sea
Submerged and sunk beneath its bottom, comes
By whirlwinds trumpeted. Nor did they doubt,
Who heard the sound, that, for these atheist scoffs,
God, as not seldom in their impious den,
Had bared his terrible and still lurking hand.

At once for flight, the ethereous army formed
Their hovering ranks, and on delayless wing
Sought a near mount; and on its farther side
Descending, perched, as on a leeward cliff
The ominous flocks of ocean wait the storm.

BOOK VIII.

In earth above, on the celestial round
Open to heaven, and clad with air and wave,
And on that side of the great polar stream,
Where the bold Genoese touched the strand, till then
The virgin of the sea, a marble stands,
Whose shape by old Ilissus many a one
Might equal, none excel; a fresh antique,
Birth of the old world and the new, that shows
How Orpheus at the twilight doors of hell,

Fast by lulled Cerberus, with forward stoop
And hand above his patient brow, explored
The hushed and awful deep. And thus, arrived
To where he left of late his numerous league,
With standards fixed and warlike sheen and din,
To find it silent now and void and dim,
Gazed Cecrops: and the hindered Titans stood
Expecting when his voice should clear the cause
Of their delay. But nothing heard or saw
The infernal pilot, whom conjecture strange
Held dreamy mute, and fixed on leaden foot.
For them dispersed upon the battered field,
Like fear possessed of heavenly argument
Proved perilous to the disputant, as those
Who brought their mischief, and on pinions fled;
And for the passion of whatever ill
Moved toward them, like a storm-predicting host
In deep Sahara, these, from sight and sound
Self-buried, lie, and wait the dismal wave.

At length he spake; concealing what he feared,
That they through paler after-thought had fled,
Doubting the dread alliance which he brought,
Of equal power to injure as to aid.
"Or have they gone, for whom I broke your rest,
O sons of Uranus, impatient grown
To seek the foe, or by a greater power
Dispersed, without a vestige fled—oh thought
Too sad, though but conjecture, for a dream
Improbable!—I doubt; nor can surmise
Which—or what else befallen: but this I know,
That in this dreary void I left a host,
Like gods in strength, and men in multitude,
And, but by you, unmatched in earth or hell."

To whom attentive Cain made quick reply.
"Fled—even sight should not convict the eye
Of one who knows us, although welcomed back
To worse affliction, than thy absence sought
With vain-successful mission to avoid.

Nor yet by greater force you find us fallen,
But by mistake and guile, thanks to the prompt
And helpful malice of inveterate Heaven."
   At this, all they who cowered beneath the storm,
Still felt, though past, of their angelic foe,
All to whom hope, undying, though shot through
With every star's malignancy, or pride,
Or curious inclination to behold
Their great allies, gave strength, uprose and stood;
Some towering straight and firm, some half upright;
And some from deep gulfs labored up, and gazed
On the large brood of Cœlus, whom their mate
Held with mute gesture and persuasive mien
Adroitly governed, yet, himself,—like him
Who yoked the lions, or who first bestrid
The snorting steed for battle, on the amazed
Confronted infantry seen moving swift,
And footless, like a god,—half awed, half proud.
   Gyes and Cottus loomed in sight, and huge
Briareus with a hundred folded hands,
Typhœus terrible with as many heads,
Each breathing storms, immense Enceladus,
Cœlus and Creus, female Themis stern,
More feared than loved, and pale Mnemosyne;
And, from behind, Hyperion looked down,
Like his rebated orb, when half beneath,
And half above, he leans upon the earth,
And on the shadowy hills and forests bleak
That edge upon his light, and the great world
About to rise above him, frowning night
And cold against his beam, casts down, from far,
One wide, last look of majesty supreme.
   These to the eye of Cain familiar seemed,
And nearer to himself, though he with those
Of younger date, and less affined, stood leagued.
And now, erect, with hoary might redressed,
And like an earth-fast oak—that stronger seems,
Its twisted fibre bared, when sacred made

To vegeance by the unvictimed bolt of Heaven,
Than when its rooted strength and verdant tower
Turned the direct north wind—before them stood
Their Elder, and undoubted paramount.

But thoughtful most the seeming shame and loss
Of his confounded myrmidons to retrieve,
Soon, at his hest, a rousing trumpet broke
With melancholy clamor through the deep.
Nor might the chains of Erebus, nor the draught,
Lethean, of unmixed despair, nor fear
Of Heaven's thunder, nor superior force
In men, or gods, or elemental powers,
Retain them idle at that summons blown:
But, to the confines of the sight, the field
Uprose, throughout, and armied all the space;
Thus, when the swooping wind a pliant marsh
Of osiers bends along, its wings o'erpast,
They rise like one, and stand with whispering leaves.
Nor did the Titans less in these admire
Each splendid feature, burnished shield emblazed,
And silver-seeming limb, and pictured crest
With shading wings or plume, than they in those
Their monstrous breadth and stature, (for their bulk,
Whether on horizontal line it poised,
Or vertical, seemed hard to tell,) and strength
And aspect, as of things in nature, hills,
Or massy clouds in the horizon heaped,
And shaped by storms, were those, as these,
Endued with life and motion. But not thus
The bearded Asar, as they frowned apart,
Or without order started from their fall,
Saw the huge ancients; and the comers deemed
The Jötuns[17] without doubt, spirits of fire
And aching frost, the native powers of hell;—
Part of their myth unrealized till now.

And soon perhaps the war had sprung anew
Between these loose allies, had not again
The airy plague, returning with worse shock,

Made manifest the common foe. But now
The assailants hovered lower, and more near
The flight of warriors to their quarry came,
Like vultures stooping on a conquered field.
And some, with bolder fury, on the cast
Of spear and javelin following, sword in hand,
Leaped down; but the main army kept the air;
And each strange foes, and stronger, finds to cope,
And not inferior, though beneath. Wide raged
Tisiphone and her fateful sisters, sprung
From parricide, or the monstered womb of Night.
Their living twine, they resting, to the ground
Hung sleeping; or, if seated, spread around;
But now a thousand serpents hissed the ear,
And from their eyes shot madness. Otus fought,
And Ephialtes, and the iron blows
Of Steropes and Brontes clashed in air.
The triple-hundred hands of Gyes leagued
With Cottus and Briareus, searched the gloom,
And dragged down wingéd squadrons, as the arts
Of fowlers in a snare surprise their prey.
And loud Typhœus, fierce, together drove
Whole armies whirled and crushed, or wide dispersed
With storms blown east and west, and north and south;
As when a tempest with the fluttering leaves
Of a stripped forest plays, and on the air
The scattered tresses of shorn Ceres strows.
    But who, though frenzied with a strength like theirs,
And by heroic meditation stern
Trained like an athlete for the mighty theme,
Would dare to sing the strife where powers diverse,
Diversely armed, and numberless to thought,
Ranged, in one field, the depths and heights of hell;
To see, if sight might be, as from the peak
Of a jarred mountain one beholds the sea
Beneath, and storm above, and vapor mixed,
In the wild clouds, with light and glancing fire,
And all the sky involved with one wide wreck

Of solid earth, in whirlwind, with torn trees
And human fabric in the darkened air:
Or as if rather the essential powers
Of water, earth, air, fire, at once should meet,
In naked elemental force, to try
Which should destroy and reign; nor might it seem
Less greatly terrible when the four chief powers
Of hell encountered, in a war that left
No second battle theirs, but one full act
Of many made, and all the lingering plot
And circumstantial march of ruin marred
With the swift access of inbreaking death.

   But suddenly on the night, the element
Of tumult now, as once of silence, fell
A vast and spreading circle of clear light,
That from the side next paradise encroached
Upon the darkness, thickened more beyond;
And soon revealed the vexed and horrid space
With all its battle painted clear, and held
Distinct in its bright orb, in depth and height
And utmost bounds; as if celestial day
Had windowed their opaque dark roof, and purged
The atmospheric dross from all the clime;
And, on its edge, swept in vast demi-cirque,
The host of angels, unconcealed, it drove
Wide o'er their foes beneath; and far beyond
Alighting, they began retreat, by these
Close followed: with what cause for fear
Behold, and wonder—One of human shape,
In simple guise, unarmed, and o'er his head
A white and hovering dove! and far behind,
On all sides flocking to this emblem fair
As to a standard, legions wide-displayed,
And deep with multitude, the prospect closed;
But without spear or martial sign or sound,
Clad in the candid drapery of peace.
Yet were their garments clear not touched, nor feet
Pained by the burning soil; for, godlike, they

In moving walked not, but came gliding smooth,
Like stars adown the sky, or clouds along
The unimprinted air moved by the wind.
As from its shores, a shining river floats,
(Such things are told) unmingled through a pool,
So came the argent host; and from the van
Of glory, seeking darkness and the shades
Of deeper regions, all the dusky bands
Before them fled, like night before the morn.
  Oh! that the voice were mine, and mine the ear
And visionary power of that inspired
First builder of a Christian song, whose speech
Prophetic, laboring things too high for verse,
Foretold the end of time—doomed at the sound
And dreadful confirmation by the hand
Of that eternal angel on the earth
And restless sea upborne—and all the scenes
Of glory and of darkness in the act
Of consummated earth, and heaven withdrawn
With awful pomp, and solemn trumpets blown,
Pouring alternate ecstasy and loud woe.
I too must sing of judgment: not thy theme,
Celestial seer, the mid-air throne and throng
Beneath, paining the eye with multitudes
From the discovered depths of earth and sea
Uprising to the world-dissolving trump,
And filling east and west and high and deep,—
But of the angels, fallen first, and so
Prejudged in him their head, and head no less
Of human faction: On whom now retired,
Before the unshadowed face of heaven expressed
In human lineaments, both friends and foes,
And monstrous things and shapes, a gloomy rout
From the extremest boundaries of pain.
Why done, or with what hope none knew; but him
They knew the greatest, and to where he sat,
Still like their god, though bowed, and by despair
Self-turned to stone, cast up an awful look

Of doubt and supplication. He his eyes
Fixed on the spectacle, like one long blind,
Who stares, suspectful of some dread approach;
Then half uprose, and thrice again made feint
Of rising, ere the strength in his pale limbs
His stubborn heart diffused to bear him up:
But stood, at length, with air supreme o'er fear,
A shape of heaven, or with such look and mien
As God himself, who now in human form
He dared confront, had rather been arrayed,
Shaped to the eye of heroes, when they prayed
To Jove the arbiter. Soon, through the ranks,
Opening in vista wide and deep, he moved
To meet the bright invasion. Armed he came,
Plutonian, measureless, and dread as night;
Whose king indeed he seemed, and fit to reign
Over all powers; and wide around he cast
A darkness at his coming, as a storm
That from the ridge of some bleak mountain torn
With all its clouds, moves down in earth and sky
To overwhelm the sun. But when his strides
Had measured half the space—with what design
Who knows but He who gave him power thus far?—
He faltered, and with haughty steps reversed,
Before the calm severity of mien
And feature in his opposite, retired;
But lingered so, and sought against the shame
Of his retreat to hold himself upstayed,
Each backward step impressed the bedded flint
Whereon he set his strength and sought to stand;
Till at the gates of the dark fort which held
The keys of heavenly access, and of that pit
Sole egress, their appointed keeper paused.
Immense they stood, shut by almighty power,
And barred secure against less force and skill
In human or infernal siege applied.
And here, at bay, the great apostate turned
Full on his enemy, and frowned despair;

And roused his strength, and to his soul, sublime
With sense of single greatness, while his host
Stood imbecile, up-summoned for this hour
The thoughts of all that he had been in heaven,
Or hoped or claimed on earth, or held in hell.

   With steady front advanced the shining siege;
The unarmed army onward, and converged,
Came, glorious with numbers: but alone
Moved their eternal leader, and from far
His aspect shone with unremitted beam
Direct on Satan: He his dusky shield—
That heretofore, thrown back, his gloomy head
Around, and on his mighty shoulders lay
Like the horizon on the earth at eve—
Cast forward, drooping his huge spear, inclined,
But not full-levelled. All the host of saints
Stood still, and fatal sympathy first moved
A murmur in his own, with slumberous stir
As of awaking war: but onward and more near
Came the celestial Man; when once again
He moved, and with a forward step shook hell.
But at the instant, as with lightning struck,
Though none perceived the stroke, with arms upthrown,
Self-hurled, on the disputed gates he fell,
And ruined down their strength; nor fell alone,
But all his host the silent thunder felt,
And smote, with wide and simultaneous roar
Of armored limbs, the adamantine floor.

   But other noise soon rung, and from the saints
Hosannah, and hosannah! sweet and loud,
In that deep cavern, from the echoing air
Sunk far beneath the roots of earth, as sung
By warbling seraphs in the top of heaven.

   Now as the golden wheel of day that climbs
The precipice of the world, on that side whence
He shines at morning—brightening, as he comes,
Forests and craggy heights and seas and fields—
To early eyes, throws high into the air,

Opaque, or formless void, his welcome light,
And shapes the dark with splendid fantasy,
While hovering glories stoop upon his beam,
And crimson clouds troop in the bannered east;
So in the gloomy steeps and utmost height,
Zenith, and all sides round, of teeming hell,
Angels on cloudy wings hung looking down;
Or in the radiance hovered; or, on high,
In peopled vistas opening into heaven,
With bosom-seraphim, transcendent shapes,
And awful cherubim, before unseen
In earth or heaven, stood creation's grand
And glittering guardians, not revealed till now,
Lest deemed allies at need; and gazed, while Christ
And all the armies beatific passed,
In bright defile, o'er Satan, where he lay
Along the heap that thundered in his fall,
Supine, with upward face: But not o'erclimbed
By men thus easily, without wings to stead,
Had been the prostrate fiend. Then rose they all
Into the air, and swift the plumy throng,
Encircling, held them in their bright caress.
And in the midst, the cloud which that old fane
Made glorious with apparition of a form
Of human aspect, by awed priests beheld,
Received its body now; and like one cloud
Together rose the whole; while from the air
A voice fell on the ear of each beneath,
But seemed in Satan's, sole to him addressed—
"The Foe is judged." And still their eyes they turned,
And still their looks hung on the rising host,
Till seen like a receding sun, and then,
In the blank height of darkness, like a star;
And then the darkness covered all, but still
They looked into its depths, nor stirred nor spake.

ANDRÉ

ANDRÉ:

A TRAGEDY IN FIVE ACTS.

BY

W. W. LORD.

NEW YORK:
CHARLES SCRIBNER, 377 & 379 BROADWAY,
1856.

PREFACE

THE Author is aware that with many whose eyes fall upon the title of this book, "the attempt and not the deed confounds" him. But the consciousness that to whatever faculty for such an undertaking he may possess, he has brought a deep interest in the subject, dating back even to his boyhood, gives him confidence to hope that he may find readers; and amongst them, some who will be attracted rather than repelled by an attempt to contribute something to our legitimate American and National literature.

The difficulty of poetic representation, in regard to the most moving and tragical event in our National history, lies mainly in adapting modern and natural language to the necessities of verse, and to preconceived notions of tragic style. It is believed, however, that there is no essential connection between obsolete forms or terminations of words, and impassioned sentiment, and even harmonious expression. Nor do either rhyme or reason forbid that dramatic verse should now approach as near to our spoken language, as it did in the age of Elizabeth to a now obsolete but then familiar diction.

He has, in all material points, preserved a strict fidelity to history, in the province of history, and in that of invention a strict consistency with it. Some poetic freedom has been used with respect to two of the minor incidents of the history. The attempt of Champe to abduct Arnold from New York has been placed before instead of after, the death of André: and Arnold has been made to land with the British Commissioners, who came to treat with the Americans in behalf of André. A letter from him was, in fact, read at the meeting, and excited the indignation, which, in the Drama, is attributed to his presence.

It is hardly necessary to observe that the friendship of André and Mrs. Arnold, and its bearing upon the destiny both of Arnold and of André, by making communication with the enemy easy to the former, and causing the latter to be chosen as the agent in the affair, are historic facts.

The few directions introduced into the action for completeness of effect, are to be considered as descriptive. The only stage on which the Author contemplates the representation of his drama is the mind of the reader.

EASTRIDGE, *Sept.* 1856.

PERSONS REPRESENTED

ARNOLD: *Major-General in the American Army.*
ANDRÉ: *Major, and Adjutant General in the British Army.*
FRANKS
VARICK } *The Aids of Arnold.*
GEN. GREEN
COL. JAMESON } *American Officers.*
MAJOR TALLMADGE
GEN. ROBERTSON: *A British Officer.*
COL. ROBINSON: *An American Royalist.*
SMITH: *An American Gentleman, and a friend of Arnold.*

PAULDING.   A CHAPLAIN.
WILLIAMS.   WOMEN.
VAN WERT.   SOLDIERS.
MRS. ARNOLD.   COUNTRYMEN.

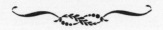

ACT I

SCENE I.

The Landing at West Point. A boat lying near. A soldier on guard. TALLMADGE, FRANKS *and* VARICK.

FRANKS. Sunset! it will be dark before we leave:
    The General forgets that you are here.
TALLMADGE. And here at his request; and for a purpose
    He has not yet explained: but let us hope
    The evening gun reminds him to descend
    From his bleak perch above there; where, you say,
    He overlooks the region like an eagle.
FRANKS. We left him standing on Bald Rock, that looks
    Quite o'er the Dunderberg; and which, like most
    Who reach its foot, you did not care to climb.
VARICK. Often, of late, he stands there until dark.
TALLMADGE. What takes him there?
VARICK.   Perhaps he plans new works.
FRANKS. He climbs there like a prisoner to his window;
    For to a spirit eager and bold as his,
    A garrison is a prison.
VARICK.   Why he asked
    For a command like this, I cannot guess.
    His wounds are a pretence, as those should know
    Who know the man.
TALLMADGE.   But many deeper wounds,
    Not got so nobly, and that take from these
    The honor and the pain, have struck his heart;
    The sentence of the Council last and deepest.
FRANKS. Since Pilate's, 'twas the most unjust, the pride
    And very insolence of armed injustice;
    The conscience, the shame rather, of the court
    Could not, upon the evidence, sustain
    The charge of peculation, nor their envy
    Acquit the accused with honor.
TALLMADGE.   It is strange
    That charges of this kind should have pursued,

Through all his life, a man, who, if not great,
Is what he is, despite them.

FRANKS.   Is it strange
That fear of his renown, so early gained,
Should, early, make the jealous, deedless crowd
Of new-made generals and their friends, who saw
How far the soldier stood above their reach,
Impeach the man?—and they are well aware
That even false and trivial charges sow
Doubt and suspicion in the public mind.
But it *is* strange, if you who are his friend—

TALLMADGE. If not his friend, I am at least the author
Of my own doubts; and what I see of him,
In his new station, does not make them less.
But when some damning fact has seemed to fix
My wavering mind, then all his wrongs and merits,
His greatness and his daring come before it;
And I must still respect him: and though all
They say or hint of him were true—we know
That the same man who fleeces his poor soldiers,
And makes the very beasts that serve us feel
His usury, is capable of deeds
As kind as just, and which might almost strike
Those charges dumb.

FRANKS.   But his accusers—never!
They know him; and they know that for their end,
His ultimate ruin, they can safely trust
A soldier's temper, and a poor man's pride,
And wronged one's rashness.

TALLMADGE.   You have felt, I hear,
His soldier's temper.

FRANKS.   And his soldier's heart
And generous nature. You, perhaps, have heard
That on this field of glory, Saratoga,
For some supposed remissness, in the heat
Of the excited hour, he struck a man
Whom admiration, and not fear, restrained

From taking vengeance: from that hour, he still
Has kept me with him, honored, and advanced me.

TALLMADGE. I doubt you not: for stronger oft than fear
Is the strange spell the brave cast on the brave;
And young and inexperienced awe of men
Renowned in action, is a stronger spell,
That of each reckless and successful soldier
Can make a hero.

FRANKS.   Yet I think I see,
Without enchantment, that whatever seems
Mysterious in this life, is the result
Of crimination, not the proof of crime;
And even that this strangest thing of all,
In such a man, his moody avarice,
But marks the eager effort to attain
That personal independence dear to one
Whose pride has suffered, and who strives to keep
His soul erect before his enemies.

[*Enter* ARNOLD. *The soldier presents arms.*]

ARNOLD. I recollect you; at Quebec you marched
Among the stormers on my left, and once,
When my foot slipped upon the broken ice,
You saved me from the fall.

SOLDIER.   Yes, General.

ARNOLD. I thank you for it now. I know each face
That I saw with me in the Wilderness;
I would that those I serve remembered me
But half so well.

        [*To Tallmadge.*]

                    We cross the river late.
And 'tis unfortunate; because I purposed
Ere you returned to Northcastle, to meet
And speak at leisure with you on the subject
Of a great enterprise, designed to end
The public troubles: but the open air
Chills confidence and dissipates attention.
You understand me.

TALLMADGE [*aside*].　　　Yes, your last assertion.

ARNOLD. I'll meet you all to-morrow—you are all
　　Each other's friends, and mine.

VARICK [*looking significantly at Tallmadge*].
　　　　　　　　　　　Each other's—yes.

FRANKS. You do us justice, General; we are.

ARNOLD. When on the heights, did you observe a ship
　　Making her way up from below?

FRANKS.　　　　　　　　We did;
　　And wondered what could be her purpose here.

VARICK. It is the same that, so mysteriously,
　　Came up the river, and dropped down again—
　　The Vulture.

TALLMADGE. A true Vulture! but what scent
　　Of prey or coming battle, from the heart
　　Of the war-region, to this distant part
　　Attracts this grim ill-omened bird of war?

ARNOLD. Ill-omened, yes—in that you may be right:
　　It has been deemed, I think, a bird of omen.

[ARNOLD *and the officers enter the boat.*]

SCENE II.

*The deck of the Vulture, a British Man-of-War, off Teller's
Point. The forts at Verplanck's and Stony Points, and
the heights at West Point in sight.*

[*Enter* ROBINSON *and* ANDRÉ.]

ANDRÉ. They little dream, who see from these redoubts,
　　Our slender armament, what danger lurks
　　Behind the slight appearance.

ROBINSON.　　　　　　Rather say
　　Behind their walls themselves, as far within
　　Redoubt and rampart, as are we beyond
　　Their cannon's range. But do you think that Arnold
　　Intends to come on board?

ANDRÉ.　　　　　　Intends! why doubt it?

ROBINSON. I know the man;—as cautious in intrigue,
As rash in conflict. I suspect he means
That you shall go on shore, and take the hazard,
Which else might fall to him.

ANDRÉ.   I hold the prize
Well worth the risk. We shall obtain a fort
Which art and nature join their hands to make
Impregnable; the key of all the roads,
Northward, and crossing from the east and west,
Which this war travels; and to gain which *now,*
When Washington at Kingsbridge, and De Ternay
At Newport, threaten us by land and sea,
Is more important, as it would prevent
The junction of the rebels with the French,
And end, we hope, the conflict. This, concede,
Offers a prospect not to be endangered
By any scruples of the when and where
Of the transaction:—I will go on shore.

ROBINSON. With my consent you shall not. In this game
Sir Henry Clinton would not risk his agent;
Although the move, I grant, could it be made,
Would take him out of check, and out of fear
Of being soon checkmated in New York.
And *you* I know he would not, if he might
In conscience, prompt to such a part. As soldiers,
Danger is our employment; and to hazard
Our lives and freedom for the King, a duty;
But not our part, where soldiers should be cowards,
To serve his cause—not ours, I mean, to dare
The dangers of conspiracy, and risk,
It may be, honor.

ANDRÉ.   There is no such danger
In this conspiracy, as you misname it.
I do the thing for honor's sake; and Arnold
Is unsuspected, and still has the power
Of his high rank and station, to assist
The hardihood and subtlety of purpose
That you concede to him.

ROBINSON.   And hate in him,
     As in the devil I do!

ANDRÉ.   Still hate them there—
     But not in him in whom they will give back
     A continent to the King, or I shall doubt
     Your loyalty; though I so much admired
     Its firmness, and the strength of that devotion
     To duty and allegiance, that could lead you
     To leave your fair domain, and the misguided
     But gallant men who call you countryman.
     For my part, I am tempted to suspect
     That had I first seen light upon this side
     Of the broad stream which king has never passed,
     I, too, might be a traitor: 'tis the clime,
     The unsubdued wild region of their birth,
     That makes them rebels; not to law disloyal,
     But to the laws that rule an older world.

ROBINSON. They were free-born, and need not be more free
     Than were their fathers.

ANDRÉ.   Birthright is not freedom;
     Free senses make free souls—and dauntless hearts.
     And here no court with enervating splendor
     Shines like a sun upon the dazzled land:
     No castled heights their feudal shadow cast
     On the tired reaper's brows, and fields of grain;
     No legendary towers, that seem as old
     As their foundation, from these rocks look down
     On the free village, and the humble homes
     And nurseries of men: the people see
     No pageantry to awe, know no prescription,
     Meet no suggestions of antiquity
     To tame their native courage to the hand,
     Far reached, and but too short, to quell rebellion,
     Inspired by every sight and sound in nature,—
     And nature its invincible ally.

ROBINSON. I sometimes have had thoughts like these—but here,
     Near my own house, and what should be my home,

Now the head-quarters of this scheming Arnold,
My sympathies are all with loyal men.

[*They enter the cabin.*]

SCENE III.

The east side of the river. A room in ROBINSON'S *house.*

[*Enter* MRS. ARNOLD.]

MRS. ARNOLD. Each day he comes back later, yet too soon.
  My love is checked, my heart is in its springs,
  And will not flow: he chills and awes it back
  With the dark shadow of unspoken thoughts,
  Or terrifies me with unwelcome bursts
  Of momentary transport, that seem madness.
  O, 'twas unlooked for! yet 'tis woman's fate,
  So ignorant of itself till fixed, and then
  So bound to its unhappiness by chains
  'Gainst which the almost bursting heart beats softly,
  Lest it should break them, while itself is breaking!

[*Enter* ARNOLD.]

ARNOLD. I was in search of you, and might suppose
  You sought to avoid me.

[*He regards her for a moment in silence.*]

                    Can it be the same?
  How changed! I know the heat about my heart
  Is withering and not warming; still you are
  My bosom friend, my wife, and you should know
  Our common fortune, be it good or evil;
  And I should have at least one friend with whom
  A secret would be safe.
MRS. ARNOLD.   Have you not many?
ARNOLD. O, yes, as close, as faithful, and discreet ones
  As ever lied by silence, could I make
  My secret *theirs*,—if not, my dearest friend,

Who thinks I hold him dearest, would reveal it
With sleepless haste, and smile to see the knife
Drink my full heart out, drop by drop.

MRS. ARNOLD.   What knife?
What do you mean? And these dark hints that fall,
Since we came hither, darker and more frequent
On my pained ear—what ill do they foreshadow?

ARNOLD. Ill to my enemies! The very shape
And substance of the fear which haunts their eyes;
Defeat and shame, felt both in my success
And their own ruin! I shall live to see
That haughty Congress, and that politic
And truckling Council, who to please a mob
Of clamorous and vulture-like civilians,
Disgraced a fellow-soldier, and themselves,
Sue for an amnesty, beg life and fortune,
At a tribunal they abhor like hell!
And my bold Countrymen, who, in their wrongs,
Find irresistible and lawful power
To right them by whatever means, shall find
That in the strength which injuries can give,
An injured man is stronger than a people.

MRS. ARNOLD. Did I not know you—had I not before
Heard words as frantic, I might think—

ARNOLD.   Well, what?
Speak freely.

MRS. ARNOLD.   That a foreign influence
Fed these resentments, and to some dark end
Directed them. O, bear with me! Our child
Makes me more sensitive to all that moves
And agitates his father. What you are,
It seems each moment to my anxious heart,
He is to be—you do not listen—

ARNOLD.   —Yes,
My son, you fear, is like me—

MRS. ARNOLD.   This once, hear me!
'Tis the world's thought, that I became your wife
Because your rank, and splendid way of life,

And consequence as governor of the city
Which was my birthplace and my world, allured me.

ARNOLD. And you'd not have me think so? Well—

MRS. ARNOLD.   O, that
Was my first grief, to find that you could think
My love such prostitution, and accept it!
I saw in you a brave, deserving soldier,
Wronged by his country, who with greater zeal
Devoted him, and with stern passion wooed
Her cold unfavoring eye; and for the hopes
By its unkindly frost cut off and blighted,
Still won fresh wreaths from her reluctant hand.
And now to see you, when, with one more effort,
To the best champion she could refuse
Her heart no longer, falter and give ear
To her insidious enemies and your own,
Might almost tempt me to forswear the vow
That did not only bind me to the man,
But wed me to his honor.

ARNOLD.   Your conjectures—
Speak out—what are they?

MRS. ARNOLD.   I have felt a doubt
Whether your frequent intercourse with André,
Begun through me, did not conceal some project
You would, but that you dared not, let me know.

ARNOLD. Then learn the secret now; by chance already
You know too much to know so little.—I,
It may be, am the first, who found a wife's
Protracted friendship for a former lover
Pleasant or profiting—but so it is:—
His fortunes are bound up with mine; through him
I gain—what else no matter—my revenge:
Through me he will get thanks, and fame;—a sentence
In the despatches, and a regiment.

MRS. ARNOLD. What riddle 's this? I see its darker meaning;
But how can you and André act together?

ARNOLD. He is to conquer me, and by assault
Take yonder fortress—aye! you wonder,—there,

Above it, float the continental colors;
And yet it is the King's—and I from Congress
Hold my commission, but 'tis for the King.
You smile—you think me jesting.—

MRS. ARNOLD.   Did I smile?
'Twas in despair then.

ARNOLD.   In despair of what?
The plot is sure—fate could not make it stronger.

MRS. ARNOLD. I meant not in despair of your success,
But in despair of you, and of myself:—
Yet you will fail.

ARNOLD.   Had you the smallest knowledge
Of military matters—

MRS. ARNOLD.   You will fail—
I speak from higher knowledge—call it faith,
Yes, faith in the just cause you would betray,
And in the unconquered faith and fortitude
Of a free people. You may yield this fort,
Though I forebode disaster to the plot;—
But who can to the King deliver up
That best stronghold of liberty, the heart
Of a great people, garrisoned against him
By the twin passions, hope and stronger fear,
And his injustice? Hear me, and be warned!
This moment may be free from destiny,—
The next, and it will seize, stern, unrelenting,
On all your after life; and with success,
As surely as defeat, the blighted name
Of him who sold his countrymen, will be
Its bearer's infamy, and to no child
Even by your children shall be given!

ARNOLD.   Woman!—
But I will not be moved;—though well I might,
I'll not be angered. My rash confidence
Gave you the privilege to misuse it: Madam,
Your taught and tragic eloquence was inspired
By the dull parrots of dead books and men,

That prate in Congress. Men of action know
A different creed: one written, not in words,
But deeds; and by the cannon's mouth confessed
And ascertained, at last. And, to predict
Whether my name or that of Washington,
Is destined to be pilloried in phrases
Like renegade and traitor, is to know
Whether his treason to the King succeed,
Or mine to him, if to betray a traitor,
And one in arms against his king be treason.

MRS. ARNOLD. O, flatter not yourself with the injustice
Of partial times or men: should his star set,
Yours would not rise above it: even they
Who should call him a traitor, would think you
A double traitor; and the ill-bought praise
Of a whole age, or world, could it be yours,
Would be but fuel for the quenchless flame
Of a just human instinct, in the end
Sure to break forth and blacken you with shame.

ARNOLD. Enough! I'd hear no more; you have my secret;
Think it your life. I cannot think you will,
And yet I half suspect you would, betray me.

[*Exit.*]

MRS. ARNOLD. I *should* betray you! O! let not that woman
Think to be surely blest who joins her fate
And makes her life one with another being.
None can be safe; let her elect the man
Whose office is a virtue, or whose bread
Is piety, and she shall find in him
Who sits in ermine a most spotted felon,
An atheist in him who kneels in lawn.
Or let her choose, my heart! my heart! that man
Of men—a soldier, a time-tried and scarred
And laurelled soldier, she shall find a traitor!
And all the wretchedness and shame of both
The child inherits—yes, my child—O, wo!

[*Exit.*]

SCENE IV.

An apartment in Robinson's house. ARNOLD, TALLMADGE,
FRANKS *and* VARICK.

ARNOLD. And that was why I'd not command the left?
    The southern army was not offered me!
    Well for the country and the coward, Gates,
    Had I obtained it—but in that they lie;
    This is the place I asked for.

TALLMADGE.   It is plain
    They do not understand your motives, nor,
    Permit me to be frank with you, do we.

ARNOLD. Once know my wrongs, and you know me; for I
    Am all made up of them; they are my senses,
    Through which I feel, and hear, and see all objects.
    They have possession of my brain, and day
    And night they work there, think and act for me;
    And from my heart they run like a disease
    Through all my blood. All that I loved I hate.
    There is a mockery in the mere respect
    Paid to my rank; the soldier's prompt salute,
    The deference of subalterns, seem now
    A sarcasm or a favor. The wild stir
    Of field and camp, which pleased me once, is dull,
    And tiresome as a town parade; the shock
    And boom of the near gun, the fife and drum
    And bugle call—are painful to my ears
    As to a branded coward's: and my heart
    Turns even from old friends; but, in one beat
    Of its most feeble pulse, it has not yet
    Turned from old enemies—not one!

FRANKS.   It might
    Dismiss them freely, for their enmity
    Is better friendship, in the end, than ours.

ARNOLD. What?—I am dull.

FRANKS.   The sense of gratitude,
    Against injustice slowly rises up,
    And, irrepressibly reacting, bears

The injured, in the people's mind, above
The injurer: if not at once—hereafter.

ARNOLD. Hereafter—yes, could I be satisfied
With that hereafter; which as yet is not,
And, therefore, nothing; and in which the present
Will have become the past, and, therefore, nothing!
It might be something, could my ashes hear
My vindication, or could marble feel
The flattery of sculpture; or the voice
And hand of retribution reach my dead
And buried enemies, lying undisturbed,
Invincible and silent in their graves.

TALLMADGE. And yet this *nothing* is the test of fame,
Namer of men, and ordeal of glory;
And even of the glory gained by war.
And the true great, and true heroic minds
Most prize posthumous honors; and have died
Poor and in misery, that their fame might live
In human memory, and their very name,
And dust, be more revered than living men.

ARNOLD. Let such as find the motive, waste the brain
And drain the vital blood, to have their relics
Embalmed and honored. 'Tis not my ambition
To be a worshipped mummy, but a man
Respected amongst men: and this has been,
Since the rash spirit of my boyhood left me,
My day and night endeavor, my sole aim.
But from that hour when to New Haven came
The news of Lexington, and men, unmanned
And nerveless, saw the first red drops of war;
And I, while orators stood dumb, turned back
The trembling crowd that fled before the shadow
Of the dark war-cloud their own breath had raised,
And bade them stand, and arm, and, when aroused,
Offered to lead them forth to instant action,
Only to hear the authorities who held
The keys of the arsenal refuse me arms—

From that first check to this late reprimand
My whole career has been a studied series
Of checks and insults.

TALLMADGE.   To resist so long
An adverse influence, and advance against it,
Gives proof of strength, which is itself the pledge
Of ultimate success.

ARNOLD.   If I resist,
It is but as a swimmer in a stream,
Who strikes and gasps for life, and does not think
How strong he is, but only in what danger.

TALLMADGE. But it is noble to possess such strength.

ARNOLD. 'Tis well—but its possessor only feels
The stress, the struggle, and exhausting effort
That calls it forth; it is for the beholders
To see how noble; but the real actor
In the great scenes of life at which they wonder,
Dares and confronts their dangers, not because
'Tis noble thus to do, but necessary.

TALLMADGE. Yet there are some at least to whose stern thinking,
To dare, is needful when the cause is noble.

ARNOLD. I have not met, thus far, with one of them—
You'll pardon me—if you be not that one.

TALLMADGE. You jest—but yes, by Heaven! I am that one.

ARNOLD. I have an act in view that has, indeed,
The strength of both inducements to persuade
To its performance, had it not too much
Of the alloy of interest—did it not
Promise too much and fair, for men who act
From sublimated motives.

FRANKS.   Let us hear;
We can best judge of that.

ARNOLD.   Of that I'll speak
Hereafter; it is, first of all, important
We understand each other in the grounds
Of the cooperation I propose:
And here I'm confident we shall not differ.
You all concede that what with want of men,

Through short enlistments, a twice bankrupt Congress,
And late defeats, but for this French alliance
We all might ground our arms, and fall to prayers
With our good general, George—to be—the First,
Who leads us in this war on George the Third.

FRANKS. 'Tis even so.

TALLMADGE.   But I cannot concede this:
Not to be vanquished, is success—

ARNOLD.   I know—
And know that we have, even, called defeats
Successes; and have turned escapes, retreats,
And countermarches into victories,
To keep the spirit of the people up.
But this you must concede;—the threadbare words
For which we fight in rags, and scarce make out
Upon our tattered banners, Liberty
And Independence, and the hopeful phrases,
Stale as the war, and ancient as the Rump,
God for the people's rights, and hope in Heaven,
Now changed to France, awake, from year to year,
A fainter answer in our hopes and hearts.

TALLMADGE. Why, Danbury and Saratoga, fields
Won by yourself, might keep our courage up.

ARNOLD. That matters not; 'tis of the French I'd speak:
A few years since they were our enemies.

FRANKS. The General himself acquired the credit
Through which he has attained his present rank
Serving against them.

ARNOLD.   Can we be quite sure
That in this family feud it is discreet
To drive out friends—

TALLMADGE.   —Friends?

ARNOLD.   Our own race, at least,
And bring in enemies? You know the fate
Of the old Britons who against the Scot
Called in the Saxon. Our attempt to gain
The independence an usurping Congress,
Not the still loyal people, have decreed,

May leave us more dependent—may, in fact,
Make us a French dependency, than which—
Will no one speak the rest?

FRANKS.   I'd rather wear
Hereditary chains.

TALLMADGE.   I'd rather die;
And rather live dishonored, and the slave
Of the remotest and most barbarous race
Acknowledged to be human, than to see
This soil, our native and true mother-land,
Again subjected to unnatural England.
The ground, which so much filial blood has drunk,
To tillage would be barren, and yield thorns:
And our proud ancestress, who would usurp
A mother's power but cares not for our love,
Would give us scornful stripes, too well deserved
By voluntary bondmen.

ARNOLD.   Bravely said!
But how, my friend, if to avoid the clutches
Of cruel grandam with her rod, we fly
To the protection of the wolf? There's danger,
Depend upon it, in these crafty French.

TALLMADGE. Pardon me General, it is difficult
To think you quite in earnest: hostile France
Would cripple England by sustaining us,
Not undertake herself the hopeless task
Of our subjection; and we, unendangered,
May use their rivalries to our advantage,—
With the great ocean for our strong ally
Against the stronger; and, soon, either power
Will think it easier to subdue the other,
Than either, us.

[ARNOLD, *who has listened impatiently,*
abruptly turns, and addresses FRANKS.]

ARNOLD.   You will find Smith below;
He waits to speak with me.

[Exeunt TALLMADGE, VARICK *and* FRANKS, *expressing
in their looks surprise and indignation.]*

No help from them.
I threw the bait too boldly; it is well
That it was into swift and muddy waters.
Something they may suspect, but not the truth:
That is too strange to dream—above their daring
But to conceive of.

[A pause.]

It was not their aid—
Although I need it; 'tis this solitude,
In which the uncommunicated mind
Loses itself, and grasps the nearest hand
To find reality. 'Tis old as treason
That the most dangerous secret, longest kept,
Like the shy serpent, tired of her own coil
And her dark cavern dropping deadly dews,
Will creep into the light, and seek to bask
In some approving smile; hence the temptation,
The mastering impulse, the fatuity,
That makes the mind a traitor to itself.

[Enter SMITH.*]*

The agent that would see me for the sale
Of Robinson's estate, must land to-night.
SMITH. I cannot find the men for it; not one
Whom I have sounded likes it; 'tis a secret,
And therefore they suspect a dangerous service.
ARNOLD. Bring them to me, and I will find a way
To dissipate their scruples.

[Exit SMITH.*]*

*[He unlocks a cabinet and takes out a paper
which he glances over while speaking.]*

—*Satisfied?*
Why, yes, that I shall get no more. *Our straits!*
The King's munificence—a petty sum

To buy a country and its army:—No!
I'll not be privy to their thoughts: the effect
Will be the same to them as if it were
The ransom of an empire, but I'll take
The fair construction of the case, which makes it
A compensation for the loss I suffer
In my return to loyalty; if they
Have other thoughts, for my sake, and their own,
They'll make the devil their only confidant.
I might deceive my countrymen with show
Of being taken prisoner; as, at first,
I meditated doing. But the secret
Might not be safe; if kept, would not be vengeance—
Such vengeance as I long for: they must curse me!
But few and brief have been their benedictions;
Their maledictions shall be long and loud.
They have not called me yet, with all the terms
They hate me in, a beaten General;
And their commiseration would be bitter.
They must perceive my hand and curse me; curses
Are never pleasant to the ear—but theirs
Will be far sweeter than would be their pity.

[*Exit.*]

ACT II

SCENE I.

*The river side at the Long Clove Mountain. A dark and
stormy night.* ARNOLD *discovered waiting.*

ARNOLD. Did I hear oars?—the wind.—They are too late;
The night will hardly cover the transaction
If they consume it thus.

[*A Pause.*]

This act will place me
Entirely in their power; the deed to do
Is as if done; the future as the past.
I have swum back and forth in the smooth waters,
And pleased myself with the alluring motion
Outward, in view of the receding shore;
The conscious master of the interval.
But now the current seizes me, and strong
Above my strength to breast it, bears me on,
And to swim forth with it is safety. Few,
Blind and irresolute the strokes that brought me
Across the narrow line which separates
The rush of action from the calm of thought:
And lo! an ocean, an eternity,
Lies, in effect, between me and the place
Where will and act were one. One chance I had
To gain without defection what I seek,—
One hope,—the offer made me to command
The left wing of the army. In that case
My triumph in particular, had been
That of my enemies, in general; now
My triumph is their ruin.

[*He starts and hastily retires. A boat lands, and
ANDRÉ, wrapped in a cloak, steps on shore.
The boat immediately leaves.*]

ANDRÉ.   No one here!
   They told me he was waiting. How the wind
   Roars down this mountain gorge, and on the river
   Leaps, like a baffled eagle on some swift
   And powerful serpent, that winds through his talons.
   A time so full of nature's discontent,
   A night like this, so full of mad disquiet,
   And such a wild and solitary place,
   A painter or tragedian might choose,
   Were a despairing man to meet the devil.
   Ugh! 'tis an ugly simile; the more,
   As *I* am here to play the tempter's part.
   But storm, and gloom, and mystery, might make
   The undesigning deem themselves abroad
   On some conspiracy against the sleep
   Of home-roofed innocence; and childhood's spell,
   With recollected dread of night, and shapes
   Of haggard fear and secret crimes that came
   With the hushed, featureless, and sable hag,
   Joins deeds of darkness, still, with thoughts of guilt.

[ARNOLD *re-enters.*]

ARNOLD. Anderson!

ANDRÉ.   Gustavus!

ARNOLD.   I heard you speaking.
   Are you alone?

ANDRÉ.   I spoke to exorcise
   The spirit of solitude.

ARNOLD.   A step this way,
   And we shall be more sheltered.

ANDRÉ.   If these rocks,
   That from the mass of darkness their huge crags
   Thrust forth upon the stumbling sight, have ears,
   As for conspirators 'tis said they have,
   They'll hardly catch our secret while the wind
   Deafens their hollow clefts with his loud story.
   How strange and wild! It seems as if there should
   Be always night here, and unceasing noise,

So well they suit the fixed and pictured storm
Beheld in the confused and broken lines
Of ledge and precipice, which, themselves at rest,
Disturb and threaten the unresting eye.
ARNOLD. Hem!—it were well for us if night and storm
Might be prolonged an hour or so, at least;
But day is near.

[*Aside.*]

A strange conspirator!

[*Exeunt.*]

SCENE II.

An apartment in Robinson's house.

[*Enter* MRS. ARNOLD, *with a lamp.*]

Why did I bring this light? It is clear day.
Night would not let me sleep, nor will the dawn
Awake me from this dream of settled horror!
O! to be made the sole repository
Of such a secret, which I cannot break,
Nor yet can keep. I'll not be seen. I seem
To every eye that marks me, to reveal it.
He told me all, as if it eased his heart
To tell it, even to ears ungratified.
God of heaven! This night he was to meet
A British emissary—now perhaps,
Plays with the fatal sword whose point, reversed,
Will drink his blood! Did aught retard or threaten,
I know the house that was to hide them. Thither
I might this moment fly.—But wherefore should I?
'Tis André that he meets, and I might still
Possess some power with *him!* But to what end?
He acts for others. Yet I cannot stay
And know that they together work the ruin
Of me, and of my child. 'Twill anger Arnold,
And show to André my unhappiness.

But fear like mine is bolder than displeasure;
And grief is more imperious than shame.
I see him, in the distance, blindly stumbling
Along the desperate edge of the abyss:—
Now, madly down the dizzy precipice
I see him plunge, and 'tis involuntary
To stretch the hand, although it cannot save him.

[Exit.]

SCENE III.

Smith's house. A gloomy and ill-lighted apartment. ARNOLD
and ANDRÉ *discovered sitting at a table strewed with papers.*

ANDRÉ. I cannot but be vexed that day surprised us;
  And though I felt secure, I could not feel
  At ease within your outposts.
ARNOLD.   'Twill, at least,
  Give us more leisure to mature our plan.

    [He places his finger on a map.]

  You will land here; and, following this ridge,
  You gain our rear; and here you climb the mountain,
  From whose unguarded summit, like a hawk
  On his unruffled quarry, you look down
  Upon the luckless Arnold.
ANDRÉ.   Yes, I see.
  Your force withdrawn, and in the mountain gorges
  Expecting us, on this point I march down,
  Storm it with fife and drum, and with the tune
  "God save the King" dumb-strike and take the fortress.
ARNOLD. Had I the heart to mar an enterprise
  Of such devoted daring, your bravado
  Might almost tempt me to confront you there,
  And change that loyal litany to prayer
  For your own safety.
ANDRÉ.   Ay, I understand,
  'Tis hard for an old soldier to succumb

Without one blow delivered for his fame,
As for the challenged flint to hold its fire
When struck with iron; and 'tis natural—
A colonist, and born American—
That you should be in feelings but half loyal.
Sir Henry thinks it certain that your wrongs,
Rather than change of sentiment, have led you
Back to the path of duty; but I think
Your honors and preferments far outweigh
Your causes of complaint.

ARNOLD.   It cannot be
That you have heard them.

ANDRÉ.   Some of them I have,
And those not slight; but you have seemed to rise
Higher from every fall—

ARNOLD.   To make my next
The speedier, deeper, and more infamous.
I call to mind, when in the wilderness
Through which we forced our way to Canada,
The thoughts of Allen's insolence—my shame,
And the indifference with which Massachusetts
Saw insult heaped on me, and her commission,
Still rankling with me;—as my little band
Struggled their inch-won way, while torrents roared,
And winter howled against us, and where each
Was for himself too great a burden, dragged
The means of life and warfare against streams
Whose fury made them seem themselves our foes;
Then—when I felt and knew myself their soul,
Their energy, their life, so that it seemed
Should I but shut my eyes to sleep, they all
Would fall like dead men there around me—this—
Fool! by the past unteachable—this I said,
Envy itself will honor, this accredit
As zealous service; and although in vain
We braved those horrors; vainly though we burst
Their wintry barrier, and unlooked for, fell
Upon our enemies, like men out of heaven;

My heart still said, This will win favor! Did it?
Or did I dare and suffer such things? No!
I dreamed, and woke to find myself disgraced,
Degraded, and four junior officers
Appointed over me. And when for new
And signal service I received my rank,
They held me still degraded, not restoring
My lost seniority, till on Behmus' heights,
Fighting without command, and seeking death,
I won at length that barren laurel too,
From the disdainful hand of my just country;
To see it trampled on, with all my honors,
And all my services, trampled in the dust,
By this late sentence of the army council.

ANDRÉ. But so adroitly your high-minded chief
    Administered their sentence, that it seemed
    More like a compliment than reprimand.
    Why, he said nothing—merely praised the service.

ARNOLD. Yes, yes, 'twas the *chaste service!* My dispraise
    Was praise of the profession. Let that pass:
    How view the royalists the accusation?

ANDRÉ. Why, royally; and will not think the hand
    Which holds the best and brightest sword amongst
        you,
    Soiled with dishonest gold.

ARNOLD.   My real crime
    Was lack of it—was poverty. My hand
    Held naught but iron, to the state not useless,
    But to me worthless. My opponents' hands
    Were stronger armed—with gold. I was a limb,
    They were the heart and vitals of the war,
    And could not be denied so slight a thing
    As my humiliation.

ANDREÉ.   What to me
    Seems wonderful, is their determined effort—

ARNOLD. But they are dogs, who love to lap the blood
    Of wounded honor.

ANDRÉ.   Their attempt was strange,
    Not their success in it. Gold has the power

In popular counsels fame and honor have
In camps and courts: it is in monarchies
An aid to tyranny; in commonwealths
'Tis the sole tyrant.

ARNOLD.   It is, everywhere
Alike, omnipotent and all-desired,
All-dreaded, honored. Greatness! What is greatness?
One shall be subtle, noble, strong, and valiant,
His name shall never die upon the air
For frequent repetition, and the man
Not be more powerful with his neighbor, nay,
May be the sordid jest of his own servants;
Uncivil cold shall pinch, and hunger starve
This great man in his empty house;—the slaves
Of his necessities, earth's creeping things,
Insult and terrify, till their base nature
Infects his own. But gold is present honor,
Strength and advantage:—'tis as if *that* God,
The dream of all the world, for whom they rear
And cast down altars; whom they seek and find
But to declare unfound, and seek him still,
In earth and heaven and hell,—had hid himself,
With all his power and most essential splendor,
In this bright ore; that hence compels from all
Involuntary adoration.

    [MRS. ARNOLD *enters unperceived.*]

ANDRÉ.   Mighty,
And even magical its power—divine
You say:—Indeed it is a potent idol,
Of wider worship than true Deity;
An irreligious god, the superstition
Of atheists and scoffers. Yet could I
Affirm of honor things more wonderful;
The reverence that even in shameful death
Attends it, when like an apparent angel
It strengthens him to brave and graceful patience,
Who meets a patriot's or a martyr's fate;

And, more than one pale scene's unbought applause,
The unwasted wealth of love it treasures up
For unborn time, and glory born anew
With every human birth, surviving change
In man or nature; to humanity,
Forever forth, a feeling, and a thought,
Still, on the soul, returning like the sun,
Still re-awakening on the ear, like song,—
A ray of brightness in the light of day,
A breathing of the universal air.

MRS. ARNOLD. Is *this* the honor that you speak of, this
That you now act?

[ANDRÉ *bows to* MRS. ARNOLD *in an embarrassed manner
and then turns to* ARNOLD *as if for explanation.*]

[*Enter* SMITH.]

ARNOLD [*to Smith*].   Is this your caution, Sir?
SMITH. I think you will perceive that Mistress Arnold
Was not to be subjected to restraint
By me, and in this house.
ARNOLD.   This way a moment:
They are old friends, indeed a kind of cousins.
Hark! I must see what means this noise of firing
That comes up from the river.—Will you go?
[*Exeunt* ARNOLD *and* SMITH.]

SCENE IV.

[ANDRÉ *approaches* MRS. ARNOLD *respectfully. She draws
back sorrowfully and somewhat sternly.*]

ANDRÉ. Dear Madam, by whatever chance it happens
That you are here, your coming is to me
Most fortunate.
MRS. ARNOLD.   And yours to me as sad,
Fateful, and inauspicious, as the visit
Of the executioner to one more happy
Than I am at this moment.

ANDRÉ. Pardon me,
    I am at loss—

MRS. ARNOLD.   I know it all. Oh, André!
    To you of all men living, as a sister
    Turns to a brother, with undoubting heart,
    I would have turned in trouble; from you now
    I'd turn to my worst enemy, if worse
    I have. God knows I little thought in you
    To find my husband's tempter—my destroyer.

ANDRÉ. Destroyer? Madam, this is a strange charge—
    If I have understood it: if you mean
    That as an instrument I have been used
    To advance your husband's fortune, give him wealth,
    And more than recompense whatever loss—

MRS. ARNOLD. Spread not the lying lure before my eyes.
    What compensation? Well you know, your gain
    Will be his infamy: there is no just,
    No equal bargain made. You buy his fame,
    His conscience, honor, character, his soul,
    And give him trash! It is a murderer's banquet
    At which you sit with him, already drunk
    With maddening passion; and before his eyes,
    As blind as is your conscience, drug the bowl,
    And give him poison.

ANDRÉ. Would that all my life
    Might be by Heaven held innocent, or evil,
    As I am clear of any evil thought
    Or practice in this thing! If what he does,
    He does from a pure motive, it is noble,
    If not, it rests with him.

MRS. ARNOLD. He does not care,
    And you will not: but I am ominous
    Of some approaching evil, which you see not,
    Some great disaster; not to him alone—
    Which his success would be—but to yourself
    And the whole enterprise. Mysterious grief,
    Felt for the living as if long since dead,
    Weighs on my heart; and I conceive misfortunes

Less as forebodings, than as memories.
Say I am sick or crazed—and I am both,
'Tis the despair that fills me, the deep night,
Which shows my spirit stars of destiny
Hid from your eyes, and which I cannot read.

ANDRÉ. I do not mock at such presentiments;
Soldiers too often see them verified.

MRS. ARNOLD. But you would laugh at dreams? O! we are
        wise,
Or wise can seem, till unconceived events
Make wisdom needed; then it fails us; awe
And mystery come dream-like on the soul,
We know not whence, and, in despite of reason,
Make us familiar with our earlier thoughts.
The world we left with childhood, and with all
Our trembling wonder, and too credulous fear,
For ever cast behind us as illusion,
Rises around, and mingles with the present.

ANDRÉ. Sleep is death's image; but life's shadow—dreams;
And being shadow, are, like shadows, true
To their substantial causes or distorted,
Clear, or obscure, as falls the Reason's light
Upon the dark realities that cast them.

MRS. ARNOLD. The ship that brought you here is called the
        Vulture?

ANDRÉ. It is.

MRS. ARNOLD. I stood upon the shore and saw it,
At once as ship and bird; and it flew on
Among wild rocks and hissing whirlpools, guided
By you and Arnold, till exultingly
You saw the open haven; when an eagle
Rushed, cloud-like, from her watchful cliff, and hurled
A storm from her broad wings against the ship;
And to the rocks, crouched like huge beasts of prey
Beneath the treacherous tide, cast it, to tear
And shatter into fragments. Him I saw
Swept outward, clinging to the wreck;—for whom
That mighty phantom wheeling, with wild screams,
Gazed o'er the sea with eye of fire; but you

The waves washed up, a pale corpse at my feet.
ANDRÉ. A strange wild dream; and yet most natural,
  And truthful to its cause; its threatening forms
  Incongruous, wild, improbable, and yet
  The distinct shapings of your fear preserved.
  You dread your husband's ruin and dishonor,
  But as in my case these seem not to threaten,
  Your dark forebodings take the shape of death.

[*Enter* ARNOLD.]

ARNOLD. Madam, I am not certain, but suspect
  That to your interest in me we owe
  This unexpected visit. Hitherto
  You shared my confidence, if not my counsel.
  But whether Major André would admit
  A third into his counsel, may be doubtful.

[*Exit* MRS. ARNOLD.]

The devil is surely privy to our plot;
  Beyond all forecast, our fierce patriots here,
  Have brought a gun to bear and forced the ship
  From her position.
ANDRÉ.   Ha! the ship—the Vulture?
  Speak out,—she has gone down the river.
ARNOLD.   No!
  But might as well have gone; our boatmen swear
  That they'll not board her where she lies, and threats
  And promises are vain. The stubborn brutes
  Refuse to touch an oar.
ANDRÉ.   What's to be done?
ARNOLD. Nothing with them. You must return by land,
  And take my passport.
ANDRÉ.   Land! But such a course
  Was not contemplated. I can, of right,
  Demand to be returned on board the Vulture.
ARNOLD. With all the right on earth you can demand it;
  But I shall do no wrong not to perform
  A thing I cannot. You must go by land.
                                        [*Exit.*]

ANDRÉ. My mind misgives me. Many unforeseen
    And cross events have set against me; first,
    My visit to the shore, then my detention,
    Now my return by land, and who can say
    What things as unexpected yet may happen.

                                        [Exit.]

ACT III

SCENE I.

*Crompond, a small military post. An inn in the distance.
A horse standing, saddled, before it.*

[*Enter* SMITH *and* ANDRÉ, *the latter wearing a military
cloak over a citizen's dress.* Time, *early morning.*]

SMITH. Farewell; be satisfied that you will meet
    No obstacles. Here, at the post, they say,
    The British scouts have been above the lines;
    You may fall in with them.

ANDRÉ.   Good day, and thanks
    For my safe guidance.

                        [*Exit* SMITH.]

                What a glorious sight!
Now on the dreamy world of sleep and shadow,
Comes, god-like, the great summoner of life;
And scatters beamy fire upon the clouds,
Which rise like incense at its touch, and dim
His day-creating orb with his own splendor:
For ever thus, wafting the dawn before him,
And weaving light and darkness, thus for ever
Shimmering along the hills, as he surmounts
Their wood-spired, wavy tops, he climbs the earth;
And never finds its summit:—ever rising
Through an eternal morning. Type of glory!
Bright and untired aspirant, hail! at once
Thou risest on my eyes and in my soul!
I, too, am of the morning, full of joy;
My care-worn spirits now are active, subtle,
Dewy with feeling, bright with kindling thought,
Fresh, lightsome,—I am part of what I see.
How many days now have I mined and toiled
In the dark world of human thought and passion,
And the great world of Nature, hills, and sky,

And yonder sun, have for that space looked down
Upon a dead man, a mere idiot,
Without sight, feeling, sympathy or wonder,
Blind, tasteless, and insensible to beauty.—
Hush André! If in this plain garb, and here,
Among the hills, alone with thy coy muse,
In the young making of the day, the devil
Should tempt thee to turn poet,—friend, beware!
Thou art a soldier and diplomatist.

[*He retires in the direction of the inn.*]

SCENE II.

A woody place by the roadside near Tarrytown.
[*Enter* PAULDING, WILLIAMS *and* VAN WERT.]

VAN WERT. Well, neighbors, we had best go home and sleep:
The birds we look for do not fly by daylight.
PAULDING. There!—hark!—hide in the bushes, and lie close.

[*They hide.* PAULDING *chooses a place which
gives him a view of the road.*]

WILLIAMS. What is it?
PAULDING.   'Tis a horseman; but he rides
Too carelessly along for one to think
His business any thing but safe and lawful.
We'll show ourselves, and question him.

[*Exeunt, walking rapidly up the road.*]

[PAULDING *speaks without.*]   This way;
Look to the horse, there, Williams. Now, this way, Sir,
A little from the roadside.

[*Re-enter* PAULDING *and* VAN WERT, *conducting* ANDRÉ.]

ANDRÉ.   Now, good Sirs,
Please tell me—where do you belong?
PAULDING.   Below.
ANDRÉ. All's well. I am a British officer.

[*They seize him.*]

ANDRÉ. Good God! I must do any thing to get on—
    Do not delay me. I am glad to find
    That you belong to us; ah—I forgot—

        [He presents his passport.]

VAN WERT. Paulding, you are a scholar.
PAULDING *[taking the passport, reads:]* *"Permit Mr. John*
    Anderson to pass the guards to the White Plains, or
    below, if he chooses, he being on public business by
    my direction.   BENEDICT ARNOLD."
                    —Ah! I see,
    'Twas a mistake—you thought us Tories.
ANDRÉ.   Yes.
    Do not delay me in the public business.
PAULDING. What will you give to be released at once?
ANDRÉ. My purse and this.

        [He offers his watch and purse.]

PAULDING.   A handsome toy, no doubt
    Good twenty guineas—but the purse is light.
    It is the same, perhaps, you brought along
    On purpose for us; it is not enough.
ANDRÉ. Then say what you demand, and name the place
    Where you would have it brought, and by my honor
    As—as—a man, you shall receive it there.
PAULDING. You are what first you said. You heard him,
             Williams?
WILLIAMS. We're poor, what say you? He might keep his word.
PAULDING. Yet not so poor but that we love our country.

        [To André.]

We are poor men, all three, whom this long war
Makes poorer, and still poorer; you can see—
These are not rich men's clothes; but Sir, your king
Has not red gold enough to buy us better.

      [Exeunt, with ANDRÉ.]

SCENE III.

*Northcastle, a military post. A room in the Commander's
head-quarters.*

[*Enter at opposite sides* JAMESON *and* TALLMADGE.]

JAMESON. Ha! Major Tallmadge! You are well returned,
 I have on hand a most vexatious business.

TALLMADGE. Thanks, Colonel, for your confidence. What is it?

JAMESON. A mystery; our scouts have just brought in
 A man who seems to be a British spy.

TALLMADGE. Ah! what's the proof?

JAMESON.   He called himself at first
 A British officer; supposing them
 A party from below, and then retracted;
 But what is most mysterious, we found
 Papers in Arnold's hand upon his person;
 And still more curious, they were views and plans
 Of West Point Station, with exact details
 Of all our means and forces.

TALLMADGE.   Strange enough!
 Where is he?

JAMESON.   I have sent him on to Arnold.

TALLMADGE. To Arnold! What could prompt you to this step?

JAMESON. I thought it a contrivance of the British
 To blast his fame, and shake the confidence
 Reposed in our best soldier.

TALLMADGE.   Confidence?
 Judas Iscariot! Yes, I see it all.
 Is it too late to bring the prisoner back?

JAMESON. He has this moment gone—if yet set out,
 And it might still be done, in case you know
 Aught of the mystery—if you can give
 Good reasons—

TALLMADGE.   I know nothing, but suspect—
 In cannot tell you what. I have not time
 To shape my thoughts, and give you all my reasons.

You know me, Jameson; will you, on my word
That I *have* reasons for it, call him back?

JAMESON. Yes, go yourself.

[*Exit* TALLMADGE.]

What can he mean? The papers
I have despatched to Washington himself,
And what harm could it do, in any case,
To send the prisoner where, in fact, my duty
Requires me to report him? Now perhaps
Arnold will take offence; 'tis most vexatious!
There's some accursèd mystery at the bottom.

[*Re-enter* TALLMADGE, *with* ANDRÉ *guarded*.]

ANDRÉ. Now pray Sir, why am I recalled?

JAMESON.   I think
This officer has reasons for it.

ANDRÉ,   You, Sir?
What might they be?

TALLMADGE.   Your name is Anderson;
Are you a soldier, or a citizen?

ANDRÉ. I answer to no questions. I demand
That either you permit me to proceed,
According to the tenor of my passport,
Or take me to headquarters.

[*While speaking he walks up and down impatiently.*]

TALLMADGE [*apart to Jameson*].   Mark him,—look!—
His step, his bearing—he was bred to arms.

JAMESON. Pardon me, Sir, the apparent fickleness,
But I have changed my mind. You will remain
Till I report you, and receive instructions.

ANDRÉ. In common justice, then you'll give me leave
To write to General Arnold to clear up
The mystery, and free me from confinement.

JAMESON. Yes, you may do this.

TALLMADGE.   But he should not do it.

JAMESON. The devil is in you, Tallmadge:—'tis but fair
That he should have the privilege he asks,

And clear himself if possible,—and soon;
For such would be the wish of any man.

[*Exeunt* JAMESON *and* TALLMADGE, *and* ANDRÉ
and his guard, severally.]

SCENE IV.

A room in ROBINSON's *house.* MRS. ARNOLD *discovered
sitting with her face concealed, and marks of
disorder in her appearance.*

[*Enter* ARNOLD.]

ARNOLD. Might I disturb your dream, in which, no doubt,
My image plays its usual pleasing part,
I would impart some tidings.

MRS. ARNOLD [*rising*].   News of André?

ARNOLD. No. Washington will pass this place to-day,
And visit us; each moment I expect him—
Heard you?

MRS. ARNOLD.   How can we look him in the face?

ARNOLD. Why, for yourself, 'twere well you did not look
With that strange countenance you turn on me,
Or he'll not know you. I shall look at him
As one who may, hereafter, look and say,
You, Sir, of all engaged in this rebellion,
I found, when of your faction, the most just,
The only just, sincere, and generous man;
And to relieve you of the penalties
Laid on your head as leader in the war,
My claims on royalty are freely yours.

MRS. ARNOLD. What fatal veil wove by your evil spirit,
What garland blinding the vowed victim's eyes,
What scaffold bandage rather, from your sight
Hides the true nature of the thing you do?
'Tis not return to allegiance, but the mode
Of your return, the bargain, and the sale,
The cheapened perfidy, the double acting—
All that a man of honor breaking off

As you do, from his party, would avoid—
These are the things that make it infamous.
I tell you, should it prove, in the event,
As you predict; the humbled Washington
Would rather touch the hangman's hand than yours,
And sooner lay his head upon the block
Than it should nod to you, or bend for favor.

ARNOLD. You *were* my wife; and I would not forget it;
A woman, which I will not—but, by God!
If my accusing angel should speak thus,
I would—would—

MRS. ARNOLD.   —A blasphemer, too!

ARNOLD.   A fiend,
A devil from hell!—if you will have it so.
How pious always is an angry woman!
If you believe in God and devils, tell me,
Do you remember whom you swore to honor?
Whose fortunes to make yours?

MRS. ARNOLD.   What noise is that?
Would I were dead!

ARNOLD.   A thing none ever wished,
And lived. What's this—what ails her now? Wife! Wife!
Her eyes are fixed and wide—if 'twere a swoon
She would sink down. Our guests are at the door.
Here, lean upon me;—do you hear me? Wife!
The General and his suite are here; be calm.

MRS. ARNOLD. Yes, they are here. The honest and brave men
Will enter their betrayer's house, and meet
A friendly welcoming—with swelling hearts
Will greet their ancient comrade, and with smiles
Grasp the bribed hand that holds their price, in theirs.

                              [*Exeunt.*]

SCENE V.

An apartment in Robinson's house, a repast set out.

[*Enter* Mrs. Arnold, *several* Officers *of rank, and* Arnold.]

Arnold. The absence of the General in Chief
    Deprives us of much honor; but 'tis like him,
    Ever regardful of the public service,
    Even to neglect of his necessities.
    I think you said he had gone down the river
    To examine the redoubts.

An Officer.   He has; but begged
    That no delay or trouble might result
    From his remissness.

Arnold.   Gentlemen sit down;
    You find, I fear, an ill-prepared repast.

      [*As they sit down, enter* Franks. *He presents
            a letter to* Arnold.]

Franks. I take the freedom to present this, brought
    By a special messenger, and marked, I see,
    "Important, and with haste."

Arnold [*carelessly*].   From Northcastle.

    [*While he reads,* Mrs. Arnold *watches his countenance.*]

Mrs. Arnold. What is it? what has happened?

Arnold [*aside to Mrs. Arnold*].   Nothing—Silence!
                [*To Franks.*]
    Where is the messenger? No matter;—pray
    Be seated, gentlemen—let what I do
    Make no confusion—business of importance
    Requires my absence.

         [*He leads* Mrs. Arnold *apart.*]
                Leave that staring look;
    Be calm. It is, as you suspect, from André,
    And half an hour of time is worth my life.
    Eyes are upon us; do not let them see
    Aught strange in your behavior. For our child's,
    If not my sake—forgive—forgive! Farewell!
    It may be we shall never meet again.

                             [*Exit.*]

MRS. ARNOLD. Stay! I will go—will follow you. Where is he?

[*She turns to the company.*]

O Pity! he, and Heaven abandon me.
AN OFFICER. Quick! quick! Look to the lady there, she swoons.

[FRANKS *supports and leads her off.*]

Why this is strange! or, are we dreaming?—here,
This moment, stood our host and hostess, well,
And in the act of hospitality;—
And now,—they both are gone! 'Tis like a story
Of sprited travellers. We shall next see harpies
Light on the table, and snatch off the food.

2D OFFICER. I do not know—that which is past, at least,
Was not a fiction. From the first, she looked
Disturbed and strange—and did you see how pale?

3D OFFICER. The table still is here; but though I feel
A fasting hunger, I've no mind to eat.

1ST OFFICER. Nor I—let us go meet the General.

[*Exeunt.*]

SCENE VI.

The same.

[*Enter* FRANKS *and* VARICK.]

FRANKS. What mystery hangs over us, and casts
Its shadow on all faces here? Our guests
Are gone, as strangely as our chief. Their looks,
Like his, were dumb, and distant as their voices,
Which scarcely said farewell to us. What is it?
Bad tidings from the army?—or some new
Affront to Arnold?

VARICK.   After his return,
Too long for parting, Washington remained

Alone with Mistress Arnold. As he left
He met me at the door, and eyed me sternly,
Then left in silence, with a sad, grave face,
Such as one asks no questions of.

[*Enter* Mrs. Arnold.]

Mrs. Arnold.   —You here?
I thought, save me, no one attached to him
Would stay a moment in this place. O, tell me,
Do they yet know,—the world, does it yet know it?
Franks. Madam, as yet we do not know what means
This strange excitement. Where is General Arnold?
Mrs. Arnold. Do you not know, then? I must not betray
    him;
For it were treachery to breathe the thing
To a new listener's ear, though as a secret.
The ignorance of those who not as yet
Have heard it, is a moment's respite for him.
But 'tis upon the common air already,
And the wind waits to whisper it in your ears.
You were his friends, and you will call him Traitor,
But I will not, though we are the betrayed ones,—
I and my child. O how could I so long
Have left it! Something mad within my breast
Prompts me to wander forth with it, and find
Some secret cavern, and there live unseen
By all the world. It looks like *him*—we called it
The little General, for it had his smile,
And in its peevish moments frowned like him—
And therefore men will hate it. O, 'tis heir
To an untold inheritance: the orphan
Of a surviving father, and my child!

[*Exit* Mrs. Arnold.]

[*Enter an* Officer.]

Officer. I may congratulate you. We half feared
That you were implicated in the plot.
But Washington has given me leave to say,
Arnold himself exculpates you expressly,

    In his communication from the ship
    In which he hides his treason.

FRANKS.   Arnold! Treason!

OFFICER. What, is it news to you? He has deserted,
    And is this moment with the enemy.

FRANKS. I hardly seem to hear it! Did you say,
    Arnold had carried all his wounds and glory
    Over to the enemy, and given them back
    To them he won them of?

OFFICER.   Not given—*sold* them;
    A messenger from Jameson brought the proof.
    'Tis not without example that great soldiers
    Should fail to be great men. The broad-winged vulture
    Has many outward aspects of the eagle,
    But he will stoop to carrion.

                                   [*Exit.*]

FRANKS.   He scoffs,
    But I could weep; I feel *myself* disgraced.
    Oh, Varick! When a great man dies, the world
    Pretends to mourn; and he is more than dead.
    That which was great in him, his manhood, strength,
    And his indomitable soul, and all
    That was the man, are dead; and but a man,
    One of the herd, now trampled by the herd
    Into the common mire of men, survives him.
    They will not rest—he was above their heads
    And is beneath their feet—they will not breathe,
    Nor laugh for joy, till they have called him Villain!
    A hundred times have called him Villain! Traitor!
    Now will the meanness, jealousy, and malice
    That dogged his whole career be justified;
    Now secret envy from its slimy coil
    Lift its low head and hiss; now littleness
    Be great in its own eyes; and now, each ass
    Will bray to deafen Heaven. Deserter! Traitor!
    I shall go mad to hear it—and from them!
    Come, curse them with me, Varick;—drones and fops,

Mere men of family and feathers—men,
Whose whole of life, with all the good and evil
From infancy to manhood done by them,
Would not make up a single act of his,
Will hate and scorn him for the only thing
In which they could be like him if they would.

ACT IV

SCENE I.

Tappan, a military post. A room in the place of
ANDRÉ's *confinement.*

[*Enter* FRANKS *and* TALLMADGE.]

TALLMADGE. And she has followed him? I cannot say
  It was not right she should.

FRANKS.   If 'twas a part,
  'Twas acted well;—but she has gone to Arnold.
  What of the prisoner? Have you learned as yet
  More than his name and rank?

TALLMADGE.   He is, it seems,
  A man in high repute; with friends and fortune
  A growing favorite, and has been advanced
  In rank and trust beyond all precedent.

FRANKS. How does he bear the new and startling shape
  His future has put on? Is that his voice?
  He sings a cheerful air.

TALLMADGE.   When he had heard
  Of Arnold's safety, such an instant change
  Came on his aspect, that 'twas then we seemed
  To see him first; and smiling, half in scorn,
  And with a kind of haughty eagerness
  He told his name and rank; and still he seems,
  Without the least surmise of the black name,
  And blacker fate, we write against his name,
  To hold himself a prisoner of war.

FRANKS. But he should know the worst.

TALLMADGE.   And shall be told it;
  Deception here is cruelty—not mercy.

[*Enter* ANDRÉ *at an inner door; his dress that
  of a British officer.*]

ANDRÉ. A captive's welcome to you, gentlemen.
  Trust me, I shall think better of your party

For having been its prisoner. It might seem,
But for these guarded doors, that I was here
The willing guest of countrymen and friends.

TALLMADGE. You meet misfortune with a cheerfulness
That would disarm severity in tyrants.

ANDRÉ. Why I have been in reasonable temper,
Not sad, if not quite gay, since I threw off
That irksome and detestable disguise,
That like a wet and aguish cloud hung round me,
Dripping black melancholy.

FRANKS.   But does not
The failure of your enterprise depress you?

ANDRÉ. No; why should I of my misfortune make
My punishment? We played for a high stake,
And lost it,—that is all.

TALLMADGE.   But I fear not;
I fear that is not all.

ANDRÉ.   I cannot say
What view your countrymen may take of it—

TALLMADGE. Yours have decided for them. Hear the story:
We had a man amongst us, young like you,
Like you endowed with every gift that Nature
And Fortune, in matched rivalry, bestow.
He, like yourself, upon his party's service,
Was found disguised among the enemy.
I do you no dishonor when I say,
His motives were as pure, his aim as high,
And his soul noble as your own. That man
Was put in fetters, and his youth made old
With cruelty; and when in his dark hour
He would have set one last fond word on record
For his dear mother's eye, it was denied him.

ANDRÉ. The villains!

TALLMADGE.   This, my countrymen to you
Will not do, even in revenge; and yet,
One thing was done to Hale, which they will do,—

I must be open—understand me,—He
Was sentenced as a spy, and hanged.

[A short silence.]

ANDRÉ.   You said
    He had a mother?
TALLMADGE.   A fond, aged mother.

[A longer silence.]

ANDRÉ. Pardon me, Sir, I fear your last few words
    Received but poor attention. I suppose
    That he was executed.
FRANKS [*aside to Tallmadge*]. Let us leave him.
    In your narration you have touched some chord
    On which his whole life's music slept; and now,
    For the first time, awakes with sounds of pain.

[Exeunt FRANKS *and* TALLMADGE.]

[ANDRÉ *continues standing in the same atttiude.*]

SCENE II.

*The same. A public room. A number of General Officers, con-
tituting the Board of Commissioners met to investigate the
case of* ANDRÉ. ANDRÉ, TALLMADGE, *and a guard of
soldiers. General* GREEN *sitting as President.*

GREEN. The evidence is before us: If the accused
    Have aught to say, he has permission now.
ANDRÉ. I have not much to say, and in that little
    I feel myself prejudged. Your charge is this:
    That I was near your outposts found disguised,
    And on my person, some intelligence
    Of value to our army. This is true.
    You know the tale too well to make it needful
    That I should show by what necessity
    I was thus found. At the request of one
    High in command with you, I came on shore,
    And *I came* undisguised.

GREEN.   Did you conceive
        Your landing had the sanction of a flag?

ANDRÉ. I came at night, and on a secret mission,
        And yet I came not as a spy. I harbored
        No thought of treachery,—had no design
        To palm myself upon you for another,
        And steal your secrets. When, against my will,
        Forced to return disguised, the information
        Found on my person, your own officer
        Committed to my keeping. And if this,
        With no intention, of myself, to gain,
        Or use my borrowed habit to acquire
        Such information, is to be a spy,
        Then am I one—if not, then am I not.

GREEN. Your noble candor, Sir, concedes the facts
        That will control our verdict. I will add,
        That had it been a common British soldier,
        Who, one of like condition in our army
        Had aided in betrayal of his trust,
        And had been found disguised, with written proof
        Of his own practice and the other's treason
        Concealed about him,—none on either side
        Had hesitated to call *him* a spy.
        Where higher rank is compromised, to aid
        In the betrayal of a higher trust,
        The turpitude is greater: and although,
        Without intention, doubtless, to subject
        Yourself to the great danger that now threatens,
        You made yourself the agent, to become
        The victim of another's crime—our duty
        Is to pronounce you an undoubted spy;
        And subject to be dealt with as the laws
        Of war require; and our clear conscience adds,
        May God be merciful, where man is just!

        [*The court rises. Exeunt all but* TALLMADGE,
                ANDRÉ, *and the guard.*]

ANDRÉ. Come hither, Major Tallmadge. You have been

A kinder keeper to me than your warrant
Or my desert could justify; and yet
You owe me something. 'Twas your interference
That on my first detention, at the crisis
And turning point of all my destiny,
Prevented my return to Arnold's quarters,
And so procured my death.

TALLMADGE.   Was I to blame?

ANDRÉ. You did as I should do by you. Come near,
Survey me. Do you see the marks of fear
And weakness in my aspect? Has the blood
Betrayed my cheek? Do I grow pale and tremble
At the stern face my destiny puts on?

TALLMADGE. You look as usual; and no doubt confront
Your natural fears with manly fortitude.

ANDRÉ. But I am weak. O God! no child is weaker.

[*He approaches, and leans on* TALLMADGE.]

Tallmadge, I know your nature stern, and therefore
Believe it strong, and one to lean upon.
Yours is a true heart, a true manly heart,
I feel—I felt it from the first; and now,
Because you owe me something, as I said,
Though I accuse you not, in recompense,
Your heart must taste the bitterness of mine.
I have—this tightness at the throat prevents—
I'd say—

[*He turns to the guard.*]

May these men go?

TALLMADGE.   Retire a moment,
And stand without the door.

ANDRÉ.   I sought to say
That I have sisters and a mother. Now,
Even while I speak, they wait for news of me,
And smile, and speak, with hopeful fond conjecture,
Of some new honor lighted on the head
Of their hearts' idol—whom they've learned to think

Is that of fortune too. And they will hear—
O! were it of my death alone, I might
Be cheerful. Had it been my fate to fall
In arms and honor on the open field,
Where life-blood shed, is a serene libation
Poured on a country's altar, in the sight
Of all mankind, I had not felt these pangs,
This wild disturbance, this keen shuddering chill
At the fore-tasted cup of death; nor they
The agony that they will feel to hear
The ghastly tidings soon to fall on ears
That never more will hear a joyful sound.

[*He turns from* TALLMADGE, *and stands for
awhile, as if lost in thought.*]

I was obscure and happy; O, too happy!
I broke the sacred human ties that bound
My wildly restless wishes to a life
Of peaceful humble joy. And I have found,
O yes, I may say fame—I shall be famous!
A death of shame—a shame that makes death mean,
A death that makes shame ghastly—is the end
Of all my inspirations of success,
My hopes that blushed to know themselves for hopes,
My cautious daring, and my ardent thought.
Dreams! dreams! It is all darkness now before me,
That was so late a scene lit up and splendid
With bright deceitful torches, waving on
To farther glory. High-aspiring André!
One sentence will tell all, and be your record—
Hanged as a spy, will be your history!

[*A pause.*]

They came, they crowded round me, the illusive,
The treacherous visions—they allured me on,
The blooming spectres! garlands waved around,
And music stirred my pulses. Silently
They pointed to the future; yet methought

I read a glorious promise in their eyes.
But suddenly they change; each wears a shroud,
And scowls on me with looks of death; they crowd,
They press upon me from behind, they urge,
They thrust me on; and there, before me, stands—
O God! I cannot speak it, cannot name
To my own ears, the thing which threatens me
With more than pain of dying; and beneath it
I see a felon's coffin; and beyond,
A lonely, naked, and dishonored grave.

[*He covers his eyes with his hands, and stands motionless.* TALLMADGE, *as if afraid to disturb him, also remains
motionless, and regards him with a look of sympathy.*]

SCENE III.

The same. A street.

[*Enter* FRANKS *and* VARICK.]

FRANKS. A soldier, of the name of Champe, has ventured
    To go, disguised, into New York; the plot,
    Thus far, has prospered. Arnold can be captured
    By a small number of determined men,
    Whom Champe will meet there.

VARICK.   Now, may Heaven, or Congress,
    Send him an epaulette! I'd give my own,
    Although it was through Arnold that I gained it,
    To see his frowning face beneath the gallows,
    Instead of smiling André.

FRANKS.   Secret friends,
    Of both sides, in the city, will assist us,
    Being assured that by this means alone
    They can save André. Thus, we have discovered
    The house in which he lodges—are to find
    A boat moored in the river, and disguised
    As strolling sailors, favored by the night
    We shall surprise him, seize, and bind him fast,
    And bear him off in triumph.

[*Enter* TALLMADGE.]

VARICK.   Here comes one
Who should know something of the secret game
In which ill-fortuned André's life is played,
With little doubt, against the higher card.
What news of André?—

TALLMADGE.   Washington is steadfast.
Commissioners from both sides are to meet:
But that you know.

FRANKS.   And with what hope we know;
There's better even in my hair-brained plot;
And if that fail, why then the hapless André
May, as his mood is, frown, or smile, or weep
His farewell to the world. I did believe,
Nay would have sworn, that Washington would save him.
But he is much too faultless to feel pity;
Too good and great to be more great and better.
He is all justice, rigid, iron justice,
Untempered by the gold alloy of mercy.

TALLMADGE. Why, he is merciful to you and me,
And to the many thousands of brave men
Who venture life and fortune in this war.
Before mankind, and Heaven, we have asserted
Our independence,—these four bloody years
Maintained it with the sword; and we must show
The hesitating world the free commission
We hold from God, at our own will and peril
To do all acts that may pertain to nations.

FRANKS. He dies, then, not because his death is just,
Although it were so, nor because he ran
Intelligently upon danger. No!
We need, state policy demands—a victim.
To me, I will confess, this policy
Seems but a mean assassin, hired to stab,
Where justice hesitates, and feels no strength
To lift the sword. No, no. If we must be
His executioners, let us say at once,

It is because the man himself deserves,
Not that we need, his death.

TALLMADGE.   But policy
Did not condemn, although it will not save;
And if it be of force to turn the edge
Of a judicial sentence, as it is,
In every case of pardon, then why not
Of force sufficient to prevent a pardon?
We do not plead the policy of justice,
But the impolicy of mercy.

FRANKS.   Oh!
If it has come to pleading—I am silenced.
I have no skill in casuistry: compassion
Is not a function of the brain, nor can
The wiser heart that leans on its own instincts,
Refute the processes, which, of a thread
Of policy, can spin a cord to kill
An innocent, brave man.

TALLMADGE.   The heart that trusts
To its own instincts merely, often errs,
And mistakes feebleness for strength of feeling.
I have no feeling, doubtless,—no compassion
To temper sterner thoughts? And Washington,
Who from the very first, because determined
By an example it would heed, to quell
This British tampering with our discontent,
Would never see him, fearing lest at sight
Of the brave stripling, his large father's heart
Should feel relentings,—he, too, has no pity!

                         [*Exeunt.*]

SCENE IV.

New York. A room in ARNOLD's *quarters.*

[*Enter* MRS. ARNOLD.]

MRS. ARNOLD. At last!—and it has come to this: *his* hands
Have raised the gibbet, and prepared the cord.
Inhuman laws, as stern and blind as war

That made them, claim their victim, and another
Must be the sacrifice! There is one way,
Forgive me Heaven that I think of it!—
I do not will it—no! no! God, thou knowest
I would not have my husband yield himself
To save this man; but I cannot but feel
That I would have him capable of this.
O, it would wipe out half the infamy!
Truth to humanity, and private ties,
Would expiate his treason to the state,
And military perfidy; such stern
Fidelity to one, make good the want
Of public faith; and 'gainst the citizen—
In the severest patriot's heart—the *man*
Would rise and plead for him. But will they, then,
O! can they take his life, thus freely offered
To save another's? No! They will not, cannot.
A light breaks in on me—they surely cannot.

[*Enter* ARNOLD, *in the uniform of a British officer.*]

ARNOLD. Your too prophetic bodings, in the end,
Have proved but half inspired. My new allies
Seem to conceive that, of myself, I am
A full equivalent for what they offered:
They give me rank quite equal to my higher,
But less substantial title, won from Congress
With greater effort. Trust me, you shall find
That though the hurricane has torn the oak
Out of its rooted place, it has again,
By the same wind, been planted broad and deep
In firmer soil, and still can give you shelter;
Only upbraid me not, nor think to call
The irrevocable back, by tears and frenzy.

MRS. ARNOLD. Because you were my shelter—while the storm
Hung doubtful, writhing on the hand of Heaven,
Reluctant, and still waiting for repentance,
I did accuse and pray.—It has begun
To unfold its bosom peril, and its lightnings

Look in the face of Death, and watch his eye
To see on whom it turns: I pray no more.
Who ever prayed to Fate?

ARNOLD.   Prophetic still!
And still a skeptic to my stars, although
I stand here safe, where others have been ruined.
But if you yet fear evil, you have friends:
They hate me in their hearts; and doubtless, *now*,
They curse me with their lips: return to them;
You will be praised for it. As I have dared,
I would bear all—alone.

MRS. ARNOLD.   And can you bear,
Do you bear all alone? Is there not one
Who suffers more? One, on whose life has fallen
The sword that glanced from yours? One, too, whose death
Will leave the name of murder to avenge it?
I recollect, when of my native city
The British army held possession, he,
In his first bloom of youth, scarce soldierly,
And yet more hero-like than veterans
Scarred in the field, won every heart to him
By his fair looks and manly courtesy,
Tempered with fine and undisdainful pride.
It seemed, to look on him, that he might pass,
Like a young warlike deity, admired,
And praised, through battle, and no hand be found
To strike him with disfigurement or death.
And now they dig for him a felon's grave;
And he must die a death so much abhorred,
It taints the hand that deals it—by a means
From which the haggard orphans of all hope,
Despair's wild victims, who run eagerly
On self-destruction, would shrink, shuddering, back,
And choose to live.

ARNOLD.   Your fears, then, are for André?
But still you start at shadows; on my life,
These threats of the Americans are such.

MRS. ARNOLD. Yes, shadows, fearful, as they will be found
 Faithful to the dark purposes which shape them.

ARNOLD. Their generals have sentenced him, 'tis true;
 And just as plain that 'tis for some advantage
 They hope to gain by way of compromise.
 Perhaps—at once, they will demand that I
 Shall be delivered up to them!

MRS. ARNOLD.   And how,
 If tempted to make void a barren contract,
 And save a favorite, the commissioners
 Should listen to them?

ARNOLD.   I still wear my sword.
 It is a toy, here, by my side, at present,
 But was, and may be more. At Danbury
 It saved my life, and therefore may well serve
 To take it; I might rather say again
 To save it—more than save it! Can you dream
 That I would live to die beneath the eyes
 Of my old enemies,—and new ones—friends
 That are no longer friends—I almost die—
 By the great God in Heaven! it stops my heart
 To think of it; to save the world, I could not.
 'Twould be to taste damnation, and not death!
 I tremble, but it is not fear. The thought
 Even of the cord does not unman me—no!
 It is the hands that hold it; 'tis their grasp
 Upon my throat that makes me weak and faint
 With hate that is like death.

MRS. ARNOLD.   But, if you freely
 Delivered up yourself for André's sake,
 O, could they, would they dare to touch your life?
 I will go with you; Washington is noble,
 I'll fall down at his feet—

ARNOLD.   You at his feet?
 And I—it strangles me to speak again
 The thing you uttered, and my loathing soul
 Tastes its own poison: What! It looks well—I,

Of him, proud, cold, impassive Washington,
A beggar for an hour's existence longer!

MRS. ARNOLD. But the alternative of this may be
A far worse thing.

ARNOLD.   What worse thing, out of hell?

MRS. ARNOLD. What more humiliating can be feared
Than that which will befall us in the event
Of André's death? By that we shall be thrown
As life-long pensioners on enemies,
Whose scorn will be our safety. O, be warned!
This is your second peril—this the rock
On which your new-embarked adventure drives,
With fatal swiftness; the still treacherous pilot,
Your evil spirit, laughing in the shrouds,
And wild eyed shipwreck standing by the helm.
The living can be met, their life itself,
Subjecting them to what they would inflict,
Gives power to opposition. But the dead
Are dreadful enemies. At every point
In your career, some viewless influence
Reaching from André's grave, will thrust you back,
Powerless, from fortune. On the very step
And threshold of preferment, will your feet
Slip in his blood: his name will be a curse,
Heard, like a mind-born echo, in all ears
At sound of yours—and to your own, his fate
Be Heaven's mercy.

ARNOLD.   Feeling takes you far!
I might suspect, aye, and I partly do,
That personal motives lead you to prefer
My honor to my life. This youth, this André,
Has claims upon your gratitude, perhaps,
Which I have not established, though your husband.
Your family are loyal, very loyal!
And if they, more than ever, hate me now,
As I suspect they do, I know 'tis not
Because of my defection, but my failure.

> They doubtless favored him, as you, in heart,
> Though not in your ambition, may have done.

MRS. ARNOLD. Neither in my ambition nor my heart,
> Nor in my views. I liked him—not his cause,
> And saw you both, ere I chose one; and now,
> Even for the preference' sake which then I showed,
> O, save him!

ARNOLD.   Were it in some other way!
> O, were it but to spring, as I have dreamed,
> When in my sleep he seemed to call for help,
> Into the storm-blind sea—what man would dare
> Leap in before me? Were it in the field
> To rescue him, and all my enemies
> Stood, armed, around him, frowning death and shame;
> No league of desperate madmen to bring off
> Their king or colors, ever dared as I
> Would dare for him. But now, what can I do?
> I have the power, indeed, nor lack the daring
> To do what you advise; but strong repugnance
> Masters the weaker motive, and the will
> Lies bound in its own chain. And if his death
> Will arm the invisible and restless hands
> Of coward slander 'gainst me,—let them strike!
> I am no novice in that kind of warfare,
> Not weak, nor imbecile, nor to be hurt
> By such like shadows as they wield, nor wounds
> That words can make; though they should be such sound
> As Traitor, Murderer, and like epithets,
> Whose hateful meanings men like basilisks shoot
> One at another—their sharp, viewless points
> Dipped in the killing poison of their nature.

MRS. ARNOLD [aside]. His sullen mood is on; and I but stand
> Upon the shore of his chafed mind, and see
> The turbid waters dash themselves in foam.

                                     [Exit.

ARNOLD. Yet she speaks truth; she is inspired to give
> A shape to my dim fears; I see already

That André is a cloud upon their favor
To keep its rays from me. He saved my life;
That is his crime with my old friends, as is
My want of power to save him, with my new.
I pity him: the warning that saved me
Has proved his own death-warrant. But to throw
The game into their hands; to give my throat
To my own knife! It is not fear deters me,
No! I can say to my own heart, not fear.
What should I fear? I shall not seem a wolf
With broken fangs, clutched by the throat and strangled,
But as a lion that stalks freely in,
And dares the amphitheatre. By Heaven!
I've half a mind to do it. I shall still
Be free, because self-offered; and unconquered,
Because I yield myself without constraint.
Then, let them seize me, let them pierce and tear,
Like Indians, their stake-bound foe; each blow,
Each stab, will give the lie to their fond notions
That I am treacherous, selfish;—and my blood
Will blot the record in their lying annals.

[*Exit.*]

ACT V

SCENE I.

Dobbs' Ferry. A room in an inn. General GREEN *and other* OFFICERS, *constituting the American Commission. To these, enter General* ROBERTSON, *Colonel* ROBINSON, *and other officers of his suit; and, behind them,* ARNOLD, *wrapped in a military cloak that conceals his person.*

ROBERTSON [*to Green*]. 'Tis understood that all who land
    with me,
  Are equally protected by the flag.

GREEN. It is; I only wonder at the question.

ROBERTSON. Our powers are ample; and I think that you
  Are not such willing executioners,
  But that some way may be devised to spare
  Your sense of justice its distasteful office
  On our young countryman.

GREEN.   Our hands are tied
  By our commission; yet we have some hope
  In your success—which we should feel as ours.

[ARNOLD *discovers himself, and advances.*]

SEVERAL AMERICAN OFFICERS [*speaking to each other in
    confusion*]. What! He? Yes—No—So like him!

1ST OFFICER.   It is he.
  'Tis the King's scarlet that has changed his looks.
  Heaven! so unblushingly to wear it here,
    And flaunt it in our eyes—

2D OFFICER.   It blushes *for* him.

1ST OFFICER. But it shall not protect him—he's an outlaw.

GREEN. To us, but not to them. Respect the flag.

ARNOLD. You, General, I ever have regarded—

GREEN [*abruptly to Robertson*]. If that man has a share
      in this commission,
  I do not treat with *him*.

ARNOLD.   Ha! When we stood
   On the same ground, and when our swords might reach,
   You dared not use me thus.

ROBERTSON [*to Arnold*].   Have you gone mad?
   [*To Green.*] We are empowered to give you in exchange
   For Major André any officer,
   Though of the highest rank, whom we retain
   A prisoner of war.

GREEN.   There is one man
   Amongst you, who is not a prisoner,
   Nor yet one of you; there he stands, and him,
   Him only, we are authorized to accept
   As an equivalent for your countryman.

ROBERTSON. To this we cannot listen; British honor
   Is dearer, in our eyes, than British life.

ARNOLD. And now hear me. For all that André did,
   I only am, of right, responsible
   To them who sent you hither,—as I am,
   In some degree, to others, for his safety.
   What they will do, 'tis not for me to say
   Although I know that at their mercy lie
   A multitude of prisoners, whose lives
   Stand fairly forfeited in this rebellion:
   But I am to command a British column;
   And at the moment André dies, from me
   Tell Washington—he knows me—that till then
   I still retained some sense of ancient ties:
   But thenceforth I am changed. No foreign wolf
   That ever from his floating lair leaped down
   On a defenceless shore, but had more mercy
   Than I will have on my own countrymen.
   All shall be held participators; all—
   To my own kindred—guilty of the crime.
   Cities and villages shall burn by daylight
   Around their silent bells; and fire shall hiss
   Along their streets against the stream of slaughter.
   They would have *me*, would buy *me*, life for life!
   Go back, and tell these cunning barterers

Of their own bloody verdict,—As they write
The fate of André upon this war's record,
And in the self-same character, shall all
Its history be written: if in blood,
Then let them look to see no other color
Where'er my hand appears; and, by my word,
Red shall not seem to stain it!

GREEN.   What you do,
Those whom you serve must justify. To us
The daylight howl of the uncaverned wolf
Portends no harm; 'tis night and treachery only
That makes him dangerous.
[*To Robertson.*]   Sir, farewell; 'tis clear
That conference is useless.

              [*Exeunt* GREEN *and the* AMERICANS.]

ROBINSON.   Wrong! all wrong!
Our purpose is to save, not to revenge him;
It was no time for threats.

ARNOLD.   No, nor persuasion.
I had a surer means. 'Twas my intention,
My full determination, when I came—
Nor is it now too late—to act a part
That I've rehearsed to no one. But to hear
This man make the demand!

ROBERTSON.   But you should first
Have seen if 'twas his pleasure to know *you,*
And not addressed him else.

ARNOLD.   And you too think
That my return to loyalty degrades me?
This is the blossoming of royal favor,
The flower of that sapless parasite,
That grew so rank upon me, while my roots
Still grasped their native soil, but perishes
With my transplanting! But I find no fault:
'Tis well—'tis natural—it is both royal
And human nature. No—no fault, no fault!

[*Exeunt* ROBERTSON *and the others:* ARNOLD
  continues speaking, as if to himself.]

It is a child, whose ignorant impatience
Complains of the inevitable—cold,
And fickle heat; and he a weaker child
Who rails at human falsehood and injustice.
Beasts to each other are more wise: the tiger
Knows, if not loves, his kind; and does not start
To see the treacherous blood-thirst in the eye
Of his own image; doubtless also serpents
Who share one bane, are innocent to each other.

[Exit.]

SCENE II.

New York. A street. SEVERAL PERSONS *in the garb of of sailors
discovered waiting before a house; with them,* VARICK *and*
FRANKS: *the latter wearing a cloak, but not otherwise
disguised.* Time, *night.*

FRANKS. I hear a step! keep back, within the shadow.
1ST DISGUISE. It moves another way; it is not he.
VARICK. I see the break of morning; if not now
    Within, he's safe, and only we in danger.
FRANKS. 'Tis time we knew; let's try his castle's strength.
    Make but one stroke of it; the less we fear
    The noise we make, the less we make, to fear.

[They burst the door.]

VARICK. Stand all—Franks only, and myself, will enter.

[Enter the house FRANKS and VARICK.]

2D DISGUISE. I would as lieve they did so: I conceive
    An honest man will sometimes dread to look
    A villain in the eye, just as a villain
    Is thought to shun the other's.
1ST DISGUISE.   It is so.
    Your conscience acts for his; and makes you feel,

In virtue of your common nature, shame
That he feels not, perhaps, at sight of you.

[*Re-enter* FRANKS *and* VARICK.]

VARICK. The game is up: to-day he left the city,
    Not to return to-night. What noise is that?
FRANKS. Fly! the Philistines! Each a different way!

[*Enter a* BRITISH PATROL.]

SEVERAL VOICES [*in confusion*]. Which way! I heard them
    here—this way! where now?
FRANKS. Here—yonder—every way. I am the hindmost,
    And so fulfil the proverb! I surrender.

[*Exeunt* PATROL, *with* FRANKS.]

SCENE III.

Tappan. A room in the place of ANDRÉ's *confinement.*
The scene shows a table, on which lies a book,
a plumed hat, and a sword.

ANDRÉ [*before a window*]. The sun once more!—but once!
    To others now
    He rises, but he sets to me. What still
    Remains to me of day, is like the pale
    Imprisoned daylight of a dream—a lamp
    Within a tomb, a light enclosed in darkness.
    There is a greater and eternal glory!
    I know there must be—or this would not be.
    But still my eyes turn from it to the sun,
    The bright, warm sun! And even that is made
    To act a part in my low, wretched doom.
    At noon—the time when sentenced murderers die—
    It silently but certainly will strike
    A night-hour—strike my hour of death; and shine,
    And still shine on; and earth and sky will smile
    As brightly as before. Just there to-morrow
    That line of light will fall as it does now;

And I—O darkness! darkness!—Death and darkness
Are but one thing; and even now the twilight
Is on my soul, and I see nothing clear.

[*Enter a* CHAPLAIN, *in his robes.*]

CHAPLAIN. I trust that, in my absence, you have sought
 The consolations of this book; well named
 The Book of Life; for it is that alone,
 Whose words have power against the power of Death.
ANDRÉ. I feel what they express—yes, I would hope
 All, all they mean. But they are words, though awful—
 Are still but words; of which the power and meaning
 Are less than in my thoughts; or clearer there
 Than in these ill-seen symbols.

[*A pause.*]

      Ah! how many,
With any one of whom to part were pain,
And now I part with all! They little know;
They little dream of it! The sea, that was
A few months' barrier to our meeting, now
Is an eternity between us! Yonder
They breathe, they move; but death has come so near,
And stands so in my vision, that it throws
Shadows on all things. Still they rise before me;
I cannot make them absent when I would:—
The past, that I'd shut out, blends with the future;
Familiar looks come mingling with strange faces,
That with the anticipated spectacle
Of shame and death flow in, and stare at me
With wonder and with pity. 'Tis not I
But they that are to die, if I should trust
This feeling of distressful nothingness,
This emptiness around me, when I grasp
For substance in the forms that paint themselves
On the dim air, and bend half-breathing toward me.

[*Enter* TALLMADGE.]

O, welcome! What says Washington? But tell me

    I am to die by any other mode,
    And you will give me life again.

TALLMADGE.   I cannot.

ANDRÉ. This is so bitter—so unnecessary!
    I did it all in honor—had no thought
    Except of honor. I could meet, though sentenced,
    A soldier's death, with soldier's nerve; but this
    Is more than death!

TALLMADGE.   The view which makes the thing
    Seem necessary, also makes the mode.
    Don't think of it—'tis nothing: the aversion
    Men feel for it will not attach to you,
    But add to the compassion felt by all.

ANDRÉ. 'Tis your compassion, my kind friend, that seeks
    To make me think so. Have you lately heard
    Of them—of General and Mistress Arnold?

TALLMADGE [*bitterly*]. He lives, and prospers!—but 'tis just
        to say
    Has made great efforts in his way to save you.

ANDRÉ. And she—think you she knows that I saved *him?*

TALLMADGE. She doubtless saw your letter; that, to you,
    So fatal message!

ANDRE. [*takes a miniature from his bosom, and puts it in
    Tallmadge's hand*]. This is a poor likeness—
    There—thus—a picture, taken by myself,
    Of her of whom I told you—of Honora.
    I lost her.—And I now have lost her name—
    The name for which I better loved her—Honor!

TALLMADGE. Your honor is not lost: it lives, untouched,
    In your pure motives—in itself! 'Tis like
    This picture, which is fresh and bright, although
    The gilded case is tarnished.

ANDRÉ.   Sadly tarnished;
    When wounded once, and taken prisoner,
    I hid it in my mouth.

    [*He takes it back, and regards it for a moment in silence.*]

It is in pity
To *me,* you do not say 'tis fair! Please see
It buried with me.

[*Martial music without, and at a distance.*]

ANDRÉ.   Now, how soon?

TALLMADGE.   An hour.

ANDRÉ. Ah! I feel wondrous calm: 'tis said, in drowning,
    That, at a certain point, the distressed life
    Gives up the struggle, and the full deep quiet
    Of death sets in, while one yet lives; and thus
    It seems with me.

TALLMADGE.   Nature is merciful;
    'Tis the unwilling soul that makes death painful.

ANDRÉ. O, but not that alone! It is the love
    Resisting death—the unwillingness of others.
    I had a dream last night, my last, at least
    My last one with a waking interval.
    I was in England: all was as of old,
    Too fresh-imagined to seem less than real,
    Yet for reality too fair; and I,
    Glad to be rid of all the cumbrous show
    And wild excitement of unresting war,
    Walked homeward through the quiet villages,
    And praised the blissful and soft face of peace,
    Unscarred by fire and sword. Joy was full-blown,
    And like a rose within me; and sweet fancies
    Hovered around and fed upon the flower.
    So I passed on, until the blooming precincts
    Of home embraced me, and the very air
    Whispered low welcomings to the wanderer.
    I saw them, all together, and unchanged,
    Sisters and mother, and the one I loved.
    They smiled, and all seemed happy, and I said,
    Ere I could hear them, Now they speak of me!
    I entered full of gladness. My fond greeting
    They did not answer, but gazed strangely on me:
    I took the hands of her who was my love,

Each in a hand of mine; she shrank from me,
And pale, and shuddering, sank down like snow.
My sisters turned to stone: only my mother
Came slowly toward me, and in such soft tones
As I in childhood heard, and with such sad
And questioning eyes, she said to me—My son!
What ails my son? what have they done to thee?
And then I knew it all, and horror waked me!

TALLMADGE. You should not think of such things at this moment.
It will unman you. I and all—forgive us!
We could not, dared not, trust our hearts in this.

CHAPLAIN. No, could not; to be always merciful,
Is Heaven's best privilege—might not I say
Its sole prerogative, to be *always* just?

TALLMADGE. The escort!—Be prepared.

ANDRÉ. [*who has not attended to the remarks of Tallmadge
and the Chaplain*].   Oh, I have heard it,
More often than the jarring axe and hammer,
Whose sounds have told me where I am to die—
"What ails my son? What have they done to thee?"

[*Enter the* OFFICER *in command,* GREEN, JAMESON, *and
other* OFFICERS, *who approach* ANDRÉ, *and take his proffered hand in silence. In the meantime, soldiers enter and
fill the back-ground.* ANDRÉ *takes up his sword and hat, as
if prepared to go.*]

TALLMADGE [*throwing his arms around André, and embracing him*]. O mine is the worst fortune, in this way
To part with you!

ANDRÉ [*returning his embrace*]. My friend!—Ah, it is when
Life's torch burns clear—though pale, yet strong and
        clear—
Against death's shadow, that the shadows vanish
Which stood between our spirits, and thenceforth
There's no chill in the touch of heart to heart.
        [*To the* OFFICER *in command.*]
Sir, let me not delay you: shall we go?

[*As they go out, a plaintive air commences in the street.*]

SCENE IV.

Tappan. A street.

[*Enter a number of* WOMEN *and* COUNTRYMEN.]

YOUNG WOMAN. Oh! and so young he is, and they say the hand-
somest man!—and if it were not that General Arnold
can't be taken, as innocent as the babe unborn!

OLD WOMAN. There'll be some disappointment or other, I've
made up my mind to it. A pardon, or something of that
kind 'll come just at the nick! If it wasn't for a hangin' or a
buryin' now and then, Lord knows, I see little enough
of life!

3D WOMAN. Well, I never saw but one man hung, and he had a
cap drawn over his face, so 'twas but little good it did me;
but he yerked, and yerked.

OLD WOMAN. How can you try one's nerves so, and the hangin'
to go through with? I warrant you, it makes me as weak as
a cat!

[*Enter* 4TH WOMAN.]

4TH WOMAN. O, the young Englishman won't be hanged, after
all! They've got the traitor, they've taken Arnold. Up there,
now—this moment, they're hanging him in the place of
André.

COUNTRYMAN. Up there? Why the gallows is yonder—there they
are hanging Arnold in effigy.

[*They pass over, and enter* PAULDING, WILLIAMS,
VAN WERT, *and several* CITIZENS *and* SOLDIERS.]

1ST CITIZEN. To each of you two hundred dollars—faith,
A very good reward! Now, brother Paulding,
Show us the medal, come; it warms my heart
To see a poor man's merits thus rewarded.

PAULDING. Well, here it is; FIDELITY on this side—

1st Soldier. Which means that you behaved like honest
    men;
    But on the other side—what's this?
Paulding.   'Tis Latin;
    And means—eh, Williams! that we love our country.
Williams. Yes, so they told us; and 'tis curious, Paulding,
    That this should be the very thing you said
    In answer to the offers André made us;
    Which shows me that a poor man's words may be
    Put into Latin, just as a poor man
    Into fine clothes, and look as grand, and seem
    As strange to old acquaintances as he.
Citizen [of Dutch descent]. We shall be late; I see them
    coming yonder.
    Poor fellow! well, a fever might have done it.
    Some say that he's not English; make him English,
    Or make him French—I say that he is Dutch:
    My wife has cried for him as much to-day,
    As for our Hendrick, after Saratoga.
3d Citizen. And mine has been more exercised, I guess,
    Than she will ever be for Jacob Thomson.
2d Soldier. Perhaps when you are hanged, she will regret it,
    Though you are *not* a soldier; but to André
    The women are so pitiful, I think
    In place of him they'd see their husbands hanged.

[*A drum is heard.*]

Eh comrades, hark! that calls us to the ranks.

[*He looks at* Paulding *and the others.*]

I wish these Minute Men, who have had all
The pay and glory, had this business too—
This gallows work: I'd rather, for myself,
Again be beaten at the Brandywine.

[*Exeunt in the same direction as the others.*]

SCENE V.

The same: an open place. A gallows in the distance—
a company of soldiers drawn up on each side, leaving
an interval, through which it is seen from the front.
Behind them a miscellaneous crowd.

[*Enter to these a body of soldiers, and arrange them-*
selves with the others; then the OFFICER IN COMMAND
and ANDRÉ *(in the full dress of a British Officer)*
walking between TALLMADGE *and the* CHAPLAIN, *and*
accompanied by GREEN, JAMESON, *and other* OFFI-
CERS. *Behind these, another small division of soldiers.*
As ANDRÉ *comes in sight of the gallows, he*
stops suddenly.]

CHAPLAIN. Sir, why this pause?
ANDRÉ.   'Twas all in loyalty,
    All, all in honor—and I die by *that!*
CHAPLAIN. We thought you reconciled.
ANDRÉ.   And so I am:
    It is not that; I am reconciled to death,
    But O, not to the mode!
OFFICER IN COMMAND.   If Major André
    Has aught to say—
ANDRÉ [*looking firmly around*]. I would but say, let all
    Who see my death, when they shall speak of me,
    Bear witness that I died like a brave man.

    [*They move on toward the place of execution.*]

SCENE VI.

New York. A room in ARNOLD'S *quarters.* ARNOLD,
ROBERTSON *and* MRS. ARNOLD.

ROBERTSON. I still feel hope; yet their commissioner
    Was plain and frank; and Washington is noted
    For his direct and open policy.
MRS. ARNOLD. There is no hope. Even from the first, I felt
    As when one reads a guilty tale, and knows
    The end is horror.

ARNOLD.   Fear as frequently
Deceives as hope; though its presentiments
Are like religion to the mind of women.

ROBERTSON. Have you no fear?

ARNOLD.   Yes; but the more they threaten,
The less I fear. While they've the card in hand,
It tells upon the game,—once played 'tis worthless.

ROBERTSON. There's reason in that view.

[*Enter* ROBINSON.]

ROBINSON.   I shall be pardoned
My abrupt entrance, if this letter's contents
Confirm its bearer's tidings.

ROBERTSON.   With your leave.

[*He reads the letter.*]

He is dead!

MRS. ARNOLD.   Is dead.

ARNOLD.   Why he is dead then—dead!
And, once again, say dead—then let him rest
In silence, and be silently avenged.
He died, himself, but once; and why for us
Should he die oftener? There's no help for death.

MRS. ARNOLD. Nor for the living dead. The end has come—
We should be glad. Our evil destiny
Is consummated, perfect; and hereafter
Has no misfortune for us, and no fear.
The past makes all the future.—God in heaven,
I do not even ask help of Thee!

[*She sinks down, unnoticed.*]

ARNOLD.   He risked,
In every petty skirmish, no less danger
To do less service. Yet 'twas damnable!
Mere butchery and bloody-mindedness;
A dastard and disguised revenge on me,
For my defection. Yes, to sprinkle me
With innocent blood, they plunged their hands in it.
The hour is theirs—they have a moment's triumph:

But in achieving it they have begun—
Where tragedies end—a drama whose first act
Is murder—but whose last shall be as pale
With retribution. They shall have no cause,
Like common murderers, to start at spectres.
Shapes of substantial evil, real horrors,
Shall be the conscience of their homicide.

ROBERTSON. That will not give him life again; our André!
The young, and brave!

ARNOLD.   But, Sir, the royal cause
Shall be no loser. It has lost one friend,
And gains in me another, pledged to vengeance.

ROBERTSON. Sir, we can judge of that. 'Tis not your office,
And ill becomes one in your place, to rate
The consequence of André's death to us.

ARNOLD. But you mistake me! There lives not the man
Who more desired his safety than did I;
And had I once conceived his death so near,
Or known it certain, I'd have shown the world
That no man cared for it as much as I.
It was my full intention, my fixed purpose,
To give my life for his, or cast myself
Into the hands, at least, of those who seek it.

ROBERTSON. Had we but known it, you should not have wanted
Our countenance to the act.

MRS. ARNOLD [rising].   What stroke like this
Has André suffered? This is worse than death!

[Exit.]

ROBERTSON. 'Twere best you understood me, General Arnold,
And your position, which you might mistake,
If unexplained. Henceforth our intercourse
Must be official, simply such;—Adieu.

[Exit.]

ARNOLD. Ha! am I Arnold still? or have I changed
My nature with my party? Has my heart
Grown white beneath this scarlet livery,

That I should hear these insults, and my sword
Rest in its scabbard, and not leap to meet
His insolent tongue! My God—it must be so!
For once my brain seethes, and my blood is cold.
He bears the King's commission, and is higher
In rank than I am, and has equal power
To ruin as insult me, an unfriended
And helpless man; but had the King himself
Stood in his place, with death upon his lips,
I should have struck the dastard who insulted
My helpless fortunes! Coward! coward! coward!
I have no courage to resent, no will, no power.
They have me at their mercy, and they know it,
These old, new enemies! I am a man
Without a home, a country, or a friend.

[*Enter* FRANKS.]

Franks! you? Why this is strange. A prisoner?
FRANKS. Yes, of my own design I have been taken,
  Have given my parole, and now am here;
  And to meet you once more was my sole purpose.
ARNOLD. My old, tried comrade! my true friend in need!
  Never in all my life felt I such want
  Of a true-hearted friend. The death of André
  Has set the stream against me, on whose bosom
  I trusted all my fortunes. They insult
  And slight me here: or, if at times more gracious,
  Their faces are but painted with their smiles,
  And frowns lie under them. My faithful Franks!

[*He approaches, and leans on* FRANKS.]

Let my heart feel you, thus; forgive the weakness:
It moves me at this time beyond my nature,
To know there's one man who still clings to me.
My wife is alienated; and my path
Become a solitude, on which no being
Sets willing foot. I needed such a one,
One bound by former ties—I will not speak

Of favors now—who brings unaltered feelings
To my reversed condition—and he comes!

FRANKS [*disengaging himself*]. Sir—General—Your
        confidence in me
Is, as was mine in you, misplaced. I came—
I must out with it—General—I came not
To be your confidant.

ARNOLD.   Did you not say
You came to meet me? Of what other man
Could I believe this? but of you I did.

FRANKS. I came to right myself—but thus to see you—
In that red coat, unmans me with mere shame.

ARNOLD. Make not all quarrels yours; but tell me now,
What have I done to undo all the past?
I mean—what done to you?

FRANKS.   At Saratoga
You struck me with your sword; but 'tis not that—

ARNOLD. Did I not make amends, and you forgive me?

FRANKS. Yes, the brave soldier fully, freely, did I;—
Not the hired traitor!

ARNOLD.   Ha!

[*He draws his sword, and advances a step towards*
FRANKS, *then drops the point and seems to muse.*]

FRANKS.   It is not that;
I said it was not that; although the blow
Now seems as vile as once I held it light,
Nay, almost honorable! But it is,
That you deceived me—made me the blind tool
Of your designs, your dupe, your trumpeter;
Beguiled me, with the fable of your wrongs,
To hate just men, whom you had wronged, and boast
And swagger in your cause, and make myself
A fool or villain in the eyes of others.
Nor is it only that you cheated me
Of admiration, service, and affection,
But you have robbed me of my trust in manhood.
Undoubtingly I leaned upon your honor—

With my whole soul. It broke, and wounded me,
And I shall halt even to my grave, and find
No second man that I can lean upon.
ARNOLD. Here, take my sword, and strike! wipe out the blow,
And all dishonor; after all I know—
And 'tis a joy—that I meet death from him,
Of all who hate me, my least enemy.
FRANKS. General—I—I—
ARNOLD.   Take it, and strike! Return
To loyalty has branded me a traitor;
A death I would have perished to prevent,
Stains me with murder,—'tis but right, my friend
Should be my judge and executioner!
FRANKS [*speaking under strong excitement*]. Give me the
          sword.

> [ARNOLD, *with a look of surprise, but without*
>   *hesitation, gives him the sword.*]

                    You stand there firm, undaunted,
There is no shrinking in your mien; your eye
Is powerful and calm: no one can doubt
Your courage, or the unconquerable force
Of a great mind, that ever on itself
Built for attainment of its ends; and yet,
A life passed in great deeds, now shows but one
Poor, common virtue—that you dare to die!
'Twere no fit vengeance for the death of André,
That you should fall, self-sentenced, on the sword
Grasped by a soldier and a man of honor;
But in my country's name, and in the right
Of my untainted honor, as a hireling,
A renegade, and traitor—I degrade you.

> [*He breaks the sword, and throws down*
>   *the pieces at the feet of* ARNOLD.]

UNCOLLECTED

POEMS

INTRODUCTION TO THE
UNCOLLECTED POEMS

DR. LORD at one time seems to have contemplated publishing a volume to be called *Poems and Sonnets*. He himself assembled all but three or four of the poems in the following section, which includes all the fugitive poems by him now known. These are taken from leaflets, clippings, old proofs, and manuscripts. Where more than one version survives, the later version has been chosen.

The following poems were printed separately as leaflets or broadsides—and in periodicals as well: "The Attributions of Mary"; "The Old World" (first version only, the text follows a copy with MS corrections by Lord); "Constant Angels"; "Silent Life"; "Lines on the Banner Song"; and "The Waiting of Judah" (which later was published in the *Churchman* New York, March 7, 1903).

The following are from periodicals: "A Rhyme," *Godey's Lady's Book*, July, 1844; "My Three Loves," *Godey's*, October, 1845; "Prouder," *Charleston Mercury*, May 13, 1868 (a MS dated May 9 being also preserved); "Agnellus Dei," *Charleston Daily News*, June 23, 1868; "Infant Life," *Charleston Daily Courier*, October 2, 1868; "The Lost Spring," *New Orleans Daily Picayune*, November 8, 1868; "The White Rose," *Charleston Daily News*, April 21, 1869; "The Gorgon's Secret," *Charleston Daily News*, September 29, 1869; "The Great Ascidian," *Vicksburg Herald*, May 18, 1871 (the year not sure from the clipping—a MS is also preserved); "Sonnet on Fox," *Cooperstown Freeman's Journal*, about August, 1899. "The Stand at Princeton" is preserved in proofsheets, believed to have been intended for the Princeton *Bulletin*, and the "Lines altered from Bryant" come from Lord's *Sermons*, Cooperstown, 1882.

The other poems are from MSS alone. That of "To Sylvia" is written on a back cover of *The White King of Africa*, published August 8, 1899 by Street & Smith. There is a draft as well as a fair copy of "The First Columbus." An earlier draft of the "Poetical Plea for the Daisy" called "The National Flower" survives. "Hearts-Ease" is preserved only in an old typescript copy, and the "Inscription" is taken from the monument referred to.

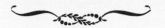

SPRING FLOWERS

O FAINTLY smiles spring as 'twere half a-cold,
   And winter is weeping itself away,
But who heeds the tears of a dotard old,
   In the faintest smile of a maiden gay!

And a maid, with drooping flowers in her hair,
   Hath asked me to sing, why the flowers that spring,
Hardiest and first in the cold bleak air,
   Are the soonest of all seen withering?

Sweet maiden! believe me, spring even now,
   While your heart the death of her flowrets grieves,
Breathing on thousands just open to blow,
   Kisses the winter's cold tears from their leaves.

And flowers! wild flowers! at her whisper, your hue
   Is deepen'd with blushes, but say, O say!
Why bloom ye soon, and then shrinking from view,
   Ah! why so soon do ye perish away!

Ye are not of earth! she owns nought so bright—
   Spring coming from Eden, brought you away,
The guardian angel frown'd at the sight,
   But she smiled—and how could he say her nay!

And wild flowers of spring, 'tis from pride I fear,
   That timidly shrinking, ye droop so soon:
For ye feel, sweet flowrets, degraded here,
   And will bloom in spring's brief visit alone.

1844.

MY THREE LOVES

My Boyhood's Love! Oh, not more sweet
   Are the first wood-bird's notes in Spring,
Than the sweet thoughts that in my heart
Make music wild, beyond the art
   Of even love-taught lips to sing!

No laughing, romping hoyden she,
   With rosy cheeks and eyes of jet,
But still and mild, and in her cheek
(Its only rose) the white rose meek,
   In scarcely fairer lilies set.

Her forehead parted locks of gold,
   And though 'tis long, long since we met,
From heaven's softest, clearest blue,
As when they look'd their last adieu,
   Her eyes seem looking on me yet.

I feared no rivals in her love,
   And, save the angels, had not one:
Not hers the glance which young eyes seek,
Not hers the laughter-dimpled cheek
   That young eyes love to look upon.

Nor as *I* loved, could angels love;
   Young hearts—their love is worship sure!
And she was as a saint to me—
Both saint and lady-love was she,
   That pensive little maid demure.

O sweet, unconscious innocence,
   That *feels,* but *sees* not, beauty's lure;
As buds before the flowrets birth—
As snow-flakes ere they touch the earth—
   As she herself—that love was pure.

Well I remember in the play,
  When mimic wedlock's knot was tied,
And I, O bliss! stood hand in hand,
With her sought out from all the band,
  And heard them shout, "Salute the bride."

How I, who ravished kisses those,
  For every forfeit kiss I won,
(The rudest boy, they said, alive!)
Now shame-faced stood, and could not give
  The little blushing trembler one.

And when, long passing round and round,
  Her hand touched mine with gentle thrill,
And I, with sudden leap, should spring,
And catch and kiss her in the ring,
  Ah me! my very heart stood still.

And though since childhood's heaven we left,
  I and my dream have never met,
Or met in life's dark ways unknown,
Sweet as the breath of roses blown,
  Her memory lingers with me yet.

Like morn upon the morning star—
  Like day-light on the peep of morn,
Rose a New Love upon my First—
It must be so—at morn's full burst
  The brightest star grows dim and lorn.

Fancy and Love! gay bridemaids, these,
  To deck the heart's elected bride;
All that seemed bright to me before,
She like a sparkling Cestus wore,
  And her own matchless charms beside.

Who looks at drifted snow may see
  Her neck and dawning shoulder fair;
Who, watching stars, hath stood and dream'd,

Hath seen the eyes that, star-like, beam'd
   In the night of her raven hair.

I shame to speak—what dreams, what dreams
   Passed through my brain! what fantasies!
How oft I saved from fire and flood
My pale fray'd love—how oft my blood
   Pour'd forth to save from enemies.

And these wild feats of daring done—
   I sheathed my sword—my harp I strung
And gave her name—back mantling shame!
I gave it to immortal fame!
   With names by deathless Poets sung.

I woke at last—she lov'd me not;
   But 'twas not that—the love unprized
Is no less love, but (strange that eyes
Like hers could glass deformities)
   My angel loved where I despised.

Like noon upon the dreamy morn—
   Like the full breathing of the day,
Or Memnon's sigh—like music heard,
Rose, on my Second Love, a Third—
   But not like that to pass away.

I loved thee, Kate—I know not why;
   'Tis death of love to question why;
I know but this—thou didst impress
Upon my soul the loveliness
   Before but mirrored in my eye.

Few think thee fair—I little care,
   Nor well can judge—for when I saw,
First saw, those tranquil eyes divine,
They triumph'd, and thenceforth in mine,
   Thy looks, sweet Kate, gave beauty law!

And when to add another grace,
   And beauty's self to beautify,
As through the frozen marble broke
Warm, blushing life, beneath the look
   Of that old Sculptor's frenzied eye,

I saw a fond, warm heart rush up
   Into those pallid cheeks of thine,
To hear a tale of love and pain—
I falter'd in the plaintive strain,
   And felt the blood deserting mine.

O, fickle heart, I hear them say—
   Hush, maidens! simple that ye are;—
The needle, touched, turns east and west,
Before the charméd wire doth rest,
   Due pointing to its own bright star.

'Tis fabled that at Love's light step
   Spring roses, blushing into sight;
Not so springs Love itself to birth,
Nor at one day-burst, on the earth,
   Breaks the unclouded soul of light.

Love hath, like light, its silver dawn—
   Like light, it hath its golden morn—
Then comes the full, clear flood of day,
Which drinks up in its glowing way
   The clouds, of its own brightness born.

Dear Kate! and should thy closing eyes
   Bring on my soul the shades of even,
Nor long nor starless is the night,
And thou, a day for ever bright,
   Wilt rise upon my soul in heaven!

1845.

PROUDER

"I am prouder" said the old Duke of Ormond
"of my dead son than any man in Europe
of his living son."

PROUDER to-day, said the stern, grey man,
Than any sire of his son can be,
Lord of an Earldom or chief of his clan
In England, or Ireland, or over the sea—
Am I of my hero, my Bayard, my Mars,
Who, wrapt in his banneret's bloody fold,
Lies, pale, in the darkness, his face to the stars,
And whose sword in its scabbard is cold.

And with prouder eye we mark, to-day,
These low, dead ranks of the ever Free,
Than her living men, in battle-array,
The proudest Nation on earth could see;
And prouder than they, in their lives, are those
Whose Cause, though buried, with them, in the grave,
Stirs even the banner that floats o'er their foes,
And lives, with their life, in the hearts of the brave.

Memorial Day, May 9, 1868.

AGNELLUS DEI

I.

"O LOVE, look there! is that a smile?
    Or thus can wild despair
The pain of deadly grief beguile
    With phantoms of the air?"

II.

"Like light around the Babe Divine
    In Holy pictures set,

I see a tender glory shine—
   Jesus our babe has met!

III.

The beam that on an infant's birth
   Shone like a wondrous star,
Still leads the child-like of the earth,
   To Him, in regions far.

IV.

It shines upon the martyr flowers,
   The Virgin Host in white,
Around the Lamb, now leading ours
   Amongst the fields of light.

V.

O'er purple hills, through valleys low,
   They keep Him still in sight,
Where'er the Bright One moves they go,
   With ever new delight.

VI.

Yes 'fainter now,' for farther on
   He follows, farther goes
Into the land where shines no sun
   That ever set or rose.

VII.

It fades—and on that pearly face
   The shadow grows, as far
He passes through the shining space
   Where is no sun nor star."

VIII.

"O love, look not!—the smile is fled,
   Yon dazzling troop and He
Into the light are farther led,
   Into the darkness, we."

Charleston, May 22, 1868.

INFANT LIFE

WHY vainly, with fond eyes that never tire,
Watch we this infant? She has guardians higher
   In office, mightier in power than we;
That life, that seems so fragile, has the powers
Of infinite reason, and the hours
   And years and cycles of eternity!
Why, fearful, do we hear her troubled cries,
And mark each change with sweet or sad surmise?
   Nature her mother is, and Heaven her sire.
Life seems to fade from paling cheek and eyes—
Fear not—yea, though from lip and heart it flies,
   It is a spark of that immortal fire,
That paints the flowers and feeds the flaming skies—
The pure celestial fire, that never dies.

Charleston, October 1, 1868.

THE LOST SPRING

"The year has been robbed of its spring." Pericles,
on the death of Athenian youth in battle.

I.

TRUE words and tender strain,
Immortal Greek!—again
Tired *Summer* faints; for oh, with dewy rain
And rosy dawnings clear
Though all thy months were here,
Rejoicing Spring, we missed thee from the year!

II.

Hence, *Autumn* is not glad;
Grey heads are bowed and sad,
Her scanty crown reminds them what she had
Ere War and Spectral Fear
And Love, to deck the bier
Of youthful heroes, spoiled the vernal year.

III.

And *Winter* is more stern;
Prone on his chilly urn,
Earthwards he mutters, She will not return:
Our youth sleep far and near,
Like them, she does not hear
The loud March wind, the birth-cry of the year.

IV.

The skirting poplars fling
Green banners of the *Spring*
High on the air; the Hours their offering bring,
Pale flowers to Sorrow dear,
And many a shining tear,
But thou, where art thou, Glory of the year?

V.

The briar, at noon, is sweet,
And cool to cloven feet
The way-side grass feels not the climbing heat:
But lo! when, stark and sear,
Hands, like a shattered spear,
Some leafless signal of the stricken year.

VI.

The stream in splendor flows,
Nor shrinks when Taurus glows;
Her bosom is still cold with mountain snows:
O Youth, serene, severe!
O Shining, swift career!
Gone, is the grace, the glory of the year.

VII.

Upon dead Freedom's breast
Bright, curly heads are pressed,
Ah! many a fiery heart is here at rest:
True words old Greek! how drear
Without her tones of cheer,
Without her smile how sullen is the year!

VIII.

Forever art thou fled
Spirit that smiling, bled
By Athens' Wall? How late we saw the tread,
With Hope thy fair compeer,
In haggard Battle's rear,
Flower-footed Spring, nor missed thee from the year.

IX.

O God, bring back the spring;
In vain the Thrushes sing,
In vain wild harps in leafy forests ring:
Their music in our ear
Is harsh till she appear,
Till Thou, at last, reclaim the perfect year.

Charleston, October 1, 1868

THE WHITE ROSE

WHITE little hands, white face, white rose!
    Though roses bloom of brighter hue,
Thou art the only flower that blows
    Summer and winter through.

White flower, white rose, how well they chose
    Who culled thee, flower of death!
Thy thorn is in our heart, white rose,
    Thy sweetness dims our breath.

Tears drop upon thy leaves, white rose!
  Tears are their only dew;
As fits the only flower that blows
  Summer and winter through.

Charleston, April 10, 1869.

THE PLACE NEAREST HEAVEN

WHAT spot of earth is nearest heaven?
Great Mount unclimbed! is that the place—
Thy highest peak, that, lone and riven,
  Stands sentinel on space?
Or is it some high tropic Isle,
Close to the path the planets run,
And wound with seas that flash and smile,
  Set full against the sun?
Or some great Minster, on whose spire
Angels light down, or take their flight,
And upward like a flame of fire,
  Mount to the source of light?
No! it is here—the nearest place,
This gate, this grave (my tears fall fast)
Through which a form of deathless grace,
  A little maiden passed.
But few steps—and she reached the gate
Which opens to that world above
That gives what each would ask of fate,
  Or vainly asks of love.
Here to the old, eternal youth,
To youth, eternal years are given,
Here all the erring find the truth,
  And all the wretched, heaven.

1870?

THE GORGON'S SECRET

FROM GOETHE—AN OFFERING TO THE MEMORY
OF BYRON

Chor (zu Phorkyas.)
"Schweige, schweige!
Missblickende, missredende du!"
[FAUST, *Zweiter Theil, Dritter Act.*]

I.

HUSH thee, Hag! be silent, thou
With eyes askant and hissing brow,
Mouth deep and black, with lips that hang
Dissevered by one ghastly fang—
　　Fit birth-place for a tale
　　At which the sun turns pale,
While Nature sickens in his glare—
Such horror as to upper air
Came never till this fated hour,
　　Came never yet from earth or sea,
Save when their dark and stormy power
　　From some deep cavern sent forth thee.

II.

　　Inly malevolent,
　　Seeming benevolent,
She-wolf, under thy snowy fleece
　　More to be dreaded
　　Than the Three-Headed
Whose barkings break the Hell world's peace;
Though foulest of the shapes of dread,
The gray, gaunt dog that bays the dead.

　　Eager, trembling stand we now,
　　Breathless, await the when and how;
　　Shadows from the cave of night,
　　Bring ye darkness?—bring ye light?
Secrets, the dead have kept so long,
How broke ye prisons deep and strong?

Spectres that lurked in the lives of men,
 Deeds that were done without the sun,
Have ye a voice?—say where and when;
 And your tale be told, your task be done,
  And back no more
  From Lethe's shore,
Unseemly phantoms, in our ken
Moping and mouthing, come again.

III.

But thou, as oft in other days,
 With mind elate and bosom free,
For eager falsehood waiting praise—
 Hear the earth curse thee: earth and sea
Shall make thee hateful; starry night
 And mountains rosy with the morn
All thou hast sullied that was bright
 Shall shame thee, babbler, with our scorn—
Shall make us hate thee with the might
 Of banished love and hearts forlorn.
For when upon the fated strife
Of gloomy passions, darkening life,
Came peace—and all the stormy fight
Fell weaponless, as, with dawning light,
Lethean hopeful words were cast
 Backward, with many a soft alas!
Into the darkness which holds fast
 The shades that into its shadow pass,
The shame, the blame of all the past—
 Unblest one! thou, in evil hour,
Hast found a nameless word to blast
 The splendor in the grass and flower,—
To earth and air hast breathed a story
 That, staining beauty in its birth,
And tearing all the scroll of glory,
 And making all of vilest worth,
The star-crowned head of Heaven hoary,
 Brings down with shame to the dust of earth.

IV.

Silence, silence! and leave us still,
    Ere yet thy tale be done,
Though pale with doubt, with horror chill,
    The image of the sun:
The world that reels beneath our feet,
    The forms of things that from us flee,
But wait until our lips repeat
    Earth's malediction upon thee.[1]
Ere thou thyself fly, winged with fear,
Back to the stormy ocean, hear
Thy mother curse thee: "By the night
    And this avenging sun, and me
The eldest, and not less in might,
    Now to thyself a 'terror' be!
Till watched by fear, and worn by flight,
Thou start from sleep, and hiss with fright.
Of all the furies latest born,
With all their fury, hate and scorn;
Accursed inheritrix of strife,
A sister-terror, sprung to life
From dire Medusa's blood—for thee,
Mortal like her, I see, I see
The bright steel gleam, and drops that fall
Red on my bosom, and appall
The hideous train of fear and pain
Gorgons, Erinnyes, that remain,
To fly the strong—the weak to hound
With phantoms, while my sun goes round.[18]

THE GREAT ASCIDIAN

*"In the dim obscurity of the past we can see that
the early progenitor of all the Vertebrata must
have been an aquatic animal. This animal seems
to have been more like the larvae of our existing
marine Ascidians than any other known form."*
DARWIN's *Descent of Man.*

(Bibulus loquitur)

I.

AND this the Cause! and here all life began!
  Primordial stomach, in the tadpole found,
Thy leather bottle was the type, the plan,
Which Nature worked on when she moulded man;
  Ere Adam made a track upon the ground.

II.

I thought it strange that nothing touched the chord
  Of natural feeling when, perchance, I saw
My grandsire of the woods, baboon abhorred;
Yea, truly, as a creature of the Lord
  I loved him better than by Nature's law.

III.

Did something queer about this mute freemason
  Hint trouble on his own side of the question—
Frog, lizard, newt, from whom by variation
Came our four-handed, nimble poor relations,
  Made odious to us by too much suggestion?

IV.

But this small mollusk, this half-inch ellipse!
  I only smile to think of native man
Drifting about, attached to weeds and chips,
  Till a high tide, in cyclone or eclipse,
  Left on some rock the future Caliban.

V.

'Tis not, I grant, a question of chronology;
    Form loved by Nature! in its oval curves
She hides the secrets of her dim biology;
Seeds, eggs, and worlds, and facts in physiology
    Point to a purpose that the shape subserves.

VI.

Nearer the cause, the simpler, forms are found,
    And hold! Ascidians older than marine;
Why stop at ape or oyster?—to the ground
Of life organic let the plummet sound
    A man I am—a vegetable have been.

VII.

Nature leaps nothing—on the word of sages,
    Which no one dares (though he may not as they do,
Evolve the world through many thousand ages
While form from form its embryo disengages)
    Looking a Zoophyte in the face say nay to.

VIII.

Thy *phyton* simplest, lowest form is seen
    Down in the rocks, through all the ages gray;
Dim shadowy bulb! since in thy tender green
My germ I saw, no slimy thing obscene,
    Nor hairy monster, fills me with dismay.

IX.

Ringed, rib-nosed, howlers, climbers, ugly links
    In nature's chain, would more of you were missed;
One fact would still remain the *Man* who thinks
Began his being in the *Man* who drinks,
    The infant *Mammal*—here I must desist.

X.

I call them links—they are in fact but kinks;
    The true link is most perfect in each kind

Of what it joins, and never blurs or sinks
The one kind in the others, a true sphinx,
  Both and yet neither, medely undefined.

XI.

And is there such a link? and is this he,
  With hookéd hands and feet and devilish tail
By travellers seen disporting on a tree,
By me, sometimes, oh, horror! in a spree?
  I tremble at the thought, my spirits fail.

XII.

Avaunt, begone, thou fearful ape and brother,
  Batrachian, polyp, any form but thine,
I would say swine or dog, or any other,
But for some slight respect I owe thy mother,
  Of distant kin, through that first bulb, to mine.

XIII.

The onion is not meant, but let that pass,
  Though Egypt worshipped it with Thot and Pthah,—
Bulbous in form I mean, in substance grass;
And such is man, and such, to man and ass,
  Ascidium N. distillitoria.

XIV.

The Autocthones sprang up with Attic mint,
  And he whom attic-bards still build upon,
The sage who said it was a heart of flint
That could eat beans, beheld, he seems to hint,
  His grandam in a *dicotyledon.*

XV.

Organic life, he means, is that perfected
  Which in a single cell or thread begins;
The simple stomach in the sponge detected,
By much selection into man erected,
  Becomes a thing that walks and talks and sins.

XVI.

But great Ascidian, vegetable bottle
  Aught might I venerate it would be thee;
The thirsty ape who held thee by the throttle
Could know no more than I, or Aristotle,
  He held the father of all apes, and me.

XVII.

Capacious pitcher-plant, I see thee now,
  Thy fair round stomach bibulous of dew;
And I a stomach, bibulous as thou,
A walking stomach, which, I must avow,
  A moist night often fills, like thine, anew.

XVIII.

See here the spheric form by Nature loved,
  See here the centre of the human frame!
By correlation altered and improved,
Through hairy generations, far removed,
  Till hardly Science knows it for the same.

XIX.

Life from a leaf? and does that seem too low?
  The Bible says our origin was dust;
And dust is dry, and I am dry, and so
A clear case of reversion; but you know
  We give such stories up to "Dryasdust."

XX.

Dodona's talking tree, and that of Polo—
  Was it of our "arboreal" sire a fable?
(But if he speaks, we know 'tis strictly solo,)
Or did it hint of "library" and "folio"
  And thought impressed on matter vegetable.

XXI.

But back from our digression; though we could,
  With high example, follow this suggestion

From "bark" and "leaf" into the very wood,
Of which so many heads are made as should
   Put man's botanic origin out of question.

XXII.

Plato knew something of the soul and he
   Had motives for the region where he placed it
And Nature errs, Nepenthes, or I see
A rudimental abdomen in thee,
   Or first rude sketch with which her hand prefaced it.

XXIII.

Life without brain is found—but stomach, never,
   The Soul means Life, as that old trifler knew,
And life is in the lowest form that ever
Possessed a paunch, or made its first endeavor
   To drink the rain-drop, or distil the dew.

XXIV.

As life, to change the formula, is *thirst;*
   Earth drinks the sky and the sky drinks the sea
Buds drink the dew, and germs with moisture burst,
And the old mosses, arid as at first,
   Hang out their stomachs upon rock and tree.

XXV.

Nay, stunning thought! the now Ascidian race
   Must grow to mew by constant evolution,
And fish, or phyton, sitting in our place
Will hob-a-nob with quite as good a grace,
   About the world's ten millionth revolution.

XXVI.

Startling discovery! Rabelais touched thy bound;
   The Holy Bottle to which pilgrims went
With questions deep, and in its gurgling sound
"Trink, trink" all first and final causes found,
   What question but the great Ascidian meant.

XXVII.

See everywhere unconscious imitation,
  Vase, pitcher, jug—which (sure as man is hay
And by reversion feels a foolish passion
For flowers and weeds) was not in its first fashion
  Fitted with handles, nor yet made of clay.

XXVIII.

Well?—Adam, I suppose was an exception
  We'll class him, if you like, with fictile pottery,
But the Ascidian, in its first conception,
Lived, male and female, long ere Eve's deception
  Had proved that wives are *not,* alas! "a lottery."

XXIX.

The tale 'tis now the fashion to gloss over;
  But mark how life is bound up with a tree!
And that old reptile—viewed by a philosopher,
Was, in some age, all grown with fossil moss over,
  A bottled imp, or loose fish, in the sea.

XXX.

And mark—with Science came the sense of shame,
  For truth is naked, as at first were we;
Let Science blush, let fools her rashness blame,
But *Homo bibax,* by that oldest name,
  Drink to the great Ascidian with me!

1871-6.

FERNS AND THE CROSS

FERNS and the Cross! What memories of the past;
  What shadows of the dim and future years,
Like silent leaves in autumn falling fast,
Throng on my heart, still hoping that at last
  The Cross shall triumph over mortal fears!

But when again its shadow shall be seen
  Upon the ferns, although in heaven appears
The light that casts it, and though intervene
Long years of happy life and hope serene,
  I know it will again be seen through tears!

HEARTS-EASE

INSCRIBED TO FRIENDS OF OTHER DAYS

IN simple words what subtle power!
  Hearts-ease, what is it? and O where
To find the true, the mystic flower?
  Ask them who on their bosoms wear
The costly blossoms of an hour,
  To glow in hope's enchanted air
And wither in the heart's despair;
With tears they say, It is not there

In banquet hight, in bridal bower,
  In captive coils of beauty's hair,
By cottage door, or gate and tower,
  On altar step, or palace stair,
In field and garden after shower.
  In wildwood and the bramble's lair
Where sweetness harbors unaware,
Look for the flower: it is not there

Shy leaf! is thine some Alpine flower
  Sole growing where not foot may dare,
Or dost thou in deep forests cower,
  Where feet of men might never fare.
Or hide where darker shadows lower
  And Lethe's poppies nod and stare,
While sunny banks thy namesake bear,
A name for balm that is not there.

1884?

POETICAL PLEA FOR THE DAISY

For commonwealth a common flower,
Proof to pierce sun and pelting shower,
    Suits best, and in the land
    Thick as the stars doth stand
That simple flower of humble station,
Hardy and fair, the flower of the people,
    True flower of the nation.

The daisy, day's eye, glint of the day,
The starlike flower with circled ray,
    Be our symbol of light,
    Be our emblem of right,
Our shamrock, our thistle; in all creation
No flower shall match thee, flower of the people,
    True flower of the nation!

The rose, the lily, the violet sweet,
Others have claimed; in thee we greet,
    Unclaimed among flowers,
    The one flower that is ours.
No Old World history, hint or relation
Spoils thee for us, white flower of the people,
    True flower of the nation!

1889.

WHY BROWNING'S VERSE
FINDS SCHOLARS

Surprise to find it is not nonsense, first;
Next comes upon us doubting a cloud-burst
Of song, bold, free, triumphant in the power
Of a sun-quickened, sea-born thunder-shower
Breaking on green fields, gutters garbage-filled,

Street, garden, lane, with muddy rivulets rilled;
Then to the song-bird's notes and chirp of sparrows
Struck to the heart by sunlight, as with arrows,
Lo! in the sudden shining after rain
God on his England paints the sky of Spain.
Great Pan is dead! with every poet dead
From whose clear-piping reed the sound is fled,
Yet ever lingers upon land and sea,
Waiting for echoes from Eternity:
But thee, deep-breathing giant, on our shore
Aloud lamented by that voice of yore,
Heard from Arcadia by the wandering Greek
Thee, Delphic bard, what words, but thine can speak
—Seek to grasp stars in water, seize and hold
Shadows in darkness drowning, Proteus old
To marble turn! Yet metaphors there be
In thy own bold, untaught metonymy
For thee, expressing, in just sequence terse,
The poet's trinity, Thought, Feeling, Verse.
Hermes-Hephaestus this, wings on lame feet;
This, breath of Dawn, and odors of the street;
And this a deep drum, rattling and unstrung
With cymbal's clash and sound of trumpets flung
Along the discords.
                But Hist! hark! heard I,
Saint John, thy eagle from its islet cry?
Or Jove, from lightning-lit Olympus, thine?
Or bird of Freedom, from some blasted pine,
Thy shriek defiant? Poet in thy dreams,
Like nature mingling what exists, and seems,
Do we the obscure, grotesque, fantastic see
In her, or bold interpreter, in thee?
But if, nor yet her jester nor her seer,
Each changing mood's inspired interpreter,
Mere histrion art thou? actor before all,
David and Achish, and in Naioth Saul?
"O serpent King!" from thy cross-bar come down,
In words articulate, say, art king or clown?

Or both? as Shakespeare and thy Rabelais are:
For men too wise, "motley's the only wear."
Enigma, problem, god or druid stone,
Nay, Sphinx! dead Egypt's signature, unknown
Vast hieroglyphic! fill thy broken nose
And battered lips with sound like that which grows
In Memnon's statue as the slanting sun
Leaps upwards, and ere mental life is done,
Tell us the secret of thy mighty Nile:
While we the lotus eat, and dream and smile
In drowsy wonder, asking with a start
Is discord music? or has Art lost art?
And still this verseless verse upon our ears
Strikes in swift thoughts, like music of the spheres
Splintered to fragments, and in star-showers thrown
Wide through the air from one great central tone
That welding heavens to heavens, and earth to sea,
Binds God to Nature with its harmony.

New York, February 1890.

SONNET

ON THE FIRST SIGHT OF THE MEDITERRANEAN

OCEAN, at last! blue deep, with splendor crowned,
    Old Homer's sea, the Ocean-stream which drank
    Diurnal sun and stars, and rose and sank
With the Moon's bosom: and whose mighty sound
    Was heard by gods and men, when all was blank
    Beyond the pillars in the West, and found
    For the unknown immensity no name:
    And Neptune with his white-maned horses came
Only to Atlas, and shook all the ground
With suppressed fury at the narrow bound,
    O were thy gods no dream! thou crimson-stained
    Old battle-plain of freedom, lost or gained,
What murmurs in thy billows might we hear
Of Salamis, Lepanto, Aboukir?

THE FIRST COLUMBUS

His heart was iron, it of old was said,
   Who first, Poseidon, thy wild horses rode
   Into the darkness and the vastness, the abode
Perchance of gods and demons and the dead
To whom the earth denied sepulchral rite:—
   How fared it on that desert without road
   When the last mountain-top sank out of sight?
   Did the storm waver and the vanished earth
   With native lance and wife and children seem
The shadows of a half-remembered dream?
But oh, what joy by Greek or Phrygian hearth,
   What civic glory, when from ocean's girth
Came the first Colon and of Etna told,
Stromboli and Hesperian lands of gold.

THE WAITING OF JUDAH

   "Beautiful thou for situation,
      Mount Sion, joy of the whole earth"—
   Here stood the bard; the invocation
      Is to the harp that gave it birth,
   An echo from three thousand years,
      As thus—white crown of Sion's hill,
   Seen through a mist of gathering tears—
      Jerusalem, I greet thee still.

   So rose thy battlements to them
   Who saw the first Jerusalem:
   So looked Jerusalem to Him,
   Whose eyes, beholding it, were dim
   With sudden tears, that hallow yet
   Jerusalem from Olivet.

   On yonder height, what visions rise!
      What sees He, mortal passion worth?
   Siege, slaughter, famine, agonies,

Years of forgotten joy and mirth,
And wearing, still, before the nations,
  Thy sorrows like a diadem,
Thee, to the end of desolations,
  Bound to His cross, Jerusalem.

And surely, yet, some mighty spell
  Is on thee, captive stern and lone,
Waiting for exiled Israel,
  And monarchs upon David's throne,
When Nineveh can no longer name
  Her ruins; Tyre hears not the sea;
And Babylon is but the fame
  Of Judah in captivity.
In pity and in pride, or shame,
  For guilt and grandeur of the past,
The silent-footed ages came,
  Unseen, and buried them at last.

And Sion, wherefore not for thee
Sweet peace, and end of tyranny?
Martyred, in hate, or veneration
Of the Cross and its oblation,
Scorned, mocked, or pitied, must thou be
Forever on thy Calvary,
Awaiting from a heathen race
Deliverance, or the stroke of grace?
As once, held up to heathen scorn,
Waited thy Christ, the virgin-born,
Whose birth-cry, heard in Bethlehem,
Shook Herod and Jerusalem!

Yet more in wonder than in pain
  Thou hast waited—thou must wait
Until He comes to thee again,
  Thy meek King comes to thee in state;
Like a monarch to his throne,
Banners waved, and trumpets blown;

Or warrior with his armor on,
Triumphant from his battle won
Against all human tyrannies,
Of race or creed all cruelties.

Messiah, Shiloh, Christ, is He
Whose spirit made the nations free,
And to that sacred spot of earth
Returning, where it had its birth,
Down-trod Jerusalem, in thee
Uplifts the chant of victory.
Judea's hills the pæan swell,
Immanuel! Immanuel!
God of God—Messiah's name
Flashes o'er the earth like flame;
Like a leaping tongue of fire
Minaret answering to spire,
Muezzin's cry, to Christian bells;
From East to West no infidels!

Lift up the chant, ye tents of Shem;
The King from royal Israel's stem,
In whom the nations should be blest,
To give His wandering people rest—
Who throng to touch His garment's hem—
Sits on thy throne, Jerusalem.

Mount of Olives, 1890.

THE ATTRIBUTIONS OF MARY

THE sweetest name for woman, sounding
   In human ears,
Mother and maid, with grace abounding,
   Is thine, *beata.*
So Heaven fulfils its benediction;
   But Earth endears,

And Calvary crowns thee with affliction;
  Commiserata.

On Israel's night, O virgin queenly,
  Foretold by seers,
Rose a meek star, and burned serenely—
  Thine, *consecrata.*
To thee—so high, with heart so lowly,
  And maiden fears—
Came down an angel from the Holy,
  O *salutata!*

Never was yet, to mortal, greeting
  Like that which hears
Thy virgin heart, with wonder beating;
  Ah, *consolata!*
Born is the King, the superhuman,
  Ring out ye spheres!
And hail the long predicted woman,
  Bethlehem Ephrata!

Wake, dreamer—lo! the Jews have crowned
 Him.
  And see the throne
On which their hands have raised and bound
 Him;
  O *dolorosa!*
Is this the Christ? gray, ghastly, gory—
  Thy son, thy own?
For this came *Ave* from the Glory,
  And *gratiosa?*

What is, to thine, the grief of others?
  To hear thy moan,
Sad Rama hushed her weeping mothers;
  Ah, *desolata!*
The sword, with which thy son was smitten,
  O pang unknown!

Pierced through thy soul, as it is written;
　　　　Praedestinata.

Now, with the mystic spirits seven,
　　　　Burns, through all years,
Thy star before His throne in Heaven;
　　　　Immaculata.
Till earth and Heaven all ties shall sever,
　　　　Midst angels' tears,
Of thee, shall tongue of mortal never
　　　　Say *obscurata.*

Cooperstown, N. Y.

THE OLD WORLD

　　　　I. *(humanus.)*
OLD world, where life was young,
　　And we first live, and not—
In soul—not there, whence sprung
　　Dumb races, long forgot!

Thine were the race divine—
　　The bards, who saw in air
And mountain-top the sign
　　Of higher presence there.

Thine were the song and lyre
　　And art, that first began,
From sleep and low desire,
　　To wake the god in man.

The grandeur of what line,
　　The story of what hand,
That is not part of thine—
　　Or written on the sand?

Old is the world called new,
    But thine the mighty past,
And memories that in view
    Stand like thy mountains fast—

And cast on earth the grand,
    Unmoving form sublime
Of an invisible hand,
    A shadow thrown on time.

To disappear at last,
    When time itself shall be
A shadow of the past
    Cast on eternity.

            II. *(terrestris.)*
New world, by men called old!
    The stars that hymned the birth
Of earth and heaven told
    Of older heaven and earth.

And what if told to thee
    That in the silent West
Deeper on earth and sea
    Creation's shadows rest!

Thine are the gates of day,
    Hills older than the morn,
Peaks that first caught the ray
    In which the world was born.

What, if on new worlds rise
    The sun that sinks from sight?
Thy offspring name the skies,
    Thine is the world of Night.

And small, unnamed by thee,
    The realm of Ocean old;

And ours, a nameless sea,
  Had still for ages rolled:

When, lo! to Ocean's name
  Thunders the world of waves,
In tides of which there came
  No whisper to his caves.

But *gloriam dei* flame
  The heavens; Him the seas,
Him, unawares, proclaim
  Their pagan deities.

THE OLD WORLD

[ANOTHER VERSION]

I.

Not, in my transient thought,
  The world beyond the seas,
Nor "Ind" that, westward, sought
  The daring Genoese;

II.

Old World, where we were young,
  Aye, and, in spirit, born,
(Not then, thy harp unstrung,
  Nor yet, thy creeds outworn);

III.

World of the past:—our Sires
  Who stormy ocean crossed
To light new household fires,
  Thee, neither left, nor lost;

IV.

High birthright:—Ours, this great,
   Fair land, and seat of might,
By birth alone, and fate,
   But thou, by older right;

V.

Our child-world, full of joy
   In fear, and fearful deeds,
And faith, without alloy,
   In wonder's infant creeds;

VI.

World, where, in youth, before
   We knew how great and fair,
We dwelt, and in its lore
   First breathed immortal air;

VII.

Large world, and unconfined
   To classic shores and skies,
Dominion of the Mind,
   Realm without boundaries;

VIII.

Each freeborn soul on earth,
   Thou grander Rome, in thee,
Wherever casual birth,
   Can claim nativity.

IX.

What walls thy State confine?
   The story of what land
That is not part of thine,
   Or written on the sand?—

X.

As "men articulate"
  Have left us, with their bones,
Their story (haply great)
  Silent, on Aztec stones.

XI.

Theirs, the old world called New,
  But thine, the mighty past,
And memories that in view
  Stand evermore, and cast

XII.

Upon the earth the grand,
  Unmoving form, sublime,
Of a conjectured Hand,
  A shadow thrown on time,

XIII.

To disappear, at last,
  When time itself shall be
A shadow of the past
  Thrown on eternity.

1892?

CONSTANT ANGELS

A CHRISTMAS AND EASTER SYMPHONY

[*Inscribed to Mrs. F. U. J.*]

Two angels who remain are these;
  That man, to whom they still appear,
With joy, but not with wonder sees,
  And greets, with each returning year.

One comes with winter bleak and wild,
  In saintly robe of shining white,
And brings again the Holy Child
  To light the dark, terrestial night.

And one, in vernal sunbeams clad,
   When life in waking nature yearns,
And puts forth flowers, and voices glad
   Exclaim, The Lord is risen—returns.

This, to the human heart appeals,
   The simple thought, the childlike heart;
The other to the soul reveals
   Its own celestial counterpart—

The higher, the immortal part,
   That lived in God, ere Christ was born;
Lily, that bloomed in Mary's heart,
   Rose of the Resurrection morn!

Known are they? Have they place and name?
   Who brought the Virgin joy and doom?
What angel, clad in lightning's flame,
   Kept watch by Christ's deserted tomb?

Is *Gabriel* in that shining stole,
   To bid the Virgin Mother hail?
In Easter's Triumph of the Soul
   Stands *Michael* in his dazzling mail?

Bright visitants! returned ye not,
   Deep were the pagan winter's gloom,
Sweet greetings, loving gifts forgot,
   And in *no heart for Mary room*.[19]

THE STAND AT PRINCETON

A LAY OF THE REVOLUTION

[*That Washington exposed himself to great
personal peril in his efforts to rally the Continental troops, checked by the British stand
at Princeton, is matter of historic record; but
the particular incident, on which this poem
is founded, depends on local tradition.*]

I.

In chronicles of other days
  What ashes, that were once a flame!
What deeds of arms, that miss their praise
  With mute reproach to silent fame!
But what of all that stands in sight
  In this new world, or that the old
War-wrinkled ages tell of fight
  Made famous by an action bold,
Surpasses this—a deed unknown
Or told, as heard, in speech alone,
Where shadows of unwritten fact
  Lingering around a mighty name
Dwindle and fade: because the act
  Is lost in history's grander claim:
Or that the action seems less great
In one to greatness consecrate:
The star that in the morning grey
  Was seen and marked, thus hides its light
In deeper splendor, when the day
  Rolls its great orb upon the sight:
Thus war and peace in song and story
  Drop all the titles that he won,
For the one name he gave to glory,
  And got from Heaven—to be by none
Raised higher, and to none passed on—
Its own great title, Washington!

II.

Harp that has long in silence slept,
Hast thou the shaping spirit kept
To tell how one great deed imparts
Its impulse to a thousand hearts?
Or what a heaven-born hero dares,
Defiant, while his soul despairs?
But pause: of what grand tale retold
Seems this the echo, onward rolled?
Of heroes in their dust, what forms,
   Warlike but calm, like men who long
Have dwelt in regions above storms,
   Called by the poet's magic song,
Or touched by hoary History's wand,
Start forth, as if by Glory's hand
Reclaimed from death!—the Attic king
   Who to his subjects, doomed, in strife,
Ignoble victory to bring,
   Fighting, put off his crown and life;
The Jarl, whose banner bore, foretold,
Death, wrapped with victory in its fold;
The youth, who held the bridge for Rome;
The Swiss, who made his Alpine home,
Scene of a drama beyond art
For power and pity, and his part
A terror to the human heart—
Stern archer, who before the eyes
   Of gloomy tyrants stands forever,
While each unerring shaft that flies
   Sings of its brother in the quiver!
And, in the same wild eyrie born,
And with his eagle soul of scorn,
The knight, who rode on victory's crest,
Borne by the spears that in his breast
He gathered to make Freedom way:
Heroes! but not the heroes they,
Realms wasted by the sword and flame,
Condemn to everlasting fame:

Greek, Roman, Goth—in each we see
The same great form, superb and free,
Of victim, vowed to Victory!

And though in fable's misty light
It gains in stature to the sight,
Was never form to that more true
Than this, which consecrates anew
The man, in whom mankind has known
Its greatest, by the tokens shown;
But never on his brow serene
Shadow of martyr's crown has seen.
Yet, doubt me not; without the name
    Martyrs have lived, in thought and will
Like those whom death gave palms of fame;
    And in the same grand circuit still
All things come round, from age to age—
So said the King; so reads the page;
Men but bequeath their heritage;
And heroes live, and men are free
By the soul's grand heredity.
And in what country or what day,
Be faith or faction what it may,
Lived hero, sung to Freedom's lyre,
    But had—though not upon the roll
Of men who died by axe or fire—
A martyr's faith, a martyr's soul?

III.

And this the tale: no fiction spun
    On Fairy wheel in days of old,
But what in Freedom's war was done,
    And brave Hugh Mercer saw and told—
Borne from the field and staying death
By that last use he had for breath—
And gave to those who leave to me
The right its chronicler to be,

And hero's tale of hero give
Place in a nation's narrative.

'Twas in a crisis of the strife
Of infant Freedom for her life,
Threatened by Britain's glaive, in scorn
Of birthright and of title torn
From monarchs by the iron will
Of men whose dauntless spirit still
Wrought in wide lands beyond the sea
The giant tasks of liberty.
Their voice her sleeping spirit woke;
A Sidney in her Adams spoke;
As finished, by a sculptor bold,
From block defaced or broken mould,
The work a master's hand begun,
So, Hampden, thine by Washington!

But little for such service then
He thought to have the thanks of men,
Or of a country that in fame
Snatched from a Continent its name;
And, as it first-born nation's right,
    Will bear forever on her shield
AMERICA, although in spite
    Of older claim and larger field.
Far on the land, the invader's power
    Impending cast a shadow grave;
And fear grew bold and croaked the hour
    Of coward triumph o'er the brave.
Forced backward by an iron hand,
And leaving naked all the land
From Blue Ridge to Atlantic strand,
On the Colonial arms a blight
Fell, like the rust that came by night
On blade and bayonet. Backward still,
    Still Southward, fell the patriot force.
What courage, or what strength of will

Can fill the ranks of foot and horse,
Feed, clothe, inspire a starving host,
Half conscious that their cause is lost?
Thus by the fireside said, in thought,
Brave men: the women prayed and wrought—
Then through the Delaware's crashing ice
  The unexpected hero came,
To cast again the iron dice,
  For life or death, in war's grim game.

IV.

As oft, when his predestined track,
Re-entering, the sun turns back
On the stern realms of cold and frosts,
A wave of summer smites the hosts
Of icy vapor into rack
Of rain and mist, and drives the pack
Of winter's tyrants from their hold,
So back on the invaders rolled
The tide of battle, and before
The Colonies' ragged columns bore
The British and their Hessian corps.

O, sweeter than the voice of fame
  Or vows when parted lovers meet,
Is glory snatched from threatened shame,
  And victory following on defeat!
Nor then divined they that their feet,
  Ill-shod and wounded in the march
Would, later, press the flowery street,
  And under the triumphal arch
Of Trenton's civic pageant pass:
Nor yet how few the feet, alas,
That soil again would proudly tread—
But sadly, for it held the dead
Who, sleeping there in glory's bed,
Through summer's heat and winter's snow,
Shall never of their victory know!

V.

And now, though winners of the day,
Well knew they that before them lay
An army stubborn as the best
That ever yet, in east or west,
Held field or fortress: for the rest,
Briton or Teuton, theirs the race
Of which a Roman who in face
Of fiercest battle met the Franks,
Said, there were red cheeks in their ranks.
And the redcoats—beneath which aye
A red heart beat—no older day
Of shining mail or wolf's rough fell
Their hated wearers could excel
In valor's evidence; as knew
The hearts to touch of kindred true
That beat beneath the buff and blue.
Nor lacked they proof: from day to day
Skirmish and feint renewed the fray;
Till, in superior force of men
And ordnance, confident again,
The royal leader throws in vain
His gage of battle on the plain.
Thus stood they fronted: until—blind
Outmarched Cornwallis left behind—
On foeman, better matched in might,
The great Virginian moved, by night,
So swiftly that the morning light
Still deeper with the hue of blood
    Reddening the Royal colors showed
The hireling Hessians, where they stood,
    Holding, in force, the Northern road.
On Princeton's heights, their ordnance manned
By men with mastered eye and hand,
Stood silent; till the dusky wreath
Of marching infantry beneath
Came, winding upward, where, to sight,
In battery on the nearest height,

The cannon stand against the sky:
Then thunder!—but the death-bolt high
Above them crashed, and hurtled by,
Forward! and half the extent they gain,
Of the broad slope from hill to plain,
When falls again the iron rain
And pales the best, the boldest daunts.
The column halts: "Close, and advance,"
Said Washington, "Disarm at once
That height!"—no movement, no response;
Wavered the Pennsylvania line;
"Great God," he said, "my life is thine!"
Few heard him, but each eye was strained,
When moving to the front, he reined
His charger in, and, wheeling, right
  Before the battery held him checked;
Like some grand statue in their sight
  He sat there silent, calm, erect,
Confronting death: one moment's hush,
Then with a whirlwind's sudden rush,
Before the battery once more
Can shake the summit with its roar,
Right up the hill, upon the run,
They charged, and captured every gun
On Princeton's heights: the day was won.

VI.

Suppose coincidence, or result;
Give the old reason, *"Deus vult";*
The fact is certain: the twin days
Trenton and Princeton, in their blaze
Of native valor, mark the turn
In Freedom's fortunes; brighter burn
Her struggling stars; though clouds still lower,
No shrinking from the front of power!
Doubt and suspense, but not despair:
Lion and whelp their forest lair
Disputed still, but this, grown bold,

Feared not the giant, grim and old.
Boys marched to battle, dotards planned
High strategy, to save the land.
Women changed hearts with men, and one
Stood firm, to an abandoned gun,
Refilled with death its iron bore
Unflinching, waked its silent roar,
And lives in fame. Through hopes and fears
The war crept on, and tracked the years
With bloody footprints, till at last—
  Grandest of tyrannies overturned,
And noblest of free leagues surpassed—
  The sun of Yorktown rose and burned
In glory on the astral wreath
Of federal commonwealths beneath
The New World's banner, and—the sun
Of later fields for freedom won
Foretelling—with reflected glance
Shone on the chivalrous arms of France.

But grander is the form that stands
  Under the Princeton battery's frown
Than that which takes from Britain's hands
  The sword surrendered by the Crown
  And deathless title to renown.

VII.

To thee, old Nassau's honored Hall
  That, erstwhile, showed for many a day
The dint and scar of iron ball,
  Duteous, I dedicate my lay.
No laurel from thy wreath of fame
  It plucks, to tell how, though in war,
The Father of his country came,
  Led by his often clouded star,
To wrest from the invader's hand
  The home of Stockton, and the boon
Of new hope offer to that grand

Unwavering Scot, gray Witherspoon.
And thou, old, glorious battle-land,
New Jersey, one who loves thy sand,
And owes thee much, could he repay
The debt with this historic lay,
Might say with greater bard, and bold,
"When courage is the theme, not gold
But song rewards, nor song alone";
Nor fame I add, nor sculptured stone,
But the heart's tribute for a deed
Done in its terror, and the need
Of act spontaneous, undivined,
Forth-springing, god-like, from the mind;
As when one into flame or wave
Precipitates himself to save
Woman or child; nor stays to hold
Parley with death. Hence, from of old
Were heroes worshipped, and the strain
Heroic over warriors slain,
Or death-devoted by the will,
Shall be the world's grand music still
Rolled on and on. Not left untold,
Till memory lose its faltering hold,
A high-souled deed, forgot too long
In that great strain; and though my song
Be sung too late, or sung in vain,
And History or the Muse disdain,
Praise for the act shall live in praise
For other acts, in other days,
And Honor's self; and shall abide,
    In some memorial, with men,
While in the heart the crimson tide
    Of life shall ebb and flow again—
And glory wait on death and pain,
And speech articulate remain,
And Shakespeare live, and Homer reign.

SILENT LIFE

*Inscribed to Susan Fenimore Cooper, author
of "Rural Hours" and founder of the church
and county orphanage at Cooperstown.*

In the sweet earth, where sun and rain
  Wake silent life from slumber deep,
Until thy spring-time come again,
  Friend of the wild flowers, sleep.

There where thou liest, earth to earth,
  And they with God their secret keep,
All living beauty had its birth;
  Friend of the wild flowers, sleep.

Long in its root abides the rose,
  Spring flowers from winter's bosom creep;
He gave thee longer life than those—
  Longer than theirs, thy sleep.

And human wild flowers, to the view,
  Weeds tangled in the grain we reap,
On these thy pity fell like dew;
  Friend of the orphans, sleep.

If *vision,* in that deep repose
  Which life in Lethe seems to steep,
Be thine, I know not—He who knows
  Gives his beloved sleep.

But errs not faith, nor hope beguile,
  Thy angel hears when orphans weep,
And sees remembered faces smile;
  Friend of the wild flowers, sleep.

LINES ON THE "BANNER SONG" OF THE REPUBLIC

Inscribed to EDWARD SEVERIN CLARK, *commemorator
of Otsego's Soldiers who followed the flag,
some to death, and all to victory.*

SONG of the past, that marching thousands sing,
    What sound is this—what note, unheard before,
Blends with the stormy symphonies that ring
    From Omaha to either ocean's shore?

War for humanity! Christ, and can there be
    From Christian nations scoffs or faint reply?
Soon will the world no other battles see,
    And to no other drum-beat, soldiers die.

Live on, great song! Shall need be, let thy strain
    Call liberty to arms in future wars;
Still show, O radiant flag, on sea and main,
    Thy stripes to tyrants, to the free thy stars!

Star-spangled banner, still be borne on high,
    First, and in front of freedom's struggling line;
Though there shall be no friendly standard nigh,
    Besides, O great and kindred nation, thine!

And thou, fling out the meteor flag—once ours—
    In dreadful, or in righteous victories waved;
Sometimes in triumphs of despotic powers,
    But often o'er the cause of freedom saved.

Show the Red Cross, and read aright the sign,
    "In this," *and with it,* "conquer"; that unfurled
Above thy Christian cohort, Constantine,
    Gave Rome a Cæsar, and to Christ the world.

Cooperstown, May 20, 1898.

SONNET ON THE NAME FOX
IN ENGLISH HISTORY

MEN take the name back to the lordly Vaux,
　When sounded full and round, as in the time
　And tongue of Chaucer. Now, to nobler chime
It rings in English history, as we know
　Who read it there, by Martyr fire and flame;
　And by the strange New Light that, later, came
And shone, pure Saint, and Friend of Peace, in thee;
　But best, by Freedom's torch-light, in thy hand
　Still held aloft, great Statesman, when the band
Of trembling patriots feared for liberty;
　And thou, scion of Holland House, and heir
Of noble memories and an ancient line,
　Dared say that Freedom stained with blood was fair,
And, desecrated, not the less divine!

Cooperstown, August 7, 1899.

TO THE BISHOP OF NEW YORK
[BISHOP POTTER]

HONORED civilian, and revered divine
Looking from thee far down the mitred line
I note not the old Greek and Latin Bishops
With sometimes "too much water in their hyssops,"
But England's martyr band; and foremost thee,
Undaunted Worcester, known as bold and free
Hugh Latimer, "endued as with a sense
And faculty for storm and turbulence."
And yet, perhaps the nature his that leans
To homefelt pleasures and to gentle scenes.
But if his life of this has left no sign
We know, O kindred spirit that 'tis thine
The happy warrior thou, in whom we see
What every man at arms should wish to be.[20]

TO SYLVIA

A WOOD-NYMPH art thou by thy name,
  Or, not less fair, a forest maid,
  Like her who played in Arden's shade
A part in love's immortal game.

Which if thou play, or not, still thine
  The witchery of the poet's spell,
  The freshness of the forest dell,
The fragrance of the fir and pine.

The laughter of the brook that ran
  Past the gnarled oak where Jaques lay
  And mused on what he called a play
In seven acts—the Life of Man.

And now, O wonder! comes to me,
  In this my Seventh Age forlorn,
  A maid, who, one might swear was born
In Arden or in Arcady.

1900.

CHRISTMAS GREETING

TO A FRIEND IN CHINA

EARLIER to thee comes the Christmas morn:
  Far east of the East where Christ was born.
A Christmas greeting, young Christian, to thee,
  Amongst Pagans as pagan as Pagans can be!

And over two Oceans I make thee the sign,
   Mystical, wondrous, immortal, divine,
That with water and word I made on thy brow,
   And called thee a soldier—aye, then, as now.

Soldier enlisted and sworn at the knee
   Of Him who was conquered for thee and for me,
And for every man under the heavenly blue,
   Buddhist and Brahmin and Moslem and Jew.

INSCRIPTION ON THE INDIAN MONUMENT AT COOPERSTOWN

White Man, Greeting!
We near whose bones you stand were Iroquois.
The wide land which now is yours was ours.
Friendly hands have given back to us enough for a tomb.

LINES

PARTLY ADAPTED FROM POEMS BY
THOMAS HOOD AND JAMES ALDRICH

We watched her breathing through the night,
Death seemed on dawn to wait;
It came, and when the morning light
Illumed the eastern skies,
She passed through glory's open gate,
And walked in paradise.

FRAGMENTS ETC.

ALTERATION OF THE LAST STANZA OF BRYANT'S
"PONCE DE LEON"

"Might but a little part,
A wandering breath of that high strain (I pray),
Descend and lead my heart
To where, no more astray,
His flock around him rest, at noon of day.

THE LOGICAL ANGLERS
(Unfinished Poem)

Doctissmo Arcadio Avellamo:
 *Carmen jocosum, quod tibi admodum obscurum vide-
tur, hæc versio vulgaris forsasse illustret. W. W. L.*

*[To the most learned Arcadian Havilham (?); the hu-
morous song, which seems to you somewhat obscure,
this version in English may perchance make clear.]*

A fair dame, who and where witness
[Cætera desunt.]

"*If Milton had not written* Paradise Lost *and if Keats had not given us the 'Miltonic Inversion' of his sublime* Hyperion, *this nineteenth century epic by an American Churchman (now still living) would be the most sonorous and lofty blank verse composition in the English tongue.*" E. C. S.

[Written by Edmund C. Stedman in his own hand in his copy of *Christ in Hades,* and recently discovered by his granddaughter, Mrs. George M. Gould.]

AUTHOR'S NOTES

[1]. . . . *thoughts   To their own music chaunted.*—Coleridge.

[2]. . . . *sat Aïdoneus discrowned.* The propriety of giving Satan, as king of Hades, the classical name of Aïdoneus, needs only to be suggested.

[3]. . . . *that his pride may play at Jove.* There is perhaps no occasion for explaining why those who represent in Hades the ethnic deities, sometimes give the Supreme Being the name of Jove.

[4]. . . . . . *but in the west   The elect infernal queen, , , ,* Astarte or Ashtaroth, the Diana of the Phenicians, and thus identified with the Persephone of the Greeks.

[5]. *In the same world of demons and damned men.* It may not be thought superfluous, perhaps, to explain why Paradise and the place to which custom gives and limits the name of Hell, are made regions of the same place.

"The word Hades, which occurs eleven times in the New Testament, and is very frequently used in the Septuagint translation of the Old, never signifies in Scripture the place of torment, but always the place appropriated for the common reception of departed souls. There is no single word in our language that has this signification. Homer, Hesiod, Plato, and other Greek writers, distinguish Hades from Tartarus, which was the place of punishment for the wicked."—*Tomline's Exposition of the Third Article.*

"Our *English,* or rather *Saxon* word, *hell,* in its original signification (though it is now understood in a more limited sense), exactly answers to the Greek word Hades, and denotes a concealed or unseen place; and this sense of the word is still retained in the *eastern,* and especially in the *western* counties of *England;* to *hell* over a thing is to cover it."—*Parkhurst's Greek Lexicon; word "Αδης.*

"By *Hell* may be meant the invisible place to which departed souls are carried after death; for though the Greek word so rendered does now commonly stand for the place of the damned, and has for many ages been so understood, yet, at the time of writing the New Testament, it was among Greek authors used indifferently for the place of all departed souls, whether good or bad; and by it were meant the invisible regions where those spirits were lodged. * * * That the regions of the blessed were known then to the Jews by the name of *Paradise,* as hell was known by the name of *Gehenna,* is very clear from Christ's last words, 'to-day shalt thou be with me in Paradise'."—*Burnet on the Third Article.*

That our Lord gives the weight of his authority to the Jewish opinion that Paradise and Gehenna were in the same region of space—the place of all departed souls, supposed by them to be the under-world—is proved by the parable of Dives and Lazarus, in which a soul in torment and one of the blessed are made to converse with each other across a gulf.

[6]. . . . . . *of earthly saints   Born ere their Saviour—till that Saviour's power   Should break its shadowy door and set them free—   The sad Elysium.* . . . .

"Inferiora [Eph. IV. 9] autem terræ infernus accipitur, ad quem Dominus noster Salvatorque descendit, ut Sanctorum animas, quæ ibi tenebantur inclusæ, secum ad cœlos Victor abduceret."—*St. Jerome.*

"Nihil aliud teneatis nisi quod vera fides per catholicam ecclesiam docet; quia descendens ad inferos Dominus illos solummodo ab inferni claustris eripuit, quos viventes in carne per suam gratiam in fide et bona operatione servavit."—*Gregory the Great.*

"The end for which the soul of Christ descended into hell was not to deliver any damned souls, or to translate them from the torments of hell unto the joys of heaven. The next consideration is, whether by virtue of his descent, the souls of those which before believed in him, the patriarchs, the prophets, and all the people of God, were delivered from that place and state in which they were before; and whether Christ descended into hell to that end, and that he might translate them into a place far more glorious and happy. This hath been in the latter ages of the Church the common opinion of most men, and that as if it followed necessarily from the denial of the former: He delivered not the souls of the damned, therefore he delivered the souls of them which believed, and of them alone; till at last the schools have followed it so fully that they deliver it as a point of faith and infallible certainty, that the soul of Christ, descending into hell, did deliver from thence all the souls of the saints which were in the bosom of Abraham, and did confer upon them actual and essential beatitude, which before they enjoyed not. And this they lay upon two grounds: first, That the souls of saints departed saw not God; and secondly, That Christ by his death opened the gate of the kingdom of heaven."—*Pearson on the Creed.*

[7]. *A shape like man;* . . . "As Christ died for us and was buried, so also it is to be believed that he went down into hell."—*Article III.*

"That Christ descended into hell is not expressly asserted by any of the Evangelists; but they all relate that he expired upon the cross, and that after three days he again appeared alive; and therefore it may be inferred that in the intermediate time his soul went into the *common receptacle of departed souls.*"—*Tomline on the Third Article.*

"Several places of Scripture have been produced by the ancients as delivering this truth; of which some, without question, prove it not; but there are those which have always been thought of greatest validity to confirm this article. First, that of St. Paul to the Ephesians seems to come to very near the words themselves, and to express the same almost in terms: 'Now that he ascended, what is it but that he first descended into *the lower parts of the earth?*' This many of the ancient Fathers understood of the descent into hell as placed in the lower parts of the earth; and this exposition must be confessed so probable, that there can be no argument to disprove it. * * *

"The next place of Scripture brought to confirm the descent is not so near in words, but thought to signify the end of that descent, and that part of his humanity by which he descended. For Christ, saith St. Peter, 'was put to death in the flesh, and quickened by the Spirit, by which also he went and preached unto the spirits in prison.' Where the *Spirit* seems to be the *soul of Christ,* and the *spirits in prison,* the *souls of them that were in hell,* or in some place at least separated from the joys of heaven; whither, because we never read our Saviour went at any other time, we may conceive he went in spirit there, when his soul departed from his body on the cross. This did our Church first deliver as the proof and illustration of the descent, [*see note* 10 *hereafter*] and the ancient Fathers did apply the same in like manner to the proof of this article. * * * The third, but principal text, is that of David, applied by St. Peter: 'For David speaketh concerning him, I foresaw the Lord always before my face; for he is on my right hand that I should not be moved. Therefore did my heart rejoice, and my tongue was glad; moreover also my flesh shall rest in hope: because thou wilt not leave my soul in hell, neither suffer thy Holy One to see corruption.' Thus the Apostle repeated the words of the Psalmist (xvi. 8-10) and then applied them; he 'being a prophet, and seeing this before, spake of the resurrection of Christ, that his soul was not left in hell, neither his flesh did see corruption.' (Acts xi. 25, &c.) Now, from this place the Article is clearly and infallibly deduced thus: If the soul of Christ were not left in hell at his resurrection, then his soul was in hell before his resurrection; but it was not there before his death; therefore, upon or after his death, and before his resurrection, the soul of Christ descended into hell; and consequently, the

Creed doth truly deliver, that *Christ* being *crucified, was dead, buried,* and *descended into hell.* For as his flesh did not see corruption (by virtue of that promise and prophetical expression), and yet it was in the grave, the place of corruption, where it rested in hope until his resurrection; so his soul, which was not left in hell (by virtue of the like promise or prediction), was in that hell where it was not left, until the time that it was to be united to the body, for the performing of the resurrection. We must therefore confess from hence, that the soul of *Christ* was in *hell:* And no Christian can deny it, saith St. Augustin: " 'Quis ergo nisi infidelis negaverit fuisse apud inferos Christum?'."— *Pearson on the Creed.*

"Seeing it is a most certain truth that our Saviour's soul did immediately go into the place appointed to receive happy souls after their recession from the body, and resignation into God's hands; if we take hell in a general and common sense for the place or the state of souls departed; and descending for passing thereinto (by a falling, as it were, from life, or by going away together with the descent of the body; and thence styled descending; what appeareth visibly happening to the body being accommodated unto the soul); if, I say, we do thus interpret our Saviour's descent into hell for his soul's going into the common receptacle and mansion of souls, we shall, so doing, be sure not to substantially mistake."—*Barrow,* Ser. XXVIII.

[8]. *Magog and great Madai old.* I have somewhere met with the opinion, sustained by plausible reasoning, that the descendants of Magog, the son of Japheth, peopled northern and eastern Asia. That Madai's descendants moved toward the east, is evidenced by what seems to be a relic of the name in Media and the Medes.

[9]. *Asrael.* The angel of death, in the superstition of the East.

[10]. . . . . . *and these words Spake,* . . . . . "Being put to death in the flesh, but quickened by the Spirit, by which also he went and preached unto the spirits in prison."—*St. Peter.*

—"The body of Christ lay in his grave until his resurrection; but his spirit, which he gave up, was with the spirits which were detained in prison, or in hell, and preached unto them as the place in St. Peter testifieth."—*The Third Article, as first published in the reign of Edward VI.*

"But in them [the words of St. Peter], taken in their most literal and obvious meaning, we find not only a distinct assertion of the fact, that 'Christ descended into hell' in his disembodied spirit, but, moreover, a declaration of the business upon which he went thither, or in which, at least, his soul was employed while it was there. 'Being put to death in the flesh, but quickened by the Spirit, by which also he went and preached unto the spirits in prison, which were sometime disobedient.' The interpretation of the whole passage turns upon the expression, 'spirits in prison'; the sense of which I shall first, therefore, endeavor to ascertain, as the key to the meaning of the whole. It is hardly necessary to mention, that the 'spirits' here can signify no other spirits than the souls of men; for we read not of any preaching of Christ to any other race of beings than mankind. The assertion of the Apostle, therefore, is this—that Christ went and preached to the souls of men in prison. The invisible mansion of departed spirits, though certainly not a place of penal confinement to the good, is, nevertheless, in some respects a prison. It is a place of seclusion from the external world—a place of unfinished happiness, consisting in rest, security, and hope, more than in enjoyment. It is a place into which the souls of men never would have entered had not sin introduced death, and from which there is no exit by any natural means for those who have once entered. The deliverance of the saints from it is to be effected by our Lord's power. It is described in the old Latin language as a place inclosed within an impassable fence; and in the poetical parts of Scripture it is represented as secured by gates of brass, which our Lord is to batter down; and barricadoed with huge massive iron bars, which he is to cut in sunder. As a place of confinement, therefore, though not of punishment, it may well be called a prison. The original word, however, in the text of the Apostle, imports not of necessity so much as this, but merely a place of safe-keeping. For so this passage might be rendered with great exactness: 'He went and preached to the spirits in safe-keeping.' * * * The souls in custody, to whom our Saviour went in his disembodied soul and preached, were those who were sometime disobedient. The expression 'sometime were,' or 'one while had been disobedient,' implies that they were recovered, however, from that disobedience, and, before their death, had been brought to repentance and faith in a Redeemer to come. To such souls he went and preached. But what did he preach to departed souls? and what could be the end of his preaching? * * * If he went to proclaim to them (and to proclaim or publish is the true sense of the words 'to preach') the glad tidings that he had actually offered the sacrifice of their redemption, and was about to appear before the Father as their intercessor, in the merit of his own blood, this was a preaching fit to be addressed to departed souls, * * * and this, it may be presumed, was the end of his preaching."—*Bishop Horsely.*

[11]. *From old Iäpetus.* "The sons of Japheth (Iäpetus); Gomer, and Magog, and Madai, and Javan (Iöan), and Tubal, and Meshech, and Tiras."—*Gen.* x. 2.

[12]. *And from fair Gomer.* From Gomer, Gomeria, or Cimmeria, and probably Germania—a derivation that will seem forced only to those unaccustomed to trace the etymology of national and local names.

[13]. *. . . there, with the Asar and Asynior, sit The Einherier and Valkyrior.* The Asar (Asiatics) were the Gods, or, rather, a divine race of men. The Asynior were the females of the race. The Einherier were human heroes, raised by their bravery to sit in the Valhalla with the Gods. The Valkyrior were the warlike Houries of the Northern Paradise.

[14]. *The Berserker, who scorn armor and arms.* "The champions of the north were called Berserker, in the old tongue, from *ber,* bare, and *sekr,* a garment; because they wore no armor in battle. They are described by almost all the northern writers as men of extraordinary stature and force, subject to sudden and violent attacks of passion, under the influence of which their fury was ungovernable, and as formidable to their natural friends as to their enemies."—*Herbert. Horæ Scandicæ, Note to Helga.*

[15]. *Bleak Niffelheim from Muspelheim.* Niffelheim, the region of cold; Muspelheim, of heat.

[16]. *. . . . . the Song Of Ragnarok . . . .* The twilight of the Gods. For this specimen of genuine Norse frenzy, see *Turner's History of the Anglo-Saxons.*

[17]. *The Jötuns. . . . .* The dark, hostile powers of Nature, they figured to themselves as Jötuns, Giants—huge shaggy beings, of a demoniac character. Frost, Fire, Sea, Tempest—these are the Jötuns.—*Carlyle.*

[18]. The rest of this strophe has no foundation in Goethe. With this exception the ode, though rendered and amplified with poetic freedom, is faithful to the spirit of the original. For giving one of the Graiæ (sisters and inseparable companions of the Gorgons) the hissing locks of Medusa, and conceiving her to be Deino, "The Terrifier," the translator is responsible.

[19]. Luke ii, 7.

[20]. See Wordsworth's "Happy Warrior."

EDITOR'S NOTES

THE biographical introduction is written much as Lord's letter to Griswold suggests he would have wished it. No footnotes were added on sources. The ordinary sources have been named by Dr. O. S. Coad in his brief sketch of Lord in the *Dictionary of American Biography*. In addition many facts have been taken from the collection of manuscripts and clippings, made by Lord and added to by his grandson. Some other sources are indicated in the text, and a wide search was made in the chief public collections for material about Lord. This led to the recovery of the two important literary letters quoted, both of which are in the Historical Society of Pennsylvania; the only literary correspondence of Lord now publicly owned. Some facts about Lord are in *Charles Fenno Hoffman* by Homer Barnes, New York, 1930, and I had found several references in connection with my own studies of Poe. Mr. Reed also was able to tell me a good deal from his recollections of his grandfather. Search of the newspapers of the cities in which Lord lived was not practicable, except where we had some clue to a date. We are therefore able to say less than we could wish of Lord's work between 1857 and 1867, of his heroic conduct during the yellow fever epidemic in Memphis, and his connection with the Knights of Pythias and the Knights Templar, and the not improbable attribution to Lord of a review of Milton, in the *Princeton Review* for January, 1845.

Two poems collected in 1845 are known to have been previously printed over the pseudonym Tristram Langstaff. These are "A Rhyme" in *Godey's* for September, 1844, and "To Children" in an annual, *The Opal* for 1845, issued about October, 1844.

In addition to the printed sermons listed, I know of a fragment not identified. The broadside prospectus of Lord's school is in Mr. Reed's collection. A leaflet advertising *Christ in Hades* was once seen by the editor.

The texts of Lord's three volumes are reprinted completely and as exactly as possible, except for the correction of a few turned letters. It is true that Poe pointed out two or three instances of incorrect English in the *Poems* of 1845. But in one I am told Lord was correct, and emendation of verse by anyone save the author himself is a thankless and dangerous business; only the hypercritical deny *all* poetic license. The fourth section of the book contains all the poems now known by Lord not issued in book form previously, and in some cases now first printed.

In compiling the present edition the editor has been deeply obligated to the officials of most of the large libraries of this country. Special thanks are due to Dr. Robert S. Forsythe, for locating accounts of some of Lord's lectures. Most of all I am grateful to Mr. Robert R. Reed, the poet's grandson, without whose enthusiasm and practical collaboration, this book could not have been compiled.

Most of Lord's infrequent direct quotations, not completely located by himself, have been identified as follows:

P. [7]. The Chatterton quotation is altered from "Rowley's Letter to Mastre Canynge," line 49.

P. 19. Spenser, *Faerie Queene,* II, xii, 71, 7.

P. 21. Milton, *L'Allegro,* line 133; and Ben Jonson, "To the Memory of Shakespeare," line 71.

P. 28. Wordsworth, "On the Power of Sound," line 247.

[P. 35]. Coleridge, "To William Wordsworth," lines 47-48. See author's note [1] on page 323.

P. 36. Wordsworth, "On the Power of Sound," line 17.

P. 52. *Twelfth Night*, II, iv, 44f.

P. 60. Chaucer, *Legend of Good Women*, Prologue (second version), line 10; and Coleridge, "A Day Dream," line 1.

P. 104. Wordsworth, *Recluse*, I, i, 784; and Milton, *Paradise Lost*, VI, 835-836.

P. 191. *Macbeth*, II, ii, 11.

P. 292. *Anthony and Cleopatra*, II, iii, 244, "Octavia is a blessed lottery to him," but the phrase is proverbial.

P. 295. A puzzling quotation—the allusion is to *Numbers*, xxi, 9, but the phrase may be quoted as reminiscent of *Romeo and Juliet*, III, ii, 73, "O serpent heart" or Browning's "Saul," line 31, "king-serpent."

P. 296. *As You Like It*, II, vii, 34.

P. 297. *Psalms*, xlviii, 2.

P. 305. Not identified.

P. 315. From a translation of Burger's "Lied von braven Mann."

P. 318. Not identified.

Lord wrote rather elaborate notes for *Christ in Hades*, but few on his other poems. The following comments on a few obscure or difficult passages may be of interest. Allusions not annotated are either of a kind to be readily understood, or are referred to in the Introduction.

P. 23. Orpheus is Coleridge.

P. 24. Wordsworth was not blind, but poetically called so because Lord thought of him as a peer of Homer and Milton.

P. 35. The Locrian poet was Stesichorus.

P. 46. Lord's sister was named Sarah.

P. 78. We believe W. B. K. was Lord's friend Kinney.

P. 308. The allusion to the Jarl's banner is puzzling. The poet seems to have had in mind the Danish banner, which Asser tells us Alfred captured. It bore a raven, which seemed alive if victory was portended, but dead if defeat awaited it. Since the Danes' defeat led to conversion, Lord perhaps thought of it as a victory as well. The other heroes are Codrus, Horatius Cocles, William Tell, and Arnold vin Winkelried.

P. 309. The allusion to the King is obscure.

P. 312. The allusion to the Roman is obscure, it does not seem to fit Pope Gregory and the Angles.

P. 314. The heroine is Molly Pitcher.

P. 319. "To Sylvia" alludes throughout to *As You Like It*.

P. 320. The adapted "Lines" are a *cento*. The first line is from Thomas Hood's familiar poem on a "Death Bed," the last three from an almost forgotten poem on a similar subject by James Aldrich, which may be found in Griswold's *Poets and Poetry of America*.